Collection Development
in Libraries
A Treatise

**FOUNDATIONS IN LIBRARY AND
INFORMATION SCIENCE   VOLUME 10 (Part B)**

Editor: Robert D. Stueart, *Dean, School of Library Science,
Simmons College*

FOUNDATIONS IN LIBRARY AND INFORMATION SCIENCE

A Series of Monographs, Texts and Treatises

Series Editor: Robert D. Stueart, *Dean, School of Library Science, Simmons College, Boston*

Collection Development in Libraries
A Treatise

Edited by: ROBERT D. STUEART
Dean, School of Library Science
Simmons College—Boston

GEORGE B. MILLER, JR.
Assistant Director for Collection
Development
University of New Mexico Libraries

 JAI PRESS INC.

Greenwich, Connecticut

Library of Congress Cataloging in Publication Data
Main entry under title:

Collection development in libraries.

(Foundations in library and information science
v. 10)
   Includes bibliographical references and index.
   1. Collection development (Libraries)   I.   Stueart,
Robert D.   II.   Miller, George Bertram, 1926-
III.   Series
Z687.C64   025.2   79-93165
ISBN 0-89232-106-7 (pt. A)
ISBN 0-89232-162-8 (pt. B)

Z
687
C64
pt. B

ISBN NUMBER: 0-89232-162-8

Library of Congress Catalog Card Number: 79-93165

Manufactured in the United States of America

CONTENTS

Part B

PART IV: CITATION AND USE STUDIES

PART V: COLLECTION DEVELOPMENT BY FORMAT

**PART VI: NEW DIRECTIONS IN COLLECTION
DEVELOPMENT**

CONTENTS   Part A

PART I: OVERVIEW

PART II: COLLECTION MANAGEMENT

PART III: COLLECTION DEVELOPMENT PROCESS

CONTRIBUTORS

Baughman, James C.
Associate Professor, School of Library Science, Simmons College

*Chisholm, Margaret E.
Vice-President for University Relations and Development, University of Washington

*Clark, Alice S.
Assistant Dean for Reader Services, University of New Mexico Library

Darling, Pamela W.
Preservation Officer, Columbia University Libraries

Deal, Carl W.
Executive Director, Latin American Studies Association, and Latin American Librarian, University of Illinois

Dowd, Sheila T.
Assistant University Librarian for Collection Development, University of California—Berkeley

Dudley, Norman H.
Assistant University Librarian for Collection Development, University of California—Los Angeles

*Feller, Siegfried
Chief Bibliographer and Associate Director of Libraries for Collections and Research, University of Massachusetts

*Fitzgibbons, Shirley A.
Assistant Professor, College of Library and Information Services, University of Maryland

Hamlin, Jean Boyer
Director of Libraries, Rutgers, The State University—Newark

*Hannaford, William E., Jr.
Acquisitions Librarian, Middlebury College

*Hernon, Peter
Assistant Professor, School of Library Science, Simmons College

Hoffman, Andrea
Assistant Director and Head of Resources and Research Division, Teacher's College Library, Columbia University

Kaiser, John R.
   Coordinator for Collection Development and Area Programs, Pennsylvania State University Libraries

Larsen, A. Dean
   Assistant Director for Collection Development, Brigham Young University

*McGrath, William E.
   Dean of Library Services, University of Lowell

Martin, Murray S.
   Associate University Librarian, Pennsylvania State University Libraries

*Miller, George B., Jr.
   Director of Library Communications, University of New Mexico

Mosher, Paul H.
   Assistant Director for Collection Development, Stanford University Libraries

*Osburn, Charles B.
   Assistant University Librarian for Collection Development, Northwestern University

Rambler, Linda
   Reference Librarian (Social Science Bibliographer), Pennsylvania State University Libraries

Stueart, Robert D.
   Dean, School of Library Science, Simmons College

*Subramanyam, Kris
   Associate Professor, School of Library and Information Science, Drexel University

Ungarelli, Donald
   Director, C.W. Post Library, Long Island University

Varnet, Harvey
   Assistant Director for Public Services, Bristol Community College Learning Resources Center

Welsch, Erwin
   Social Science Bibliographer, University of Minnesota Libraries

*Authors appearing in Part A.

Preface

The need for a treatise on collection development has been felt for quite some time. Although recently a great deal has appeared in the literature about collection development and the selection of materials, there has been no systematic attempt to meld the theoretical foundations with the practical application of the art. Indeed, discussion has most often centered on the unique problems that types of libraries have in the development process, rather than looking at problems and prospects which are applicable to all types of institutions. The intent of this collection, each chapter of which is written by an expert in a particular area, is to present theories, techniques and state-of-the-art analysis which have wide application to academic, research, public, school and special libraries. It is intended not only as an information vehicle but also as a stimulus for discussion and decision. It should be as useful for the beginner as for the seasoned professional.

The editors wish to thank Herbert M. Johnson and Gayle Jerman of JAI for their patience and encouragement in the long struggle to complete this work, and to each of the authors who have contributed their expertise to make this treatise what it is. Special thanks is also extended to Jay McPherson for the indexing and to Fran Berger for her assistance on the manuscript.

George B. Miller, Jr.   Robert D. Stueart
Albuquerque, N.M.   Boston, Mass.

Introduction

According to sociologist Daniel Bell, we are moving from an industrial society into a post-industrial one where knowledge and information frame the problems (1). In such a world libraries certainly should occupy a central position in the universe by providing, as an adaptation of the old cliché states, the right bit of information to the right person at the right time, in the right location and in the right format. Under such changing and challenging conditions, librarians are charged with identifying trends which will have an impact on the way that libraries and other information centers function. Several such trends are already placing tremendous pressures on libraries to develop their collections and access to those materials in a more systematic way than had been necessary or even

possible in the more leisurely past. These trends are forcing a recon-
sideration of approaches and emphases that until very recently have
been taken for granted. One is acutely aware of the reasons: the
rapid pace of change; the steadily expanding, exploding—polluting if
you will—volume of recorded knowledge in the form of production
of books, journals and other media; the march of technologies,
including visual communication; the need for a larger portion of the
staff and others to bring expertise to the collection development
process; the spiraling costs of materials and their processing, including selecting and acquiring them; the impact of demands for foreign
language materials, both for area-studies programs in academic institutions and to satisfy the needs of non-English-speaking or English-
as-a-second-language populations; the greatly reduced buying power
of the dollar superimposed on dwindling materials budgets and keen
competition from other departments in the city, university, company
or school district for those dollars; and the demand for development
and sharing of library resources, through networking and other
consortia. To seriously ignore any one of these factors would be
devastating for a library's collection, which would soon lose some of
its interest and much of its value to patrons. But to recognize these
issues as catalysts may very well be the first step in the present
development of and renewed interest in the future of library collections. Indeed, collection development has become a hot and fascinat-
ing topic of discussion and debate. Much of the debate has centered
around previously held attitudes toward library collection development. For example, historically, one basic criterion for collection
development has been a knowledge of the community and its needs.
This mission is evident in statements by authorities over the years
who have maintained that discovering the needs of the community is
the librarian's first priority in establishing relationship with the
public. "How to select the books to fill those needs best is the
second; and this implies a third, how to judge the value of individual
books" (2). This idea is further reinforced if one agrees with the line
of reasoning that "every item acquired for use in a library collection . . . relate(s) directly to the needs, interests and abilities of the
clientele served by the institution, within the limits set by the
institution's conception of its scope and objectives" (3).

However, there has always existed some question as to whether the identified needs of present patrons or the potential needs of present and future patrons should have more influence on the development of a collection. Some writers maintain that those conditions are mutually exclusive. For example, Poole, writing about public libraries over a hundred years ago, declared that to meet "the varied wants of readers there must be on the shelves of the library books which persons of culture never read" (4), although they may want to do so at some future time. A speech, long since forgotten by most, further reflects this attitude toward the function of the library: "A good book is a permanent possession. Why should we get excited if we do not get a reader today? The book is there, it will attract a reader in due course—tomorrow; if not tomorrow, the day after. It is not of the may-fly order, which is born and dead in twenty-four hours; it is a permanent possession which sooner or later will find its reader" (5). This line of argument would lead to further questioning of whether any library could reasonably afford to or even be expected to maintain a "balanced, comprehensive" collection which is developed not only for present-day patrons but also for future potential needs whatever and wherever they may be. This conflict in basic philosophy has existed since the beginning of serious discussion about collection development and is perhaps best summed up by Andrews who, writing in the last century, stated that

> In the selection of the first book to form a new library, there is always a Scylla and Charybdis awaiting the unwary librarian or trustee. On one side is the great temptation to have the library represent the best thought and culture of the world in all ages. In the desire to fill the library with the very best, one fact is lost sight of, i.e., that it is not the abstract value of the book, but its adaptability to the needs of the reader, that make it the right book in the right place (6).

Goldhor, among others, has criticized the term *well-rounded* as being vague and open to numerous interpretations. He qualified the term by stating that "presumably what most librarians mean when they seek to make their collections 'well-rounded' is that, first of all, there be some material on every branch of knowledge and creative composition and that, second, purchases be apportioned among all the possible fields according to a rough, subjectively estimated composite of the amount of literature published in each field, the distribution of previous circulation between the various classes of the Dewey system, and what the librarian's experience indicates to him, in a general way, the registered public is likely to request" (7).

Disagreement still persists as to the desirability of "comprehensiveness" over that of recognized "need." Monroe cites what she calls a truism in librarianship as being able to create a good collection of materials related to the specific community and to develop that collection to fulfill the goals of the institution for information, recreation and education. She further states that "we've abandoned the artificially 'balanced collection' in favor of the community oriented collection with its own internal balance" (8). This point is certainly arguable if applied to all types and sizes of libraries across the board. It may be true that large public libraries must meet diverse needs and that their "subject coverage approaches the universal, selected to meet the recreational and informational, and to some extent, the educational and research needs of its readers" (9). But one must also consider that many small public libraries have the singular goal of recreation or, at the most, include basic reference materials, while academic libraries often exclude recreational materials, as do most types of special libraries. On the other hand, the "balanced collection" is still a goal of many large research libraries, both academic and public.

This concept of "balanced collection" is difficult to define and almost impossible to administer given the current fiscal realities. It is doubtful whether such a collection could ever be successfully developed if, indeed, it is even desirable. In addition, one would be very naive not to recognize that the quality as well as the quantity of a collection is related directly to the monetary support that the library receives from its parent institution, be that the college or university administration, the local town or city authority, the school board, or the management of a company or other corporation.

From the outset of any discussion a careful distinction needs to be made between selection of materials and the development of collections. "Mystery, maze and muddle" are all words which could easily be used to describe these concepts and the secret rites which have developed around the topic. Many are fumbling around in the process because little effort has been expended in finding out much about the past and little is currently being thought about the future. Collection development in its simplistic form is the systematic development of collections. The process is a standard one and includes the selection and/or rejection of current and retrospective materials, the deselection—or evaluation—of the collection as it now exists, the replacement of worn or vanished but useful materials, and the continuing process of surveying the collection to determine new fields to be developed or levels of intensity of collecting which should be revised. This process projects the future of collection development and poses certain major questions which must be answered in the process, questions such as whether the concept of access to, rather than ownership of, resources implies a change in the emphasis of an individual library's collection.

Such a task implies the broadest of approaches and the broadest of questions. We inquire into the directions our present collection activity is moving us; we examine the way in which our system functions, based on some empirical evidence; we evaluate the desirability of the results of our activity and our policies; and we examine the goals that they imply and the value they embody. This treatise, then, undertakes to explore the major issues relating to the history, state-of-the-art and future of library collection development. Although some issues relate primarily to one type of library, it is felt that the topics can be generalized to most types of institutions. The editors have chosen this treatise form to take full advantage of the expertise of individuals working in the field. Each chapter, therefore, is written by an individual who has been involved both in research and in the practical applications of the theory to the topics they have been assigned. In developing this work an outline was first prepared and then each author was asked to write on the issue with which he or she has been most closely identified. It is thought that this collective approach to a very complex subject will make for a much more authoritative and generalizable volume than would be otherwise possible. Even though most major topics have been addressed in separate chapters, certain topics out of necessity are woven into the fabric of several chapters rather than being assigned separate chapters. For example, "user satisfaction" and "mechanized information retrieval" are not treated in separate chapters but rather touched on in several chapters.

It is obviously impossible to reconstruct in such a subject manifold and varied practices and policies which have developed in all types of libraries and indeed that is not the intent of this work. Instead, what has been attempted here is to give a selective composite picture of the theory and practice of collection development. In a work such as this some overlapping is inevitable. It is hoped that the repetition in this volume is more informative than distracting because in most cases it has been necessary to repeat certain ideas so that discussion of the topic at hand can be fully developed. Also it should be recognized that authors' styles vary in a work of this magnitude.

The subject of collection development, for purposes of this treatise, have been subdivided into five broad categories: the *management* aspects, the *process* of development, the *use* of materials as a determinant to development, the *format* of certain materials, and finally a look at the *future* of collection development. Even though each of the subcategories is further divided into specific topics so that each chapter can be considered individually, the process of collection development is an integrating and ongoing exercise and therefore each chapter is only one part of the total process.

The first six chapters of this treatise introduce the basic management principles upon which the rest is developed, and set the framework for the remainder of the volume. With a broad overview in "Organizational Models for Collection Development," Dudley examines the state-of-the-art of responsibility for collection development in each type of library from university to school, from large public to special. In a thorough consideration of the budgeting process, "The Allocation of Money Within the Materials Budget," Martin discusses the reasons for budget planning, the kinds of things that must be considered, and various ways of making the allocation of material budgets. "The Formulation of Collection Development Policy Statements" explores the ramifications of a selection policy statement. Dowd maintains that a clear understanding of collection development policy is necessary for all who attempt to interpret the library's collections to users, not merely for those persons charged with responsibility for selection decisions. The chapter on "A Survey of Attitudes Toward Collection Development in College Libraries" by Baughman et al. takes a historic look at responsibilities for collection development and then, by way of a questionnaire, defines current attitudes of librarians, faculty, and administrators of colleges. The findings confirm that the library and the activity of collection development are a central part of the formal communications model in institutions of higher education. Kaiser's comments, in "Resource Sharing in Collection Development," based on work currently being done, lay down a blueprint for cooperative collection development and capstone a developing body of literature with a state-of-the-art analysis of resource sharing. Finally in this section, Mosher, in "Managing Library Collections: The Process of Review and Planning," addresses the need for collection review, how one goes about the process and the impact that a planned program can have on library services.

To understand the process of collection development one must look at the very practical everyday problems and at trends which have influenced this process. The second section of six chapters addresses those points. In "The Selection Process," Hamlin discusses, from a very practical point, the framework within which selection takes place and the structure of the selection process in all types of libraries. The chapter on "Mass Buying Programs in the Development Process" by Stueart presents the advantages and disadvantages of various types of approval plans and the "profile" definition which is so important to such an agreement. In the two chapters on "Collecting Foreign Materials from Latin America" and "Collecting Foreign Materials from Western Europe" Deal and Welsch cover the unique problems of collecting materials in non-English languages in two areas of the world where book production and distribution are at a reasonably sophisticated level. Both present problems peculiar to foreign materials and some problems can be generalized to other areas of the globe. Other "areas" have not been included because of space considerations. The chapter by Darling on "Preservation and Conservation of Materials in the Collection Process" addresses the problem that all libraries are having in preserving materials, even for limited use, and the even larger problem of conserving materials for future use. The acquisition of retrospective materials is one of the primary functions of a growing library. With this axiom in mind, Larsen's chapter on "The Role of Retrospective Materials in Collection Development" develops a step-by-step approach to developing collections through the purchase of retrospective materials.

The third section, the beginning of Volume 2, is composed of three chapters which discuss some of the techniques which have been used as indicators in the process. In a very thorough and extensive state-of-the-art survey of "Citation Studies in the Social Sciences," Fitzgibbons presents a composite picture of the broad social science areas and sample studies within each social science. It is evident from her discussions that monographs play a much greater role in citation analysis in the social sciences than in science and technology. Subramanyam, with an overview of bibliometric studies in "Citation Studies in Science and Technology" discusses their possible use as basis for policy formulation for the development of collections. An important discussion of Bradford's law of scattering, with which many librarians have little familiarity, provides a framework for decision-making in the area of development of serial collections. Humanities has not been included as a separate section since some of those disciplines are covered in the social sciences and because so little has been done with those "other disciplines" in the humanities. Finally in this section, the use of circulation data for the identification of use patterns of materials can be a useful tool in collection management operations. McGrath, in "Circulation Studies and Collection Development," addresses this issue in a solid theoretical chapter which relates well to his previous research and to those of others writing in the area.

The growth in information management has led libraries to examine and include formats of materials in their collections other than the traditional book materials. In many cases these types of materials have very important implications for developing collections. Clark considers all the advantages and disadvantages of "Microforms as a Substitute for the Original in the Collection Development Process" and suggests that libraries should be prepared to "sell" microforms as a valuable source of information. Hernon, in the chapter on "Developing Government the Publication Collection," makes an across-levels-of-government examination of the role that documents play in developing collections. Drawing on a survey that he has recently completed, he is able to develop a profile of government documents users and the intensity of that use and provides useful information concerning reviewing sources. In a chapter covering the complex subject of media, "Developing Non-Print Collections," Chisholm has woven together a unified media concept and has characterized the several models which currently exist for media selection. In "Developing the Serials Collection," Feller emphasizes the serials collection's value to the total resources.

The final four chapters take a futuristic look at collection development and address the questions facing us tomorrow. "Collection Evaluation or Analysis: Matching Library Acquisitions to Library Needs" by Mosher takes a rather unique approach to analyzing the collection according to need and makes some very valuable observations about the evaluation process. Miller, in a very insightful chapter on "Creativing in Collection Development," talks about creative ways of developing collections—including nontraditional financial sources, public relations, volunteers and gifts. After a brief look at past and current education components for collection development officers, Osburn, in "Education for Collection Development Officers," considers a rationale for expanding education for collection development in the context of library education and the evolving society. The final chapter, "Toward a Theory of Collection Development" by Hannaford explores the possibility of a theory emerging from collection development both as it relates to the normative which addresses what should be the bases of decisions and to the descriptive elements which relate to the bases of selecting items.

These chapters bring into a unified whole the importance of collection development in every type of library and point the direction to trends which are emerging.

Robert D. Stueart

REFERENCES

1. Daniel Bell, "Welcome to the Post-Industrial Society." *Physics Today* (February 1976): 46-49.

2. Helen E. Haines, *Living With Books*. (New York: Columbia University Press, 1950), p. 24.

3. Elanor Phinney, "Book Selection Theory." *Public Library Division Reporter* 4 (October 1955): 24.

4. William F. Poole, "The Organization and Management of Public Libraries." In *Public Libraries in the United States*, edited by the U.S. Bureau of Education. (Washington, D.C.: Government Printing Office, 1875), p. 479.

5. J.P. Lamb, "Books and the Public Library." *Library Journal* 60 (December 1, 1935): 913.

6. Elizabeth P. Andrews, "Book Selection." *Library Journal* 22 (October 1897): 71.

7. Herbert Goldhor, "A Note on the Theory of Book Selection." *Library Quarterly* 12 (April 1942): 157-158.

8. Margaret E. Monroe, "What Makes a Good Book Collection?" *Maryland Libraries* 30 (Spring 1964): 6.

9. *Encyclopedia of Library and Information Sciences*, s.v. "Collection Building," by Joseph C. Shipman.

PART IV

CITATION AND USE STUDIES

Citation Analysis in the Social Sciences

Shirley A. Fitzgibbons

INTRODUCTION

The intent of this chapter is to review the general area of bibliometrics, with special emphasis on the social sciences. Due to other reviews, it was decided to concentrate on the most productive time period for this area of study, from 1965 to date. Valid arguments could be made for the contention that such a state-of-the-art review should only be done by a researcher in the field. However, as a social scientist and a social science reference person, a certain skepticism and objectivity is brought to the task. The limitation of the review is a lack of a more critical analysis of the methodology of the studies themselves. To compensate for this, an attempt has been made to read the reactions and critiques of citation analyses.

The basic purpose of the chapter is to summarize citation studies in the social science areas, especially in relationship to their applicability to building library collections in large research or specialized social science libraries. The question being explored is—do citation studies in social science areas provide pertinent information for collection development? This information should be useful to those librarians who work with the social science literature—including reference, bibliography, and acquisitions work.

The coverage of this survey is restricted to research studies reported in the United States (which obviously includes much British work) using the technique of citation analysis within the disciplinary fields of the social sciences as defined for the review. Masters studies are not usually included due to their lack of accessibility. Doctoral dissertations are usually from journal articles based on that research and occasionally from abstracts. The focus is on readily available material representative of studies in the broad social science area and sample studies within each social science.

The search technique includes, first, the perusal of other recent general reviews; in this case, two comprehensive reviews were available from two of the library and information field's most important review publications: the work of Broadus in *Advances in Librarianship* (1977) (*1*) and the work of Narin and Moll in the *Annual Review of Information Science and Technology* (1977) (*2*). The pertinent work in these reviews has been included, but this review concentrates on the social sciences in more depth. However, it must be assumed that serious readers will also use these two basic review articles.

A search of the following indexes and abstracts was done from 1970 to date: *Library Literature, Library and Information Science Abstracts, Information Science Abstracts, Social Sciences Index*, and the *Social Science Citation Index*. Each of the pertinent references in these secondary sources led to articles with numerous other earlier citations to be followed. No attempt was made to examine major specialized indexing and abstracting publications due to the emphasis within this review on studies with applications to collection development. However, this is another limitation of the review.

CITATION ANALYSIS AS A TECHNIQUE

Definitions

The term *bibliometrics* was first used by Pritchard to describe "all studies which seek to quantify the processes of written communication . . . the application of mathematical methods to books and other media of communication" (*3*). Before this, the term *statistical bibliography* had been used. Information science has assumed this to be a valid research area especially in the hard sciences, contributing to the area of the sociology of science. Narin and Moll in their review conclude:

> Bibliometric research has developed a body of theoretical knowledge and a group of techniques and applications based on the distribution of bibliographic data elements. . . . The wider application of bibliometric techniques is leading to the development of new and more precise techniques. . . . The information scientist continues to make use of bibliometric techniques for more economical and efficient management of his materials and services (*4*).

One area of bibliometrics is citation analysis and, according to Narin and Moll, it is probably the most active area in the 1960s and 1970s due largely to the use of the computer, and the beginning of the publication of the *Science Citation Index* (SCI) in 1961 and the *Social Science Citation Index* (SSCI) in 1969, and the later by-product, *Journal Citation Reports* (JCR). Citation analysis is the "analysis of the citations or references which form part of the scholarly apparatus of primary communication" (*5*). Broadus defines the "true" citation analysis as one which "deals with works cited as having actually been used in preparation of, or having otherwise contributed to, the source paper" (*6*). A distinction is often made between references (made *by* articles or monographs) and citations (made *to* articles or monographs).

> The number of references a paper has is measured by the number of items in its bibliography as endnotes and footnotes, etc., while the number of citations a paper has is found by looking it up in some sort of citation index and seeing how many other papers mention it (*7*).

Broadus uses a somewhat different definition when he describes a citation study's methodology:

> a source publication or group of publications is searched for bibliographic citations. These references, generally footnotes, are copied and then analyzed in various ways. The typical study provides four different breakdowns of the total citations; the number or percentage in (a) each subject field (b) each major language (c) each form of publication (such as book, periodical, thesis, etc.) and (d) each age category by five- or ten-year intervals (8).

Background

To understand the field of bibliometrics in general—the validity of measures, the particular bibliometric laws and distributions, and general application to information science and the sociology of science—the Narin and Moll review is essential. This review will only briefly generalize from that work and other background papers.

Citation data has been analyzed since the 1920s with studies in this area beginning in the hard sciences with applications to the sociology, history, and economics of science. The procedure of citation analysis was first applied to chemistry by Gross and Gross (9), the seminal work in terms of library applications. More recently in the 1960s studies have proliferated in the social sciences, and a few studies and applications have been done also in the humanities. The results of these studies have been used to guide the selection of journals for library collections, to determine the adequacy of coverage of secondary services, and to trace the structure of knowledge and the flow of communication within a discipline. Monographs have received less attention than serials because of the low frequencies of citations in the sciences where most of these studies were conducted. These early descriptive studies were generally simple citation counts used to rank journals as the "most important" or "core" journals in a specific field. After publication of the SCI, studies became more sophisticated, exploring relationships between groups of journals or authors in studies involving cluster analysis, networking, cross citation patterns, hierarchies of journals, and identification of "research fronts." The SCI became not only an information retrieval source, but a data source itself for a citation analysis; a list of all items in X number of journals during one year with an ordering of all the citations attached to those items was available so one could determine the papers which had cited any given item. It then was possible to follow citations forward in time (as well as backward) and to see linkages between papers (by sharing citations in common). The SSCI has been subsequently used in the same way, with research implications for the sociology of the social sciences, especially sociology. A recent SSCI (January to April 1978) produced an extensive "Bibliography on Citation Indexing and Social Sciences Citation Index" containing approximately 240 citations.

Usefulness

Brittain and Line (*10*) have categorized the uses to which an analysis of bibliographical references and citations can be put. Generally, citation studies have been concerned only with the work of scholars and researchers and the literature that pertains to that work: scholarly journals, textbooks, classic or standard bibliographies, and masters or doctoral dissertations. The results of the studies therefore are limited to implications for collection building and use of this type of material in a university, research library, or specialized library setting.

Validity of Citation Studies

As Broadus states:

> Of concern here is the extent to which people become interested in publications because of bibliographical references in other works. A high incidence of such use would mean that (1) the validity of citations tends to be substantiated and (2) that citation counts have some direct value in predicting use of library materials (*11*).

A dissertation by Hodges (1972) attempts to evaluate the importance of citations to scholars with the following contention:

access through references is important, and potentially so fruitful for the advancement of knowledge that (a) more fields than are now served by a citation index should be so served, and (b) scholars would benefit from making heavier use of existing citation indexes than they now make (*12*).

Concerning the much-debated citation patterns of writers, her study shows:

> scientists and humanists both believe in attributing work they use to its originators, in giving readers what they need to check statements, and in relating their work in the same and contiguous areas (*13*).

> Finally, everyone takes the code [governing citation practice] seriously— their own work, in the comments they make on other work which they are asked to referee, and in what they demand from students (*14*).

She obviously believes that her evidence shows that "the reference structure of scholarly literature is indeed sound" (*15*). However, areas of concern about the nature of citation practices which have been delineated by several authors include: citing a widely known article even though it was not used in a particular paper, citing material merely to give weight to one's own paper, citing a paper on a subject peripheral to the main subject, citing own work which may not be central to a particular paper, and the lack of knowledge of or access to more important papers than those cited.

Broadus, as a conclusion of his review of citation studies, comments:

> It may be concluded on the basis of the evidence so far presented that citations are treated seriously by scholars; that they actually are used as leads to specific library materials; and here, it follows that they are predictors of demand. References made in journals or books widely circulated among scholars (e.g., official publications of leading scholarly and professional organizations) thus would appear to be the better predictors (*16*).

Several authors have reviewed the pros and cons of citation analysis including Broadus, DISISS Studies (*17*), Line and Sandison (*18, 19*), and Narin (*20*). Their arguments will not be repeated in this discussion; however, it is necessary to remind readers that it is still a controversial and changing area of research. Narin in his work has reviewed 24 validity studies ranging over a 20-year period. He concludes that the studies "indicate that bibliometric measures correlate highly with more subjective interview and survey-based measures of productivity, eminence, and quality of research" (*21*). A very critical approach to citation studies is taken by Line and Sandison; however, the emphasis is on the careless methodology and lack of rigor of many of these studies which consequently make the results "of little if any practical use to librarians and information system designers because of inadequate data collection and analysis" (*22*).

Subramanyam provides cautionary suggestions to be kept in mind while using citation frequency as a measure of journal significance: "the use of journals is strongly influenced by their availability," and "the importance of a journal to an individual user or a user group is subject to change with time because of changes in user interest or in journal scope and quality" (*23*).

As in any research area, the results are only as valid as the researcher's methodology and rigor; however, in this area several basic assumptions are still being challenged. For these reasons, it has been recommended by most of the serious researchers in this area that citation analysis should not be used in isolation as a measurement of quality, significance, or importance. A positive aspect of citation analysis is the fact that it is an unobtrusive measurement as compared to most information use and need studies.

Concepts and Techniques Concerning Citation Analyses
These citation studies and other bibliometric studies have introduced a number of interesting hypotheses or middle-range theories which need to be briefly listed so that later interpretation of results will be more meaningful to the reader.

Three basic bibliometric "laws" are clearly explained in the Narin and Moll review. Zipf's Law is based on word-frequency rankings in a defined set of documents; Lotka's Law is based on the number of authors publishing in a discipline or other defined field; and Bradford's Law is based on the distribution of publications in a discipline or of articles in a set of journals. Though working in the area as early as 1934, Bradford formalized his initial work in a statement called Bradford's Law (24). Briefly, the Law is concerned with the scatter of literature within a scientific discipline and states that there is a high degree of concentration of related papers in a relatively small number of journals. It has been proven that the literature of many scientific disciplines conforms to Bradford's Law.

Garfield (25, 26) first introduced the concept of *impact factor*, the number of citations received by a journal expressed as a ratio of the average number of articles it publishes each year, to measure the *impact* or *influence* of individual articles (and later of journals).

De Solla Price discussed the concept of "hard" and "soft" sciences and explored quantitative measures of these based on citations. In the early 1960s, he developed Price's Index (27) which states that: in any given year, 35% of all existing papers are not cited at all, 49% are cited once, and the remaining 16% are cited an average of 3.2 times a year. For a large n (n - number of citations) the frequency of citations decreased as $n^{2.5}$. Only 1% of all papers are cited as often as six or more times a year. This *immediacy* effect pertains to the phenomenon that recent papers are cited more frequently than older ones.

The concept of *bibliographic coupling* as a more refined measure of journal citations was explored by Kessler (28) in 1963. This involves the relationship between articles by grouping together articles with citations in common. A stronger relationship is effected with a larger number of citations in common. Price and Schiminovich in 1968 applied *clustering* techniques to citation data (29). Narin in 1972 used cluster analysis in several scientific areas to identify journals in subdisciplinary areas (30).

Introduced by Small (31) in 1973 was the concept of *co-citation* (frequency with which two documents are cited in common), which is a dynamic measure, due to changes from year to year, which generates clusters of related papers.

Very recent studies have used *multidimensional scaling* to examine the subject classification of journals within a discipline, the interdisciplinary influences, and dependency relationships between journals (and consequently, between fields and subfields).

SOCIAL SCIENCES—CITATION STUDIES

Definition of the Social Sciences

The definition of the social sciences as far as inclusion and exclusion, as always, has been a major problem in organizing this review. Several changes seem to be altering the status of the social sciences including the availability of the computer to allow handling greater masses of information and thus allowing increased interdisciplinary research among the social and behavioral sciences; and the stimulus of the availability of money for research in the 1960s partially due to the realization that basic problems confronting society are social problems, not always scientific problems.

The major study of the social sciences, "Investigation into Information Requirements of the Social Sciences" (INFROSS) (32) which began in 1967 defined inclusion within the social sciences as: anthropology, economics, education, political science, psychology, and sociology. The resulting major study, the Design of Information Systems in the Social Sciences (DISISS) which began in 1971 defined them as: "a broad one, including psychology, linguistics, and social geography as well as economics, political science, sociology, anthropology, and education" (33). Generally, the more "pure" social sciences include economics, sociology, and political science. The applied social sciences include education and management studies. There seems to be less agreement on psychology (often included in the sciences), history (often considered a humanity), and law (which seems to stand alone). There are also the newer subjects which cut across established disciplines and could be called interdisciplinary, such as information sciences, cybernetics, linguistics, communications, and criminology.

For the purposes of this review, law and history have been specifically excluded; law because it has its unique literature, and history because its literature characteristics seem more appropriate for the humanities. Geography has been excluded at a late date, partly because of a lack of extensive work in this area, and also because of the idea that the literature appears different. Though anthropology would be within the scope of the review, it was soon discovered that very little has been done in this area, and that it too is probably more like the humanities. Specifically added has been library and information sciences which seem to fit within the social sciences more than in either sciences and/or the humanities. Consequently, the social sciences included in the review are the "pure" social sciences of political science, psychology, and sociology, and the applied areas of business and management, economics, education, and library and information sciences.

Citation Studies in the Social Sciences

There are two general reviews of social science citation studies, both appearing in the early 1970s, the work of Broadus (*34*) and Brittain (*35*). At the time of his review, Broadus suggested that "enough citation studies have been completed to produce material for interesting comparison in the social sciences" (*36*). Since that time, there has been a proliferation of citation studies in individual social science areas.

On the basis of Broadus's review, the following conclusions emerged:

1. "It seems evident that English-speaking social scientists do not depend greatly upon research materials in foreign languages, and that in education and business administration they are used practically not at all" (*37*).
2. In terms of form, books or "non-serials" were found to be an important source of citation (ranging from 31% in education to 62% in sociology).
3. In terms of the age of the literature cited, percentages of materials published within 10 years or less ranged from 45% in economics to between 70 to 80% in sociology.

Brittain used somewhat different terminology for a similar area of research:

At the systemic level of analysis it is the artifacts of communication created by researchers/teachers that are the units of analysis. These artifacts of communication include citations, articles, monographs, and prepublication papers. The systemic approach is particularly suited to the study of changing patterns of communication over time. . . . The systemic approach can give data about information use patterns, and information demands, but cannot give data about information needs . . . (*38*).

His review includes studies of the growth, size, and obsolescence rate of social science literature, as well as reference scattering and bibliographic coupling. He summarizes:

areas of sociology, economic history, and political science, social scientists make greater use of the older literature than do natural scientists (Guttsman, 1966), but in the experimental areas of social sciences, the obsolescence rate is closer to that in the natural sciences (*39*).

Brittain found that "bibliometrical work is unevenly distributed across the social sciences; more is known about the parameters of psychology literature than the literature of any of the other social sciences . . . " (*40*). He encourages more studies that outline the structure of the literature of a particular discipline as a model for further bibliometrical work.

Six general social sciences' citation studies were examined: Gutts-man (1966) (*41*), Parker, et al. (1967) (*42*), Earle and Vickery (1969) (*43*), and three DISISS studies (1972 and 1973) (*44, 45, 46*). A use study of Great Britain's National Lending Library for Science and Technology (NLL) by Wood and Bower (1969) (*47*) appeared at the same time as Earle and Vickery's citation study so they were able to present interesting comparisons between use data and citation data.

The study by Earle and Vickery concerned the relationships between subjects within a discipline, and compared the social science data with that of science and technology. They found that 70% of citations from the sciences were to other science subjects with only 1% to subjects other than science and technology. However, 9% of the citations from the social sciences were to science subjects, and another 9% were to technology subjects. A closer look at these studies shows that there seems to be as many differences between the individual social sciences as between the social sciences and the sciences or the humanities. Some similarities as well as differences will be pointed out by analyzing these studies in the following breakdown: by form of literature, language, age, and distribution patterns.

Form. Though the percentages varied from study to study (due to different definitions of terms, such as serials, and a different set of social sciences), it was generally found that books were an important form of material as evidenced by frequency of citation. A range of 31% to 46% of all citations were to books, while a range of 29% to 43% were to periodicals. In all the studies, except Parker, et al., books were somewhat more important or of almost equal importance (DISISS, No. 5). This varied widely between different social sciences; for example, periodicals were reported as accounting for as much as 69% of all citations in psychology. Though no particular "other" form emerged as important overall, "other" forms in totality were important, ranging from 22% to 26% of all the citations. This led Parket et al. to conclude that citations of minor sources (newspapers, magazines, reports) is highly journal specific. Their study (which dealt with communication research) found that *Journalism Quarterly*, and the *Journal of Broadcasting* cite newspapers and magazines highly; while high citations of unpublished reports were noted for *American Documentation*, *AV Communication Review*, and the *Journal of Advertising Research*. These latter three journals, at that time, almost stood alone as representative of their field.

Language. Both U.S. and British studies found English to be the prominent language cited in the social sciences; 89% of all citations were to English publications in the Earle and Vickery study (with 64% to U.K. publications and 16% to U.S. publications). Guttsman concluded that only one-thirtieth of all citations were to non-English periodicals.

Age. In the Earle and Vickery study, citations in all types of social science publications had a median citation age of nine years; and citations to periodicals, six years. Again, the social sciences varied, with social welfare, economics, and education having a lower median citation age than this average. Guttsman identified the importance of older nonperiodical material within certain disciplines while in the experimental areas the obsolescence rate is closer to that in the natural sciences. Parker et al. again found that it varied, dependent on the discipline; for example, the *Journal of Broadcasting* drew 57% of its citations from the previous decade, while *American Documentation* drew 83% from the same time period.

Distribution Patterns. In the DISISS study (No. 5), 50% of all citations were to 15% of the titles, and 90% were to 72% of the titles, similar to a Bradford distribution. The number of "nucleus" journal titles was 12.8, with the top journals in the fields of sociology, psychology, and economics. Psychology was the social science most frequently cited, of the top 222 journals, 28% were in psychology.

Subject Dispersion and Scatter. Before leaving these general studies, it is important to note further the DISISS study (No. 5) and the Parker et al. study which both used cluster analysis to look at disciplinary boundaries. Economics "behaved very differently from the other social sciences, was a very self-contained discipline, not often citing journals in other social sciences" (*48*). This was in direct contrast to psychology and sociology. Journals in other social sciences made substantial numbers of citations *to* psychology. Psychology also is in a special relationship with the physical and biological sciences, accounting for over half of the citations recorded from all the source journals to *Science* and *Nature*; and to the social sciences, drawing upon sociology. Another unusual area was criminology which was dependent on a large number of social science journals. The cluster analysis of Parker's study resulted in the following clusters: psychology, sociology and social psychology, educational psychology, journalism, and documentation. The DISISS work also reported a relatively low degree of self-citations (degree to which an area drew upon literature of others, i.e., cited other disciplines' journals) in the social sciences, and consequently, a greater degree of scatter than in the sciences. There was a wide range of citations per article, 3 to 52, or an average of 12 citations per article. The Parker et al. study found a similar wide range across journals, from 3.7 median citations for *American Documentation* to

36.5 median citations for *Psychological Bulletin*. However, only three journals had more than 10 average citations: *American Sociological Review*, *Journal of Abnormal and Social Psychology*, and *Psychological Bulletin*.

The Parker study also looked at multiple authorships, finding an average number of authors per article to be 1.34, with a range from 1.1 to 1.8. These were surprisingly low figures as compared to the physical sciences.

Citation Compared to Use. The use study by Wood and Bower supported the contention that materials requested were published within the last decade, though this may be somewhat misleading due to use and users of the particular library. They reported a somewhat shorter median age of social science journals, 3.5 years. However, management literature received more than average use of recent literature; 69% of requests were for the last 3.5 years while 87% of the requests were for materials within the last 8.5 years. Education had a similar pattern. There was much heavier use of older literature (before 1969) in the disciplines of geography (52%), psychology (45%), statistics (45%), and sociology (38%) as compared to 26% of the whole social science sample citations. Citation distribution patterns are interesting to compare to this use study of the NLL which found that 50% of all requests were for 16% of the titles; and 90% of the requests were to 66% of the titles, an unusual similarity to that of the DISISS citation study. Earle and Vickery concluded that neither citation nor use demand is an adequate measure of literature use by a large community, but they can both serve as indicators.

1. Business and Management

Ten citation studies were located and considered; two as early as 1958, two very complete studies in 1976 and 1978. The overlap between this area and economics is considerable; for example, Hamelman (1972, 1973b), Cox (1976), and Popovich (1978) included economics in a comparative manner in their studies. The terminology is confusing; for example, topics covered by this group of studies included: operations research, public administration, management science, business management, the influence of behavioral sciences on management, subfields of business such as accounting, and the interrelationships between business and economics. The economics group of studies follows and needs to be compared with this current group of business and management studies. Though the Hamelman and Mazze studies are included with the business area, they are further discussed in the next section on economics.

Characteristics of the Literature. Intrama (1958) and Popovich (1978) both studied general characteristics through studies undertaken 20 years apart. Intrama used journal literature sources and examined public administration while Popovich used dissertation sources and examined business and economics.

Form. Over the 20-year period it appeared to be a changing picture in terms of important forms of literature. Intrama had found citations though primarily to books and pamphlets (57%), also to periodicals (25%), and to public documents (15%), and to "other" (3%). Popovich found the larger proportion of citations to periodicals (49%), but a still sizable proportion to monographs (32%), serials (9.5%) and miscellaneous (9.5%). The inclusion of economics in the Popovich study might be a factor, however, leading one to question any such comparison.

Language. Popovich found foreign languages practically nonexistent in this literature; only 0.1% were to non-English titles.

Age. Popovich's study showed more than 70% of all the cited materials were 10 years old or less, and that 85% of all sources were within a 15-year period, supporting the idea of a high obsolescence rate.

Distribution of the Literature. Popovich indicated that 78% of the references were for materials in 62 different periodical titles, in business and economics. Hamelman and Mazze (1973) found that 75% of all citations were accounted for by four management periodicals.

Subject Dispersion and Scatter. Popovich found 14.7% of all citations were from business, more than 6% from finance, and a total of 32.8% from economics (labor, production, theory, and history). Other social science areas cited were psychology (more than 8%), sociology (more than 7%), and political science (more than 4%). Science was represented by almost 5% of all the citations. Hamelman and Mazze noted the interdisciplinary tendencies of some subfields of business administration; for example, finance journals rely heavily (cite often) on economics journals; management journals do the same, though the converse is not true. The behavioral sciences influence business through particular journals in sociology and psychology. Using multidimensional scaling, Cox et al. (1976) found four clusters of journals which supported a current thesis that "the theoretical underpinnings of business have come from two fields, the behavioral sciences (less formal) and economics (more formal) (*49*).

Core Journals. McRae (1974) in his study of core journals of accounting reported three such journals which accounted for approximately 55% of all the citations.

Library Related Studies. Popovich had a second aspect of his study, to determine the extent to which the State University of New York at Buffalo (SUNY-B) Libraries owned the materials cited. SUNY-B Libraries owned 95.8% of all the periodicals cited, 89.3% of the monograph citations, 81.2% of "other" serials, and 26.2% of miscellaneous forms. The overall ownership figure was 85.7% of all citations studied.

2. Economics

According to the INFROSS study, the most frequently mentioned method for locating references among economists was *references from other sources*, consulting an expert, or a colleague. It would thus appear that citation studies are especially pertinent in this area.

Twelve citation studies were examined in economics. The majority of these studies were concerned with general characteristics of the literature: Coats (1971), Fletcher (1972), Nakamura (1972), Lovell (1973), and Quandt (1976).

Form. The rather high level of citations of journals was unusual for a social science; most studies indicated an almost equal or somewhat higher reliance on periodicals as compared to monographs. Fletcher found that unpublished materials (especially working papers) as well as government publications were becoming more important. Several authors spoke of the doubling over the last decade of the number of journals of interest to economists. Thirty-one new journals were identified in this area from 1971-1974.

> Economics is probably unusual in having a high birth rate and a low mortality rate of periodicals: it is no exaggeration to claim that more economics journals have begun in the last two years than have ceased publication in the last thirty (50).

Language. In Nakamura's study of Japanese economics literature, the data suggested that 70.8% of references cited are from foreign publications, mainly British and American. Fletcher concluded that though the emphasis is on English-language material, there is a slight change of source from Anglo-American to Asian and European. Eagley (1975) identified an international character in economics journals but still a growing Americanization from the early 1960s to the early 1970s.

Age. Quandt (1976) determined that the mean age of citations declines over time by about six months per decade; and that 50% of all references were less than or equal to six years old at each of the last turns of the decades of 1950, 1960, and 1970.

Subject Dispersion and Scatter. Eagley (1975) in his exploration of journal networks found a structure existing that suggested increased specialization, also reflected in the increasing number of economics journals since 1961. The trend would imply growing compartmentalization of the economics profession, and might also signify the coming demise of the general journal in this field.

The relationships between social science disciplines were the focus of the work by Hamelman and Mazze, summarized in several articles in the early 1970s, in their exploration of cross-citation patterns. The authors of articles in economics journals seldom cited work outside their own field, making economics almost insular (87% of the citations were *to* economics); while the management literature does, however, cite economics. General business journals are very dependent on specialized journals, especially the area of management. A new journal in 1972, the *Annals of Economics and Social Measurement*, had as its purpose to serve as an interface between economics and statistics, management science and information science.

Core Journals. Studies by Coats (1971), Billings et al. (1972), Bush et al. (1974), and McDonough (1975) identified important journals in economics. Bush's study identified the 14 most important journals and compared this result with the data of a Delphi study, finding similar results. McDonough's study compared several criteria of journal quality, including institutional affiliation of authors, peer evaluation especially familiarity, reading list citations and journal citations; she concluded that they were all related measures of journal quality. She discussed the idea that information is lost by the use of a single ranking, suggesting that the best estimate of the true ranking is provided by the order of the sums of the ranks of these various criteria. However, due to the large number of new journals in the early 1970s in this field, the relative rankings may be changing. Eagley's study showed that core journals have a degree of emphasis on theoretical fields, and serve as network feeders, i.e., disseminate information to other points in the network. The next group of most important economics journals (after the central core) are those geographical area journals in which U.S. journals predominantly cite U.S. journals (with a similar pattern for the English journals).

Eminent Persons. As with many other studies, Stigler and Friedland (1975) concluded that those authors most cited are also most prolific; a top 15 persons (most cited) wrote 46% of the total articles.

Secondary Service Evaluation. Roberts (1971) identified an 87% title coverage of his sample included in seven indexing or abstracting services; however, only 56% of the total articles were covered in these services.

Library Implications. Fletcher (1972) points out several implications for librarians: economists make more use of journal literature than previously believed; a high degree of use (citedness) of a few titles might require more duplications of subscriptions to a few titles; and the noted speed at which articles become obsolete, as well as the high production of volumes of readings, have implications for binding and retaining long runs.

3. Education

There are many background studies about educational literature; three need particular mention: the Herner (1968) (*51*) report on educational journals with survey data, the Wright (1973) (*52*) article on ERIC, and the Rittenhouse (1971) (*53*) study of information utilization leading to innovations in public school systems.

Rittenhouse concluded:

> The most frequently used information sources are colleagues in one's own school system; principals and vice-principals, contacts at professional meetings, superintendents, and curriculum specialists . . . the least used sources were federally funded R and D and information programs. . . . The most frequently used external source of information is programs in other school districts (*54*).

Only five citation studies were located.

Form. Broadus (1965) found serial literature to be most important, accounting for 57% of all citations, as compared to nonserial literature, 43% of all citations. However, Chambers and Healy's (1973) study (using dissertation literature) reported that two-thirds of all citations were to monographs. Mochida (1976) concluded that the number of references to journals and monographs were almost evenly divided; however, almost twice as many monograph titles as journal titles were cited.

Language. Broadus found almost all citations in English language journals.

Age. The median age of citations in the 1960 data of the Broadus study was 7 years as compared with a median age of 12 years for his earlier 1950 data, and was consistent for all 7 forms of literature categorized.

Distribution. Chambers and Healy concluded that 55% of all periodical citations could be supplied by one-half of one percent (.005) of the library's total periodical holdings and 75% by less than one and one-half percent (.015) of its holdings. The overall *average* citations per thesis were 42 (29 nonperiodical and 13 periodical) with an extremely wide range.

Subject Dispersion and Scatter. Narin and Garside (1971) and

Barron and Narin (1972) both studied subject clusters within and outside the educational literature. Special education was the focus of the Narin and Garside study which identified a stronger tie *from* special education *to* psychology than *from* special education *to* general education. They found the referencing structure of general education to be highly dispersed, special education somewhat less highly dispersed, and psychology not nearly as dispersed. Narin and Garside discovered the research relevant to special education is mainly in special education itself and in psychology, suggesting that an adequate special education library collection should include between 5 to 10 special education journals, 5 general education journals, and from 10 to 20 psychology journals.

Barron and Narin identified a *small* universe of "scholarly" journals in education; they concluded the field to be highly structured with well-defined subfields resting on a base of experimental and clinical psychology. Psychology was identified as the main source of commonly accepted knowledge in education. One exceptional subfield was science education which was found to be self-sufficient, drawing on science research rather than general education. Higher and general education (both highly dispersed) depend on sources of data outside the educational field, serving as a link from education to the social sciences and humanities.

Mochida (1976) found citations in educational literature to: education (34%), psychology (more than 25%), sociology (almost 10%), and political science (almost 8%); making a total of over 75% of the literature. Broadus had found a similar reliance on psychology and sociology though a major emphasis on education itself; he recommended a separate education library on a large university campus.

Core Journals. Broadus identified 7 core journals which were cited at least 13 times each. Narin and Garside identified journals of importance to special education research. Barron and Narin identified key journals in general educational research; psychology journals ranked more important than education journals especially for the 6 core journals including: *Journal of Educational Psychology*, *Child Development*, *Journal of Abnormal and Social Psychology*, *Personnel and Guidance Journal*, *Psychological Bulletin*, and *American Psychologist*.

4. Library and Information Science/Documentation

A short summary of library and information science citation analysis studies was reported in CALL (*Current Awareness-Library Literature*) in a series of articles between 1972 and 1974; (55) most of these studies are not further elaborated on in this review, especially those master's theses and studies done in the 1950s.

In order to ascertain how much citation analysis is a commonly used technique in doctoral library and information science research, the author referred to a statistical profile of library science dissertations (1925-1972) (56). Of the doctoral dissertations involving the social sciences, there were studies by Logsdon (1942) and Baughman (1971) in sociology, Stokes (1959) in education, Robinson (1973) in political science, Brace (1975) in library and information science, and Bolles (1975) in American studies.

There is a severe terminology problem in this area when trying to compare citation studies. For this reason, studies of the following areas have been included: documentation, information science, library science, and informatics, as well as recognized subfields such as library automation and library education. Twenty-six citation studies were reviewed; of this number, 9 were concerned with library science (or librarianship or library education); 11 focused on information science (and technology and/or library automation); one was identified as a study of documentation. However, the remaining 3 studies focused on both library *and* information science.

Characteristics of the Language. In the Saracevic and Perk (1973) study, literature indexed by *Library Literature* (LL) included an inordinate proportion of news-type articles. A high percentage of self-citations in the journal literature reported by Gilchrist (1966), close to 20%, shows the somewhat parochial nature of the field.

Form. Penner (1972) reported serial and nonserial items to be almost equally cited, with the nonserial category including 93% monographs and 7% reports. Brace (1975) and LaBorie and Halperin (1976) in their studies of dissertation literature reveal varying findings. Brace showed an equal division between book and journal literature while LaBorie reported that 43% of all citations were to books, 23% were to journals, and a very large percentage, 21%, to unpublished materials (largely attributed to the large number of historical dissertations). An earlier study by Fenichel (1969), which was definitely a study of information science literature (use of ARIST citations only) indicated that journals and reports are the most important.

Language. Foster (1969) reported only 7.4% of the total references to library science periodicals were published outside the United States (mostly English). Gilchrist presented a similar finding concerning documentation literature. Salton's (1973) information science literature study revealed an almost exclusive American orientation: of the top 35 authors, only 4 were British.

Age. Fenichel reported that 80% of all citations of information science literature was less than 5 years old, with journal articles and reports citing literature less than 2 years old on the average. Donahue (1973) concluded that the useful life appears to be shorted than ten years except for certain areas.

Distribution and Growth of the Literature. Dansey (1973) commented that the growth of information science literature has been relatively modest over the last 10 years as ascertained by the annual number of abstracts published annually.

Subject Dispersion and Scatter. The closeness of the two fields of library science and information science as reflected in analysis of their literatures is pointed out in the study by Pope (1975); two of the core journals in library science are also core for information science: *Library Journal* and *Special Libraries.* There were 9 journals that overlapped the two fields. The fields were somewhat less interdisciplinary than the social sciences in general. Pope concluded that information science is a relatively narrow field in terms of subject breadth, but even so, it is broader than library science while, as expected, narrower than computer science. Saracevic and Perk (1973) found education to be the largest single "other" area contributing to the literature of librarianship. The most common subject area was administration-management of people, resources, and systems.

Core Journals and Classic Papers. The studies of Gilchrist (1966), Dansey (1973), and Galloway (1977) attempt to define "core" literature using secondary service coverage as the base. All of these studies trying to identify "core" literature seem lacking due to their use of limited source items: they used only ARIST, or only dissertations, or one bibliography.

In an earlier study by Cuadra (1964), alternative approaches to identify key contributions to information science were used: the advice of experts, reliance on current textbooks (references), and current bibliographies. At that time, Cuadra concluded that the field was not in common agreement on important contributions to the field; he suggested the use of the citation indexing method as one additional method to identify such contributions, with the caution that they necessarily stress older publications that have had exposure time.

Salton (1973) found the list of "consensus" authors had changed completely in a 10-year span, with 1972 authors somewhat more of a scientifically oriented group; he felt this lack of "consensus" authors to be the sign of an immature field.

Scholarly value of the Field. The studies by both Pope and Windsor and Windsor (1973) indicated a lack of scholarliness of many of the journals, another confounding aspect of identifying most important journals in this field. Windsor and Windsor concluded that library education, as represented by the *Journal of Education for Librarianship*, is not a research field as measured by the lack of citations in more than half of the literature.

Evaluation of Secondary Services. Several of the citation analyses were concerned with the bibliographic control of the literature, especially through secondary services such as indexing and abstracting services. In a recent study, Gilchrist and Presani (1971) evaluated the first two years of *Library and Information Science Abstracts* (LISA) and then compared their coverage with *Information Science Abstracts* and *Referatevnyi Zhurnal* (in its English translation). They found a very small overlap, even though each service had about an equal number of abstracts and number of journal titles; they recommended the need for all three services for exhaustive coverage.

Summary. In one of the most recent studies, Brace (1975), using doctoral dissertations as source items, found an absence of a single core of research literature as well as a lack of citation patterns in the literature. He concluded that this finding does not suggest a lack of an intellectual base but rather that it is widely scattered over many titles making it elusive with present techniques of citation analysis.

5. Political Science

Only 8 studies involving citation counts were examined in this area; though numerous background articles from political science journals indicated that the more common research technique for studying the characteristics of the political science literature seems to be subject content analysis rather than citation analysis. Rosenau et al. (1977) is an example of this type of study.

Characteristics of the Literature/Form. Stewart (1970) found the largest part of the significant literature to be monographs: 66% monographs, 22% periodicals, and 3% newspapers. Baum et al. (1976) found a similar citation pattern (60% books, 32% journals, and 8.7% other), but with results of a questionnaire to all authors of multiple-authored articles published in the *American Political Science Review* (APSR) from 1960 to 1975, the study concluded that scholarly journals were more important than any other communication media for professional knowledge. This same questionnaire discovered a greater reliance on formal communication (books and journals) than on "informal networks" (preprint distribution and personal communication).

Language. English is the dominant language cited, with foreign languages cited about equally in both monographs and periodicals, only about 15% of the total citations. The foreign languages most cited are French, German, and Russian. Stewart found that British politics are more dependent on U.S. literature than vice versa.

Age. Baum et al. found the median age of APSR citations to be slightly more than 5½ years, and that 70% of the literature (in APSR) is no longer cited by the tenth year. About 10%, however, stays alive even after the thirtieth year, creating a "classic" or "hard core" literature in subareas such as political philosophy and the ethics-normative dimension. Stewart concluded that the last 12 years (1955-1967 data) provided approximately 63% of the total citations. There is generally a time lag of about two to three years between publication of a paper and reference made to it in another publication.

Subject Dispersion and Scatter. Martin (1952), Stewart (1970), Robinson et al. (1973), and Palais (1976) explored subject dispersion. Robinson found that interdisciplinary borrowing was integral and continuing; 70% of all information sources were non-political ones. In his investigation of the relationship between the maturity of a discipline and subject dispersion he found no significant association. Martin, almost twenty years earlier, found that 69% of all citations were to other than political science literature, 51% to related social sciences including history and law, and almost 18% to fields outside the social sciences such as fine arts, education, science and technology. Palais, working with Stewart's data, discovered citations to political science journals totaling 29% and citations to related social sciences and outside social science literature totaling 71%. Important social science areas included: economics, 7%; sociology and psychology, each 6%; and anthropology, 4%; other important areas included: law, 12%; history, 6%; and philosophy, 3%. Stewart concluded that 76% of the monograph citations belonged within the subject of politics. Journal citations were more varied, with sociology accounting for four of the first 25 journals, and law one of the top 30 journals.

Rosenau's (1977) study of a subset of political science, international relations, showed a lack of agreement on basic and introductory material in an examination of the syllabi for required and suggested readings. Only 8% of the references appeared in 5 or more syllabi and a total of 29 references appeared on 11 or more syllabi: 9 texts on international relations, 5 books of readings, and 13 conceptual or empirical inquiries, etc. He concluded this lack of agreement was due to a lack of structure within the field, as well as a lack of interest in recent research findings.

Core Journals. Martin (1952), Stewart (1970), and Palais (1976) rated journals in a hierarchy according to frequency of citations. The dominant role of the APSR was evident. Stewart found that the first 10 journals in terms of citation frequency accounted for 36% of the total citations.

Influential Scholars. Finnigan (1970) and Russett (1970) examined the patterns of communication within a subfield, international relations, with particular focus on influential scholars. Russett concluded that the image of a behavioral vs. antibehavioral split in the profession was oversimplified; he identified approximately a dozen distinct groupings or "schools" of scholars. His other major finding, the relative parochial nature of the typical scholar, was determined on the basis of the emphasis of each scholar on research in only a single area without utilizing the writings of most fellow members of the discipline. Overall, Russett saw the field of international relations as sufficiently fragmented to prevent a dominant orthodoxy, yet providing important linkages to insure communication of major advances.

Multiple Authorships. Baum et al. in their analysis of the APSR in two different time periods (1957-1962, 1967-1972) found that the publication of multiple-authored articles increased from 10% to 28%. They also found a recent trend toward three, four, and even five or six authors per paper; approximately 5% of the articles published in the APSR for 1967-1972 listed three or more authors. Baum also found a rejection rate of 84% for the two major political science journals.

Evaluation of Secondary Sources. Palais' study focused on the adequacy of coverage of secondary indexing and access tools in such a dispersed subject area. He found that two services covered all 25 of the most frequently cited journals but no service covered more than 69% of the full literature of 179 journals. However, even the two services were "haphazard" in completeness of indexing.

6. Psychology

There were approximately 27 citation studies reviewed in this area, one as early as 1936 and four from the mid-1950s.

Form. Though this did not seem to be the basic concern of any of these studies, the importance of unpublished works was discovered by Daniel (1967); 8% of the total citations of 6 journals were to unpublished works. The American Psychological Association's (APA) studies had already shown how dependent psychology was on informal communication especially from colleagues, and the greater importance of preprints and personal communications in psychology.

Language. Loutitt (1955, 1957) examined and compared language patterns in psychology, chemistry, and physics in several nations' literature. English and German scientists cited their own language almost exclusively; French scientists relied somewhat less on their own language and cited English and German as well.

Age. Age and obsolescence seemed to be the focal concern of a group of studies. Zhignesse (1967) found that over 60% of all citations were within the most recent decade, and concluded that the time perspective of psychology is short and getting shorter. Lawler (1965) compared subfields of psychology, finding an average age of 8.7 years in "soft" fields (personality and social psychology) as compared to an average age of 11.07 years in "hard" fields (experimental and physiological psychology), suggesting a more rapid growth in the "soft" fields.

Distribution Patterns. Distribution patterns were traced by Wall (1977), concluding that the top 10 most cited journals accounted for 53% of all the journal citations, with 7 out of the 13 top journals being published by the American Psychological Association.

Subject Dispersion and Scatter. The APA studies had reported a high degree of scatter in citations to psychology journals; in fact they found nearly 1,000 journals outside "mainstream" psychology. Daniel (1967) found a core psychology used endogenous citations about 70.4%, approximately the same as physics and chemistry; the remaining citation needs were widely spread over eight different fields. Zhignesse and Osgood (1967) found a 30% "self-feeding" by psychological journals, indicating high specialization. Garfield (1975) used the 1969 SCI to examine citing patterns of core journals. In comparing psychology with botany, he found the average botany journal cites itself more frequently; he also found that "subspecialties" in psychology were not as apparent as in botany. Garfield commented on the parochialism of psychology.

Scholarly Eminence. A truly seminal study was that of Clark's (1957) general survey of psychologists, comparing several methods of analysis of scholarly eminence; he suggested that eminence is more accurately measured by the degree to which a person's work is cited than by the amount of his publication. Ruja (1956), Platz and Blakelock (1960), and Myers (1970) built on the Clark study. Platz and Blakelock concluded: "The answer to the question as to whether high producers also produce higher quality work seems to depend upon the severity of the criterion used to measure quality" (57).

7. Sociology

Approximately 23 citation studies in the area of sociology were reviewed. At least seven of the studies concentrated on the general area of characteristics of the sociology literature, from an early study of Broadus (1952) through a more recent study of Baughman (1974). Baughman points out that there is a relatively small body of literature in the discipline of sociology that is cited with any degree of frequency, that is, more than once.

Form. Books continue to be the most cited form, ranging from 50 to 60% of the total citations, with periodical citations from 33 to 46% of the total citations. "Other" materials including theses, unpublished reports, etc. generally accounted for between 10 to 15% of the total citations at the most. Lin and Nelson (1969) conjectured that the book reliance on sociology might support the idea that disciplines with paradigms tend to publish their work in journals while those without publish in books. Another rationalization suggested by Lin and Nelson is that more sociological research is published in books due to the higher rejection rates of sociology journals.

Language. Almost all of the sociology citations examined were to English-language publications (90 to 97%).

Age. The studies varied in their reporting of half-life or median age, actual age, or mean age of the literature. Overall, the half-life reported was approximately 7.5 years for serials and 8 years for nonserials.

Rao (1974) reported on the exponential nature of sociological periodical growth; he claimed the number of periodicals devoted to subjects "related to sociology" increased about 350% from the 1951-1960 period to the 1961-1970 period due to a growing emphasis on research in the field.

Subject Dispersion and Scatter. Cross-citation patterns examined by Lin (1974) found a stratification pattern in the core journals of sociology. In the *American Sociological Reivew* (ASR), for example, 56% of the references were to other articles published also in the ASR. Broadus (1952, 1967) found a considerable amount of scatter in the field, even though there was a concentration in sociology and the other social sciences; other fields frequently cited included psychology, history, education, and medicine.

Core Authors, Journals, and Articles. In the Baughman work, approximately 10 core journals were found to account for almost 40% of the citations when considering those cited two or more times, and approximately 67% of the total citations. These same core journals were also core journals for several subfields of sociology. Baughman concluded that the Bradford Law of scattering holds for the total body of sociology journal literature.

Most of the studies in this area were concerned with the identification of the "most influential" sociologists (Oromaner, 1968, 1970, 1972, 1973; Bahr et al., 1971; and Lightfield, 1971). Lightfield explored the relationship between quantity and quality of publications, finding a significant relationship, with total research output published being the quantity measure and the total citations for the top three writings being the quality measure.

Quantity of Citations Per Article. Brown and Gilmartin (1969) in looking at the density of citations as an index of scholarliness found the range for citations in 1966 from 2 to 104 citations for the 57 papers, or a median of 20 citations per paper.

Use and Citations. Baughman (1974) made an attempt to explore the relationship between the highly cited "core" journals and library use; his library use study, a three-week user study of one social science library, indicated a "strong" relationship.

Citation Patterns Compared to Readership Patterns. An interesting and pertinent recent study by Satariano (1978) compared readership patterns (journals most read as indicated by a survey of sociologists) with citation patterns (using Baughman's list of core journals). Though he found "some overlap" (55% of the 20 most-read journals were found on the list of the 20 most-cited journals), he concluded that citation patterns differ by indicating a cross-disciplinary focus (while readership patterns are more disciplinary), and underestimate the importance of popular social science journals, specialty, and regional journals. These differences should be made apparent to acquisitions librarians in making decisions for sociology journals.

SUMMARY AND CONCLUSIONS

More than 115 studies in the social sciences were examined for this

review. The areas of psychology, sociology, and library and information science have been extensively studied through citation analysis,
with over 20 studies in each area; while education and political
science literatures have not received as much attention. Because of
space limitations, the presentation of each area's studies has been
skeletal. Rather than concluding with generalizations about the
studies, a few comments about the technique and its relevance for
collection development seems more appropriate.

There is much to be learned about the literature of the social
science disciplines and subfields as well as the actual use of these
literatures, both important areas of study pertinent to collection
development. Citation analysis does address the first concern and
though implications can and have been drawn concerning use, these
citation findings need to be carefully validated by comparable studies
of use in each case. Attempts have been made in rather isolated cases,
such as the study by Baughman for sociology, and Popovich for
business, to compare citation analysis results with use and/or actual
library holdings of the literature highly cited. The study and
conclusions of Scales (1976) (58) in comparing citation counts and
use data of lists of journals indicated a low rank order correlation;
she suggests that ranked lists produced by citation analyses are not
valid guides for journal selection. In this reviewer's opinion, this will
vary according to type of library and particular user groups; the
National Lending Library (her user group) is obviously not serving
the same users as large academic libraries. In fact, her differences can
be accounted for by factors that are already recognized: journals
scanned for currency are likely to be highly cited, highly used but
little-cited journals are often of an applied nature, and a possible
distortion factor of self-citation may exist in highly cited journals. It
is apparent that more comparisons of this type are needed to validate
this particular use of citation analysis—the core journal delineation.

Though most of the studies reported in this review do not directly
focus on implications for library collection building, they do reveal
important information on: characteristics of the literature (form,
languages, age, and obsolescence), as well as important subject
relationships of the basic literature (through cluster analysis and
cross-citation networks). Several cautions need to be stressed in
terms of the usefulness of such studies:

1. the importance of careful selection of source items to initiate the analysis; they must reflect the total field studied;
2. the importance of timeliness; core journals change rapidly due to editorial changes, new or obsolete titles, and changes of emphasis in the field;
3. the pitfall of becoming so engrossed in mathematical distributions without much consideration of meaning;
4. results of citation studies are useful only to predict use of research and scholarly materials, not materials for other purposes (browsing, current awareness, professional reading);
5. subareas of one discipline may have different citation patterns than the general field;
6. citation results should be one input into collection decision making, not the only consideration.

The social science citation studies reviewed here revealed important information about directions of change of subject literatures; new patterns of interdisciplinary behavior; new relationships within disciplines; and identification of most important forms, papers, authors, subfields, etc. Examples of specific decisions that might need this information include: developing a new curriculum area's collection, deciding on centralizing or departmentalizing particular disciplines' collections, decisions on adding or deleting serials vis-à-vis monographs for particular subject areas, and duplicating books of readings rather than keeping long runs of serials to make accessible "classic" papers. Certain characteristics of social science literature different than the science literature characteristics have emerged, such as the importance of monograph literature as compared to serial literature *in some areas* and a somewhat longer age span of useful materials.

Decision making for collection development requires accurate information; citation studies in the social sciences can provide valuable information concerning literature research needs. Obviously, curriculum needs, interlibrary loan analyses, and demands of faculty and students are as necessary considerations in collection building. Citation researchers have tended to draw too many generalizations about their findings which may have caused much of the current skepticism concerning the applications of this research area: "Whatever happens, it seems quite certain that we are less likely to look down upon the lowly footnote in the years ahead" (*59*).

REFERENCES

1. Robert N. Broadus, "The Applications of Citation Analyses to Library Collection Building." In *Advances in Librarianship*, Melvin J. Voight and Michael H. Harris, eds. (New York: Academic Press, 1977), pp. 299-335.

2. Francis Narin and Joy K. Moll, "Bibliometrics." In *Annual Review of Information Science and Technology*, vol. 12, Martha E. Williams, ed. (New York: Knowledge Industry Publications, Inc., for ASIS, 1977), pp. 35-58.

3. Alan Pritchard, "Statistical Bibliography or Bibliometrics." *Journal of Documentation* 25 (1969): 348-349.

4. Narin and Moll, "Bibliometrics," pp. 49-50.

5. John Martyn, "Progress in Documentation: Citation Analysis." *Journal of Documentation* 31 (1975): 290.

6. Broadus, "Applications of Citation Analyses to Library Collection Building," p. 302.

7. Derek J. de Solla Price, "Citation Measures of Hard Science, Soft Science, Technology and Nonscience." In *Communication Among Scientists and Engineers*, C.E. Nelson and D.K. Pollock, eds. (Lexington, Mass.: D.C. Heath, 1970), p. 7.

8. Robert N. Broadus, "The Literature of the Social Sciences: A Survey of Citation Studies." *International Social Science Journal* 23 (1971): 236.

9. P.L.K. Gross and E.M. Gross, "College Libraries and Chemical Education." *Science* 66 (1927): 385-389.

10. J. Michael Brittain and Maurice B. Line, "Sources of Citations and References for Analysis Purposes: A Comparative Assessment." *Journal of Documentation* 29 (1973): 72-80.

11. Broadus, "Applications of Citation Analyses to Library Collection Building," p. 303.

12. Theodora L. Hodges, "Citation Indexing: Its Potential for Bibliographical Control." (Ph.D. thesis, Berkeley: University of California, 1972), p. 213.

13. Ibid., p. 207.

14. Ibid., p. 207

15. Ibid., p. 252.

16. Broadus, "Applications of Citation Analyses to Library Collection Building," pp. 307-308.

17. Bath University Library (UK), "Use of Citation Linkages and Networks for Information Retrieval in the Social Sciences," (DISISS Paper No. 6, Bath: Bath University Library, 1973), p. 28.

18. Maurice B. Line and Alexander Sandison, "Practical Interpretations of Citation and Library Use Studies." *College and Research Libraries* 36 (1975): 393-396.

19. Maurice B. Line and Alexander Sandison, " 'Obsolescence' and Changes in the Use of Literature with Time." *Journal of Documentation* 30 (1974): 283-350.

20. Francis Narin, *Evaluative Bibliometrics: The Use of Publication and Citation Analysis in the Evaluation of Scientific Activity.* (Cherry Hill, N.J.: Computer Horizons, Inc., 1976.)

21. Narin and Moll, "Bibliometrics," pp. 42-43.

22. Line and Sandison, "Practical Interpretation of Citation and Library Use Studies," p. 393.

23. K. Subramanyam, "Citation and Significance." *New Library World* 76 (1975): 227.228.

24. L. Bradford, *Documentation.* (London: Crosby Lockwood, 1948.)

25. Eugene Garfield, "Citation Indexes for Science." *Science* 122 (1955): 108-111.

26. Eugene Garfield, *The Science Citation Index as a Blueprint of the Journal Literature.* (Philadelphia: Institute of Scientific Information, 1971.)

27. D.J. de Solla Price, "Networks of Scientific Papers." *Science* 149 (1965): 510-515.

28. M.M. Kessler, "Bibliographic Coupling Between Scientific Papers." *American Documentation* 14 (1963): 10-25.

29. N. Price and S. Schiminovitch, "A Clustering Experiment: First Step Towards a Computer Generated Classification." *Information Storage and Retrieval* 4 (1968): 271-280.

30. Francis Narin et al., "Interrelationships of Scientific Journals." *Journal of the American Society for Information Science* 23 (1972): 323-331.

31. Henry Small, "Co-Citation in the Scientific Literature: A New Measure of the Relationship Between Two Documents." *Journal of the American Society for Information Science* 24 (1973): 265-269.

32. Maurice B. Line, "The Information Uses and Needs of Social Scientists: An Overview of INFROSS." *Aslib Proceedings* 23 (1971): 412-434.

33. Maurice B. Line and Stephen Roberts, "The Size, Growth, and Composition of Social Science Literature." *International Social Science Journal* 28 (1976): 124.

34. Broadus, "Literature of the Social Sciences," pp. 236-243.

35. J.M. Brittain, "The Systemic Approach: Studies of Communication Artifacts." In *Information and Its Users* (New York: Wiley-Interscience, 1970), pp. 125-144.

36. Broadus, "Literature of the Social Sciences," p. 236.

37. Ibid., p. 239.

38. Brittain, "Systemic Approach: Studies of Communication Artifacts," p. 125.

39. Ibid., p. 130.

40. Ibid., p. 145.

41. W.L. Guttsman, "The Literature of the Social Sciences and Provision for Research in Them." *Journal of Documentation* 22 (1966): 186-194.

42. E.B. Parker, W.J. Paisley, and R. Garrett, *Bibliographic Citations as Unobtrusive Measures of Scientific Communication*. (Palo Alto, Calif.: Stanford University, Institute for Communication Research, 1967.)

43. Penelope Earle and Brian Vickery, "Social Science Literature Use in the U.K. as Indicated by Citations." *Journal of Documentation* 25 (1969): 123-141.

44. Bath University Library (U.K.), "Characteristics of Citations in Social Science Monographs." (DISISS Paper No. 4, Bath: Bath University Library, 1972.)

45. Bath University Library (U.K.), "Citation Patterns in the Social Sciences: Results of Pilot Citation Study and Selection of Source Journals for Main Citation Study." (DISISS Paper No. 5, Bath: Bath University Library, 1972.)

46. Bath University Library (U.K.), "Use of Citation Linkages and Networks for Information Retrieval in the Social Sciences," Paper No. 6.

47. D.N. Wood and C.A. Bower, "The Use of Social Science Periodical Literature." *Journal of Documentation* 25 (1969): 108-118.

48. Bath University Library (U.K.), "Citation Patterns in the Social Sciences: Results of Pilot Citation Study and Selection of Source Journals for Main Citation Study," Paper No. 5, p. 20.

49. Eli Cox, Paul W. Hamelman, and James B. Wilcox, "Relational Characteristics of the Business Literature: An Interpretive Procedure." *Journal of Business* 49 (1976): 264.

50. John Fletcher, "A View of the Literature of Economics." *Journal of Documentation* 28 (1972): 285.

51. Saul Herner, Janet D. Griffith, and Mary Herner, *Study of Periodicals and Serials in Education*. (Washington, D.C.: Herner and Company, 1968.)

52. Kieth Wright, "Social Science Information Characteristics With Particular Reference to the Education Resources Information Centers (ERIC)." *Journal of the American Society for Information Science* 24 (1973): 193-204.

53. C.H. Rittenhouse, "Educational Information Uses and Users." *AV Communication Review* 19 (1971): 76-88.

54. Ibid., p. 82.
55. "Statistical Bibliography and Library Periodical Literature," *CALL (Current Awareness-Library Literature)* 1, No. 5 (1972): 4-6; 1, No. 6 (1972): 5-7; 2, No. 3 (1973): 3-7; 2, No. 4 (1973): 3-13, 2, No. 5 (1973): 13-14; 3, No. 4/5 (1974): 3-7; 3, No. 1 (1974): 3-4.
56. Gail A. Schlacter and Dennis Thomison, *Library Science Dissertations, 1925-1972.* (Littleton, Colo.: Libraries Unlimited, 1974.)
57. Arthur Platz and Edwin Blakelock, "Productivity of American Psychologists: Quantity vs. Quality." *American Psychologist* 15 (1960): 312.
58. Pauline A. Scales, "Citation Analyses as Indicators of the Use of Serials: A Comparison of Ranked Title Lists Produced by Citation Counting and from Use Data." *Journal of Documentation* 32 (1976): 17-25.
59. N. Kaplan, "The Norms of Citation Behavior: Prolegomena to the Footnote." *American Documentation* 16 (1965): 179.

BIBLIOGRAPHY OF RESEARCH STUDIES

Business and Management

Back, Harry B. "A Comparison of Operations Research and Management Science Based on Bibliographic Citation." *Interface* 4 (1974): 42-52.

Cox, Eli III, Paul W. Hamelman, and James B. Wilcox. "Relational Characteristics of the Business Literature: An Interpretive Procedure." *The Journal of Business* 49 (1976): 252-265.

Creelman, George D., and Richard W. Wallen. "The Place of Psychology in Operations Research." *Operations Research* 6 (1958): 116-121.

Durand, Douglas E. "Citation Count Analysis of Behavioral Science Journals in Influential Management Literature." *Academy of Management Journal* 17 (1974): 579-583.

Hamelman, Paul W., and Edward M. Mazze. "Toward a Cost/Utility Model for Social Science Periodicals." *Socio-Economic Planning Sciences* 6 (1972b): 465-475.

_____. "Cross-Referencing Between AMA Journals and Other Publications." *Journal of Marketing Research* 10 (1973a): 215-218.

_____. "Of Models and Scientific Markets." In: "Special Issue: Record of the Conference on the Future of Scientific and Technical Journals." *IEEE Transactions on Professional Communication* 16 (1973b): 120-125.

House, Robert J., and John B. Miner. "Merging Management and Behavioral Theory: The Interaction Between Span of Control and Group Size." *Administrative Science Quarterly* 14 (1969): 451-464.

Intrama, Navanitaya. "Some Characteristics of the Literature of Public

Administration." Ph.D. dissertation, Indiana University, 1968.

McRae, Thomas W. "A Citational Analysis of the Accounting Information Network." *Journal of Accounting and Research* 12 (1974): 80-92.

Popovich, Charles J. "The Characteristics of a Collection for Research in Business/Management." *College and Research Libraries* 39 (1978): 110-117.

Economics

Billings, Bradley B., and George J. Viksnins. "The Relative Quality of Economics Journals: An Alternative Rating System." *Western Economic Journal* 10 (1972): 467-469.

Bush, Winston C., Paul W. Hamelman, and Robert J. Staaf. "A Quality Index for Economic Journals." *Review of Economics and Statistics* 56 (1974): 123-125.

Coats, A.W. "The Role of Scholarly Journals in the History of Economics: An Essay." *Journal of Economic Literature* 9 (1971): 29-44.

Eagly, R.V. "Economics Journals as a Communication Network." *Journal of Economic Literature* 13 (1975): 878-888.

Fletcher, John. "A View of the Literature of Economics." *Journal of Documentation* 28 (1972): 283-295.

Lovell, Michael C. "The Production of Economic Literature: An Interpretation." *Journal of Economic Literature* 11 (1973): 27-55.

McDonough, C.C. "Relative Quality of Economics Journals Revisited." *Quarterly Review of Economics and Business* 15 (1975): 91-97.

Quandt, Richard E. "Some Quantitative Aspects of the Economics Journal Literature." *Journal of Political Economy* 84 (1976): 741-755.

Roberts, Norman. "Current Control of Journal Literature in Economics in the United Kingdom." *International Library Review* 3 (1971): 123-131.

Stigler, George J., and Claire Friedland. "Citation Practices of Doctorates in Economics." *Journal of Political Economy* 83 (1975): 477-507.

Education

Barron, Paul, and Francis Naris. *Analysis of Research Journals and Related Research Structure in Education*. Washington, D.C.: National Center for Educational Research and Development (DHEW/OE), 1972.

Broadus, Robert N. "An Analysis of References Used in the 1960 *Encyclopedia of Educational Research*." *Journal of Educational Research* 58 (1965): 330-332.

Chambers, George R., and James S. Healey. "Journal Citations in Master's Theses: One Measurement of a Journal Collection." *Journal of American Society for Information Science* 24 (1973): 397-401.

Mochida, Paula. "Citation Survey of Educational Literature." *Hawaii Library Association Newsletter* 33 (1976): 29-42.

Narin, Francis, and Daniel Garside. "Journal Relationships in Special Education." *Exceptional Children* 38 (1972): 695-704.

Library and Information Science/Documentation

Brace, W. "Frequently Cited Authors and Periodicals in Library and Information Science Dissertations: 1961-1970." *Journal of Library and Information Science* 2 (1976): 16-34.

Cuadra, Carlos A. "Identifying Key Contributions to Information Science." *American Documentation* 15 (1964): 289-295.

Dansey, P. "A Bibliometric Survey of Primary and Secondary Information Science Literature." *Aslib Proceedings* 25 (1973): 252-263.

Donohue, Joseph C. "A Bibliometric Analysis of Certain Information Science Literature." *Journal of American Society for Information Science* 23 (1972): 313-317.

Fenichel, Carol J. "Citation Patterns in Information Science." Master's thesis, Drexel Institute of Technology, 1969.

Foster, Donald L. "Magazines in the Library School." *Journal of Education for Librarianship* 9 (1968): 144-148.

Galloway, James W. "The Relationships of Author Productivity and Article Readability to Journal Productivity in the Field of Library and Information Science." Ph.D. dissertation, North Texas State University, 1977.

Gilchrist, Alan. "Documentation of Documentation: A Survey of Leading Abstract Services in Documentation and an Identification of Key Journals." *Aslib Proceedings* 18 (1966): 62-80.

Gilchrist, Alan, and Alexandra Presanis. "Library and Information Science Abstracts: The First Two Years." *Aslib Proceedings* 23 (1971): 251-256.

Kuch, T.D.C. "Analysis of the Literature of Library Automation Through Citations in the *Annual Review of Information Science and Technology*." *Journal of Library Automation* 10 (1977): 82-84.

LaBorie, Tim, and Michael Halperin. "Citation Patterns in Library Science Dissertations." *Journal of Education for Librarianship* 16 (1976): 271-283.

Lehnus, Donald J. "*JEL*, 1960-1970: An Analytical Study." *Journal of Education for Librarianship* 12 (1971): 71-83.

Penner, Rudolf. "Measuring a Library's Capability . . ." *Journal of Education for Librarianship* 13 (1972): 17-30.

Pope, Andrew. "Bradford's Law and the Periodical Literature of Information Science." *Journal of the American Society for Information Science* 26 (1975): 207-213.

Salton, G. "On the Development of Information Science." *Journal of the American Society for Information Science* 24 (1973): 218-220.

Saracevic, Tefko. "Five Years, Five Volumes and 2345 Pages of the *Annual Review of Information Science and Technology.*" *Information Storage and Retrieval* 7 (1971): 127-139.

Saracevic, Tefko, and Lawrence J. Perk. "Ascertaining Activities in a Subject Area Through Bibliometric Analysis: Application to *Library Literature.*" *Journal of the American Society for Information Science* 24 (1973): 120-134.

Schorr, Alan E. "Lotka's Law and Library Science." *RQ* 14 (1974): 32-33.

Velke, Lissa. "The Use of Citation Patterns in the Identification of 'Research Front' Authors and 'Classic Papers'." *Proceedings of the American Society for Information Science* 7 (1970): 49-51.

Voos, Henry. "Lotka and Information Science." *Journal of the American Society for Information Science* 25 (1974): 270-272.

Windsor, Donald A., and Diane M. Windsor. "Citation of the Literature by Information Scientists in Their Own Publications." *Journal of the American Society for Information Science* 24 (1973): 377-381.

Political Science

Baum, William C. et al. "American Political Science Before the Mirror: What Our Journals Reveal About the Profession." *Journal of Politics* 38 (1976): 895-917.

Finnegan, Richard B. "Patterns of Influence in International Relations Research." *Journal of International and Comparative Studies* 3 (1970): 84-106.

Palais, Elliot S. "Significance of Subject Dispersion for the Indexing of Political Science Journals." *Journal of Academic Librarianship* 2 (1976): 72-76.

Robinson, William Chandler. "Subject Dispersion in Political Science. An Analysis of References Appearing in the Journal Literature: 1910-1960." Ph.D. dissertation, University of Illinois at Urbana-Champaign, 1973.

Rosenau, James N. et al. "Of Syllabi, Texts, Students, and Scholarship in International Relations: Some Data and Interpretations on the State of a Burgeoning Field, Review Article." *World Politics* 29 (1977): 263-340.

Russett, Bruce M. "Methodological and Theoretical Schools in International Relations." *A Design for International Relations Research*. Philadelphia, Pa.: American Society of Political and Social Science, 1970, 87-105.

Stewart, June. "The Literature of Politics: A Citation Analysis." *International Library Review* 2 (1970): 329-353.

Psychology

Borstelmann, L.J. "Classics in Developmental Psychology: Historical Persons and Studies of Common Textbook Reference." *Developmental Psychology* 10 (1974): 661-664.

Russ, Allan R. "Evaluation of Canadian Psychology Departments Based Upon Citations and Publication Counts." *Canadian Psychological Review* 17 (1976): 143-150.

Buss, Allan R., and John R. McDermott. "Ratings of Psychology Journals Compared to Objective Measures of Journal Impact." *American Psychologist* 31.(1976): 675-678.

Cason, Hulsey, and Marcella Lubotsky. "The Influence and Dependence of Psychological Journals on Each Other." *Psychological Bulletin* 38 (1936): 95-103.

Clark, Kenneth E. *America's Psychologists: A Survey of a Growing Profession.* Washington, D.C.: American Psychological Association, 1957.

Daniel, Robert S. "Psychology." *Library Trends* 15 (1967): 670-684.

Edwards, Allan J., Robert J. Kibler, and David T. Miles. *Journal by Subject Survey of Articles Published in Psychology From 1961 Through 1965.* Carbondale, Ill.: Education Research Bureau, Southern Illinois University, 1967.

Garfield, E. "Journal Citation Studies: Psychology and Behavior Journals." *Current Contents* 9 (1975): 5-9.

Garvey, William D., and Belver C. Griffith. "The Structure, Objectives, and Findings of a Study of Scientific Information Exchange in Psychology." *American Documentation* 5 (1964): 258-267.

Higbee, Kenneth L. "Psychological Classics: Publications That Have Made Lasting and Significant Contributions." *American Psychologist* 30 (1975): 182-184.

_____. "Where Are the Psychological Classics in Books of Readings?" *Journal of Psychology* 96 (1977): 73-80.

L'Abate, L. "Frequency of Citation in Child Psychology Literature." *Child Development* 40 (1969): 87-92.

Lawler, Edward E. "Psychology of the Scientist: IX. Age and Authorship of Citations in Selected Psychological Journals." *Psychological Reports* 13 (1963): 537.

Lawler, Edward E., and Carol O. Lawler. "Who Cites Whom in Psychology?"

Journal of General Psychology 73 (1965): 31-36.

Louttit, C.M. "The Use of Foreign Languages by Psychologists." *American Journal of Psychology* 68 (1955): 484-486.

_____. "The Use of Foreign Languages by Psychologists, Chemists, and Physicists." *American Journal of Psychology* 70 (1957): 314-316.

McCollom, Ivan N. "Psychology Classics: Older Journal Articles Frequently Cited Today." *American Psychologist* 28 (1973): 363-365.

Mace, Kenneth C., and Harold D. Warner. "Ratings of Psychological Journals." *American Psychologist* 28 (1973): 184-186.

Myers, C. Roger. "Journal Citations and Scientific Eminence in Contemporary Psychology." *American Psychologist* 25 (1970): 1041-1048.

Platz, Arthur, and Edwin Blakelock. "Productivity of American Psychologists: Quantity Versus Quality." *American Psychologist* 15 (1960): 310-312.

Porter, Alan L. "Use Lists With Caution." *American Psychologist* 31 (1976): 674-675.

Porter, Alan L., and Dael Wolfle. "Utility of the Doctoral Dissertation." *American Psychologist* 30 (1975): 1054-1961.

Ruja, Harry. "Productive Psychologists." *American Psychologist* 11 (1956): 148-149.

Shulman, Arthur D., and Irwin Silverman. "Profile of Social Psychology: A Preliminary Application of 'Reference Analysis'." *Journal of the History of the Behavioral Science* 8 (1972): 232-236.

Wall, Celia. "Use Frequency of Psychology Journals." *Tennessee Librarian* 29 (1977): 33-34.

White, Murray J., and K. Geoffrey White. "Citation Analysis of Psychology Journals." *American Psychologist* 32 (1977): 301-305.

Xhignesse, Louis, and Charles E. Osgood. "Bibliographic Citation Characteristics of the Psychological Journal Network in 1950 and 1960." *American Psychologist* 18 (1967): 778-791.

Sociology

Bahr, Howard M., Theodore J. Johnson, and M. Ray Seitz. "Influential Scholars and Works in the Sociology of Race, and Minority Relations, 1944-1968." *The American Sociologist* 6 (1971): 296-298.

Baughman, James C. "A Structural Analysis of the Literature of Sociology." *Library Quarterly* 44 (1974): 293-308.

_____. "Some of the Best in Sociology: A Bibliographic Checklist Created by the Unusual Technique of Citation Counting." *Library Journal* 98 (1973): 2977-2979.

Broadus, Robert N. "A Citation Study for Sociology." *American Sociologist* 2 (1967): 19-20.

———. "An Analysis of Literature Cited in the *American Sociological Review*." *American Sociological Review* 17 (1952): 355-356.

Brown, Julia S., and Brian G. Gilmartin. "Sociology Today: Lacunae, Emphases and Surfeits." *American Sociologist* 4 (1969): 283-291.

Chubin, Daryl. "On the Use of the Science Citation Index in Sociology." *American Sociologist* 8 (1973): 187-191.

Fliegel, Frederick C. "Reference Patterns in Rural Sociology Compared With the Major Sociological Journals, 1965-66." *Rural Sociology* 34 (1969): 402-407.

Guha, Martin. "Literature Use by European Sociologists." *International Library Review* 3 (1971): 445-452.

Lightfield, E. Timothy. "Output and Recognition of Sociologists." *American Sociologist* 6 (1971): 128-133.

Lin, Nan. "Stratification of the Formal Communication System in American Sociology." *American Sociologist* 9 (1974): 199-206.

Lin, Nan, and Carnot E. Nelson. "Bibliographic Reference Patterns in Core Sociological Journals 1965-1966." *American Sociologist* 4 (1969): 47-50.

Line, Maurice B., and Brenda Carter. "Changes in the Use of Sociological Articles With Time: A Comparison of Diachronous and Synchronous Data." *BLL Review* 2 (1974): 124-129.

MacRae, Duncan. "Growth and Decay Curves in Scientific Citations." *American Sociological Review* 34 (1969): 631-635.

Oromaner, Mark J. "Career Contingencies and the Fate of Sociological Research." *Social Science Information* 12 (1973b): 97-111.

———. "The Career of Sociological Literature: A Diachronous Study." *Social Studies of Science* 7 (1977): 126-132.

———. "Comparison of Influentials in Contemporary American and British Sociology: A Study in the Internationalization of Sociology." *British Journal of Sociology* 21 (1970): 324-332.

———. "The Most Cited Sociologists: An Analysis of Introductory Text Citations." *American Sociologist* 3 (1968): 124-126.

———. "Productivity and Recognition of Sociology Departments." *Sociological Focus* 6 (1973a): 83-89.

———. "The Structure of Influence in Contemporary Academic Sociology." *American Sociologist* 7 (1972): 11-13.

Rao, I.K. Ravichandra. "Growth of Periodicals and Obsolescence of Articles in Periodicals: A Case Study in Sociology." *Library Science Slant Documentation* 11 (1974): 92-96.

Satariano, William A. "Journal Use in Sociology: Citation Analysis Versus

Readership Patterns." *Library Quarterly* 48 (1978): 293-300.

Seetharama, S. "Documents on Survey Analysis." *Library Science Slant Documentation* 9 (1972): 384-395.

APPENDIX: CITATION STUDIES

Researcher	Date	Source Material	References/Citations	Dates of Data	Purposes of Study	Subject/Nationality
Social Science						
Guttsman	1966	8 journals	116 articles 1,818 citations	1962-65 (not inclusive)	Literature characteristics	Social sciences/British
Parker et al.	1967	17 journals	500 citations per journal	1950, 1955 1960, 1965	Literature characteristics	Behavioral sciences (communications)/U.S.
Earle Vickery	1969	BNB Guide to Current British Periodicals	65,340	1965	Literature characteristics	Social science, Science and Technology/British
DISISS, No. 4	1972	BNB, ABPR Bibliographie de la France Deutsche Bibliographie	15,000	1951, 1961	Monograph literature characteristics	Social sciences/ British, U.S., French, German
DISISS, No. 5	1972	17 journals	4,918 27,000	1950, 1960 1970	Periodical literature characteristics/ delineate subfields	Social sciences/ World
DISISS, No. 6	1973	SCI 15 "new" topics		1969-70	Journal networks	Short term memory/ Deviant behavior/ "new" social science topics
Business and Management						
Sarle[1]	1958					
Creelman Wallen	1958	Operations Research Management Science	131 50		Influence of psychology	Operations research
Intrama[2]	1968	5 journals	1,542	1964-66	Characteristics of literature	Public administration

Researcher	Date	Source Material	References/Citations	Dates of Data	Purposes of Study	Subject/Nationality
Business and Management (continued)						
House Miner	1969	6 textbooks		1962-68	Cross-citation patterns	Management science, Behavioral science
Hamelman Mazze	1972 a, b 1973 a, b	37-40 journals		1966-70	Cross-citation patterns	Business, Economics, Management Science, Marketing
Back	1974	Operations Research Management Science	900	1969-70 1954-70	Exchange of information	Management science, Operations research
Durand	1974	8 journals		1955-70	Influence of Behavioral Sciences	Behavioral sciences, Management
McRae	1974	17 journals	5,000	1968-69	Information flow	Accounting
Cox et al.	1976	38 journals		1966-70	Interrelationships within subfields	Business Administration, Economics
Popovich	1978	31 dissertations	2,805	1953-74	Characteristics of literature	Business Management, Economics
Economics[3]						
Seagly	1954					
Coats	1971	5 journals, A.E.A. Readings Surveys	1,691	1886-1959 1942-68 1948, 1952 1965, 1966	Characteristics of literature	Economics
Roberts	1971	30 journals	468	1968-69	Secondary information services	Economics/British
Billings et al.	1972	3 journals		1969-71	"Quality" journal rankings	Economics

334

	Year	Source	Number	Dates	Topic	Field
Fletcher	1972	9 journals	10,533	1950, 1960 1968	Characteristics of literature	Economics/British
Nakamura[4]	1972	1 journal	5,107	1950-71	Characteristics of literature	"Modern" economics
Lovell	1973	4 journals	960	1965	Characteristics of literature	Economics
Bush et al.	1974	14 journals		1966-70	"Quality" journal index	Economics
Eagly	1975	18 journals		1961-64 1970-71	Communications network	Economics
McDonough[5]	1975				"Quality" journal rankings	Economics
Stigler Friedland	1975	Ph.D. economists' publications	5,581	1950-68	Influence of scholars	Microeconomics Macroeconomics
Quandt	1976	8 journals		1890-1970	Characteristics of literature	Economics
Education						
Broadus	1965	Encyclopedia of Educational Research	1,525	1950 1960	Characteristics of literature	Educational Research
Narin Garside	1972	15 journals	14,148	1965-69	Structure of literature	General Education Special Education Psychology
Barron Narin	1972	140 journals		1965-69	Structure of literature	Education Psychology
Chambers Healey	1973	168 Master's theses	7,027	1959-68	Periodical value/use	Education/English
Mochida	1976	14 journals	489	1975	Subjects/materials in collection	Education

Library and Information Science

Researcher	Date	Source Material	References/Citations	Dates of Data	Purposes of Study	Subject/Nationality
Hart[6]	1950	6 periodicals, 10 books		1945-49	Core journals	Library
Barnard[7]	1957	7 periodicals	1,816	1955-56	Characteristics of literature	Library science
Cuadra	1964	6 texts 4 bibliographies	911 (322)	1961-63 1957-61	Key contributions	Information science
Gilchrist	1966	5 abstract services 9 journals	762 528	1964 1960-64	Scope of secondary services Core, languages	Documentation/international
Sumner[8]	1967	1 journal	1,543	1950-61	Characteristics of literature	Library science/U.S./international
Foster	1968	5 journals	5,443	1963-65	Core journals	Library education/U.S., non-U.S.
Little[9]	1968	50 items	12,034			
Fenichel	1969	ARIST	962 3,723	1967	Communication channels	Information science
Velke	1970	Research reports (1967)	515	1958-67	"Research front" authors, papers	Information science
Gilchrist Presanis	1971	LISA	2,567 2,858	1969 1970	Scope of abstracting services	Library and information science
Lehnus	1971	1 journal (JEL) 1 indexing service (LL)	235 305	1960-70	Key authors, papers	Education of librarians
Saracevic	1971	ARIST	1,331	1969	Role of annual review	Information science and technology
Donahue	1972	88 journals	160	1958-67	Bradford distribution "Research front"	Information science

336

Author	Year	Source	Number	Dates	Topic	Field
Penner	1972	20 journals	4,859 (310)	1968-69	"test" libraries	Library school libraries
Burwasser[10]	1973					
Dansey	1973	5 abstract services	987	1971	Scope of secondary services, key journals	Information science/British
Salton	1973	Index to ARIST IBS	12,000 5,700	1966-72 1960-71	Current state and development	Information science
Saracevic Perk	1973	Index service (LL)	4,418	1967	Characteristics of literature	Librarianship
Windsor Windsor	1973	2 abstract services	6,806 4,409	1966-71 1971	Scholarly status of the field	Information science and pharmacy
Schorr	1974	Library Quarterly College & Research Libraries	631	1963-72	Lotka's Law	Library science
Voos	1974	ISA	11,005	1966-70	Lotka's Law	Information science
Brace	1975	202 dissertations	20,298	1961-70	Significant authors Core literature	Library and information science
Pope	1975	1 bibliography	14,290	1964-70	Bradford's Law Core literature	Information science
LaBorie Halperin	1976	186 dissertations	43,500	1969-72	Characteristics of literature	Library science
Galloway	1977	LL		1965-74	Most productive journals, authors	Library and information science
Kuch	1977	ARIST bibliographies	1,263	1965-75	Key journals	Library automation

Researcher	Date	Source Material	References/Citations	Dates of Data	Purposes of Study	Subject/Nationality
Political Science						
Martin[11]	1952	46 books	3,000	1948 1949	Characteristics of literature	Political topics
Finnegan	1970	3 journals			Patterns of "influence"	International relations
Russett	1970	68 scholars		1966-68	Patterns of communication	International relations
Stewart	1970	1 textbook 1 American journal 2 British journals	1,700 895 617	1963 1963-66 1958-66	Characteristics of literature	Politics/U.S./British
Robinson[12]	1973	14 journals	sampling	1910-60	Subject dispersion	Political science
Baum et al.	1976	5 journals		1960-75	Communication research patterns	Political science
Palais	1976	25 journals 10 secondary services	398 articles	1968, 1970 1968-72	Subject dispersion	Political science
Rosenau et al.[13]	1977	178 syllabi from 106 institutions	2,038	1973	Characteristics of field	International relations
Psychology						
Cason Lubotsky	1938	28 journals	436	1933	Cross-reference patterns	Subfields of Psychology
Louttit	1955	8 journals	1,874	1952	Language characteristics	Psychology
Ruja	1956	3 APA journals		1949-52	Most productive people, most cited publications	Psychology

Author	Year	Source	Number	Period covered	Characteristic	Field
Clark	1957	APA members, PA	1,874	1930-51	"Eminent" people	Psychologists
Louttit	1957	6 journals	2,000	1952	Language characteristics	Psychology, Chemistry, Physics/International
Platz Blakelock	1960	Clark (and others) data			Most productive people	Psychologists
APA Studies[14] (Garvey Griffith, 1964)	1963	1) 5 vol. Annual Review, PA 2) 25 journals		1956-60 1957-62 1960	Coverage of secondary publications Journal networks	Psychology
Lawler	1963	6 journals	3,746	1958	Citation characteristics	Psychology
Lawler	1965	3 "hard" journals 3 "soft" journals	2,873 2,737	1958 1958	Characteristics literature Most cited people	Subfields of Psychology
Daniel	1967	PA 20 "core" journals	7,381	1950 1965	Scatter, coverage of secondary publications	Psychology
Zhignesse Osgood	1967	21 journals	4,046 6,836	1950 1960	Characteristics of literature	Psychology, Science, Sociology
Edwards et al.[15]	1969	PA		1961-65	Journal networks	Subfields of Psychology
L'Abate	1969	12 textbooks			Classic papers, most cited people	Child Development
Myers	1970	14 journals	143,260	1962-67	Eminent people	Psychology
Shulman Silverman	1972	1 journal	7,086	1965-67	Characteristics of literature	Social Psychology
Mace Warner[16]	1973	PA		1971	"Prominent" journals	Psychology

Researcher	Date	Source Material	References/Citations	Dates of Data	Purposes of Study	Subject/Nationality
Psychology (continued)						
McCollom	1973	18 textbooks	28 items	before 1932	"Classic" papers	Psychology
Borstelmann	1974	14 textbooks		before 1940	"Classic" journal articles, books, people	Developmental Psychology
Garfield	1975	SCI	77 journals	1969	Core journals	Psychology, Behavioral Science
Higbee	1975	8 textbooks	5,169 before 1970	1971-73	"Classic" books and articles	Psychology
Porter Wolfe	1975	Publications of psychologists, SCI	272 people (Ph.D.s in 1963-64) 1,354 articles	1964	Citation characteristics	Psychology
Buss McDermott	1976 a	3 journals		1973-75	"Best" journals	Psychology
Buss	1976 b	32 departments		1973-75	"Scholarly" departments	Psychology
Porter	1976	"Other" data 77 journals		1969	"Best" journals	Psychology
Higbee	1977	15 "readings" books	478 articles (through 1969)	1971-73	Availability of "classics" in "readings" books	Psychology
Wall	1977	1 journal (AP)	1,705	1973	Periodical use frequency	Psychology
White White	1977	SSCI (1974) 57 journals	993	1972-73	"Important" journals	Psychology

Sociology

	Year	Source	Sample	Period	Topic	Field
Meier[17]	1951	6 journals	2,993	1947-48		
Quinn[18]	1951	U.S.Quarterly Booklist	3,081	1948-49		
Broadus	1952	A.S.R.	1,016	1950	Characteristics of literature, "best" writers	Sociology
Broadus	1967	A.S.R.	1,448	1965	Characteristics of literature, "best" writers	Sociology
Oromaner	1968	10 textbooks	23 authors	1963-67	"Most cited" authors	Sociology
Brown Gilmartin	1969				Journal characteristics	Sociology
Fliegel	1969	Rural Sociology			Journal characteristics	Rural sociology
Lin Nelson	1969	4 journals	5,000+	1965-66	Journal characteristics	Sociology (3) Physical Science(1)
MacRae[19]	1969	2 journals	5,000+	1965 1957	Age distributions	Sociology, Natural science, Biomedicine
Oromaner	1970	2 journals		1958-62 1967-68	"Most influential writers"	Sociology/British and U.S.
Bahr et al.	1971	10 journals	4,805	1944-68	"Key" authors/papers	Race and minority relations
Guha	1971	6 journals	sampling	1967-69	Journal characteristics	Sociology/International
Lightfield	1971	3 journals 200 sociologists		1953-68	Productivity and recognition	Sociology/international

Researcher	Date	Source Material	References/Citations	Dates of Data	Purposes of Study	Subject/Nationality
Sociology (continued)						
Oromaner	1972	2 journals	39 articles / 47 articles	1969-70 / 1970	"Influential" writers	Academic sociology
Seetharama	1972	Bibliography	905 documents	1926-69	Characteristics of literature	Survey analysis
Baughman	1973	SSHI	11,130	1970-71	"Best" writings	Sociology
Chubin	1973	234 sociologists		1925-	"Collaboration" effects	Academic sociology
Oromaner	1973 a	42 departments / 2 journals	86 articles	1969-70	Quality/quantity/ prestige rankings	Sociology
Oromaner	1973 b	3 journals	258	1961-70	Citation patterns/ career patterns	Sociology
Baughman	1974	SSHI	11,100	1970-71	Characteristics of literature	Sociology
Lin	1974	4 journals	713	1969	Journal stratification (cross-citations)	Sociology
Line Carter	1974	3 journals		1960-70	Synchronous/ diachronous studies	Sociology
Rao	1974	1 journal		1910-73	Growth/ obsolescence	Sociology, Social Service and Welfare, Population
Oromaner	1977	3 journals	642	1960 / 1961-70	Synchronous/ diachronous studies	Sociology
Satariano	1978	811 sociologists journals		1970-71	Citation patterns/ readership patterns	Sociology

NOTES AND REFERENCES FOR
APPENDIX: CITATION STUDIES

1. Rodney G. Sarle, "Characteristics of the Literature Used by Authors of Journal Articles in Business Administration," (Master's thesis, University of North Carolina, 1958).

2. Abstract only.

3. Richard S. Seagly, "Characteristics of Literature Cited in Periodicals in the Field of Economics," (Master's thesis, Indiana University, 1954).

4. Hiroo Nakamura, "Citation Counting in *The Economic Studies Quarterly*," (in Japanese) Tosh-Kai 24 (1972): 125-129.

5. Not a citation study, but determines degree of association between five different rankings of journals, two by previous citation studies.

6. Peter W. Hart, "Periodicals for Professional Librarianship," (Master's dissertation, Catholic University, Graduate School of Arts and Sciences, Washington, D.C., 1950).

7. Walter M. Barnard, "Characteristics of the Literature Used by American Authors of Journal Articles in Library Science," (Master's thesis, University of North Carolina, Chapel Hill, 1957).

8. Frances B. Sumner, "Some Characteristics of the Literature Used by Authors of Articles in *LIBRI: International Library Science Review*, 1950-1961," (Master's thesis, Kent State University Graduate School, Kent, Ohio, 1967).

9. Thompson M. Little, "Use and Users of Library Literature," (Preprint of a paper presented at the Conference on the Bibliographic Control of Library Science Literature, State University of New York at Albany, April 19-20, 1968).

10. S.M. Burwasser, "Some Characteristics of Library Science Periodicals: An investigation of Authorship, Subject Matter, and Citations," (M.L.S. Research Report, University of Toronto, 1973).

11. Gordon P. Martin, "Characteristics of the Literature Used by Authors of Books on Political Topics," (Master's thesis, University of Chicago, Graduate Library School, 1952).

12. Abstract only.

13. More a subject content analysis than a citation study.

14. As reported in review articles.

15. Not available.

16. Citation data not presented.

17. Elizabeth L. Meier, "Characteristics of the Literature Used by Contributions of American Sociological Journals," (Master's dissertation, University of Chicago, 1951).

18. Edward W. Quinn, "Characteristics of the Literature Used by Authors of Books in the Field of Sociology," (Master's dissertation, University of Chicago, 1951).

19. Data collected by others.

Citation Studies in Science and Technology

Kris Subramanyam

INTRODUCTION

The scholarly literature of science and technology is a validated, public record of the progress of science and, like science itself, is incremental in nature. This means that the scholarly scientific literature is always based on literature published earlier. Acknowledgment of earlier contributions by making references to earlier writings is an established practice in written communication in science. Melvin Weinstock has listed 15 reasons why authors of scientific papers are likely to cite earlier publications (1). These are: 1) paying homage to pioneers; 2) giving credit for related work; 3) identifying methodology, equipment, etc.; 4) providing background reading; 5) correcting one's own work; 6) correcting the work of others; 7) criticizing previous work; 8) substantiating claims; 9) alerting researchers to forthcoming work; 10) providing leads to poorly disseminated, poorly indexed, or uncited work; 11) authenticating data and classes of fact—physical constants, etc.; 12) identifying original publications in which an idea or concept was discussed; 13) identifying the original publication describing an eponymic concept or term as, e.g., Hodgkin's Disease, Pareto's Law, Friedel-Crafts Reaction; 14) disclaiming work or ideas of others; and 15) disputing priority claims of others.

In view of this established "reference tradition" in scientific and technical communication, bibliographic references in the scholarly literature of science and technology may be considered as "unobtrusive measures" of document use (2). However, such a consideration is subject to certain assumptions and limitations, and these will be discussed in a later section.

The terms *citation* and *reference* are often used interchangeably, but there is a subtle and important difference between their connotations. A source document (or *citing* document) has *references* (or footnotes), usually listed at the end of the document, and appropriately linked to the relevant portions of the text. Thus each *reference* identifies a bibliographic entity cited in the source document. The term *citation* is used when one wishes to discuss the references made to a cited document in one or more citing documents. Thus, the description of a bibliographic entity may be thought of either as a *reference* (from the point of view of the citing document), or as a *citation* (from the point of view of the cited document). To clarify this distinction, let us consider the following set of references.

The History of the Royal Society of London, for the Improvement of Natural Knowledge, by Thomas Sprat (London, 1667), has been cited as a *reference* in the *Role of Scientific Societies in the Seventeenth Century*, by Martha Ornstein (University of Chicago Press, 1928), and also in *Scientific Societies of the United States*, 3rd edition, by Ralph Bates (M.I.T. Press, 1965). Sprat's book may be said to have received two *citations*, one from Ornstein in 1928, and another from Bates in 1965.

This chapter will review the basic principles and historical development of citation analysis, and the possible uses of citation measures as an aid in collection development in libraries, with particular reference to the scholarly literature of science and technology. It is important to distinguish between the scholarly literature of science and technology, which embodies the progress and results of scientific research and technological development, from the popular literature of science and science fiction. The latter types of literature are not considered in this chapter.

HISTORICAL OVERVIEW

Statistical analysis of bibliographical references in literature, or *statistical bibliography*, has been used as a research method for more than 60 years. In 1917, Cole and Eales made a statistical analysis of 6,346 writings on comparative anatomy published between 1543 and 1860 in several European countries (3). The term *statistical bibliography* is said to have been first used by E. Wyndham Hulme in 1922 when he delivered two lectures as the Sanders Reader in Bibliography at the University of Cambridge (4). These lectures were subsequently published as a book titled *Statistical Bibliography in Relation to the Growth of Modern Civilization* (5). Hulme used the term *statistical bibliography* to mean "the illumination of the processes of science and technology by means of counting documents" (6).

The term *statistical bibliography* was next used by Gosnell (7) in 1944 and by Raisig (8) in 1962. In an extensive review article, Raisig defined statistical bibliography thus:

> Statistical bibliography may be defined as the assembling and interpretation of statistics relating to books and periodicals; it may be used in a variety of situations for an almost unlimited number of measurements. Within the last forty years bibliographical statistics have been collected and explained in several fields of science for these main purposes: To demonstrate historical movements, to determine the national or universal research use of books and journals, and to ascertain in many local situations the general use of books and journals (9).

In a study of the rate of obsolescence of books in college libraries, Gosnell made the assumption that "mere masses of books (or titles) may be analyzed for certain characteristics without reference to their individual titles." He further observed that "the astronomical proportions to which some of our libraries, their catalogs, and bibliographies in general are growing, must force librarians to consider collections of books as populations" (10).

According to Pritchard, the purpose of statistical bibliography was "to shed light on the process of written communication and of the nature of development of a discipline (insofar as this is displayed through written communication), by means of counting and analyzing the various facets of written communication" (11). Pritchard felt that the term *statistical bibliography* was unsatisfactory, "clumsy, not very descriptive, and can be confused with statistics itself or bibliographies on statistics." He therefore suggested the term *bibliometrics* to denote the application of mathematical and statistical methods to books and other media of communication (12).

Bibliometric measures have been used for developing ranked lists of significant primary journals in many subjects (13-20). E.J. Crane studied the effect of war on the production of chemical literature in different countries by analyzing the abstracts in *Chemical Abstracts* (21). Parker, Paisley, and Garrett used bibliographic citations as unobtrusive measures of scientific communication in the field of behavioral science (22). A number of similar studies have been reported in which bibliographic citations have been used as unobtrusive indicators to study the characteristics of subject literatures (23-26).

Bibliographic citations have also been used as unobtrusive measures in sociometric studies on the productivity of scientists, as well as for the identification of "research front authors," "technological gatekeepers," and "classic papers" (27-30). It has even been suggested that citation data could be used to predict Nobel Prize winners (31, 32). Simon, Brookes, Bottle, and others have examined the application of citation analysis for investigating problems in scholarly communication (33-35). Stevens has reviewed the results of several bibliometric studies reported up to 1951 as a possible basis for policy formulation for the development of journal collections in libraries (36). Discussion in this chapter will focus on the application of citation-based measures for collection development in libraries.

BASIC PRINCIPLES OF CITATION ANALYSIS

Empirical bibliometric studies have repeatedly shown that in a scientific subject, a relatively small number of "core" primary journals contain a substantial proportion of the journal literature bearing on that subject, and the rest of the literature is scattered throughout a large number of primary journals. This pattern of concentration and dispersion of journal literature was observed and explicitly stated by S.C. Bradford in 1934 (*37*). Bradford observed that in a given scientific subject, beyond the "core" sources which accounted for a substantial proportion of the periodical literature, the remaining articles scattered in numerous other periodicals showed a definite pattern of diminishing returns; i.e., there was a progressive reduction in the "yield" of articles on the subject from journals that were more and more remotely related to the subject. "In other words, the articles of interest to a specialist must occur not only in the periodicals specializing on his subject, but also, from time to time, in other periodicals, which grow in number as the relation of their fields to that of his subject lessens and the number of articles on his subject in each periodical diminishes" (*38*). Bradford studied the periodical literature in the fields of lubrication and applied geophysics, and stated his law of scattering of scientific literature as follows (*39*):

> If the scientific journals are arranged in order of decreasing productivity of articles on a given subject, they may be divided into a nucleus of periodicals more particularly devoted to the subject and several groups or zones containing the same number of articles as the nucleus, when the numbers of periodicals in the nucleus and the succeeding zones will be as $1 : n : n^2$.

Bradford also plotted graphs of the cumulative number of source items (R) versus the logarithm of the cumulative number of journals (log n). The resulting graph was similar to the graph shown in Figure 1. Such a graph is sometimes called a "Bradford Bibliograph." Bradford's law of scattering has been interpreted and restated by many subsequent writers including Vickery, Brookes, Cole, Kendall, Fairthorne, Leimkuhler, Naranan, Goffman and Warren, Wilkinson, and Praunlich and Kroll (*40-51*). Vickery was the first to notice an

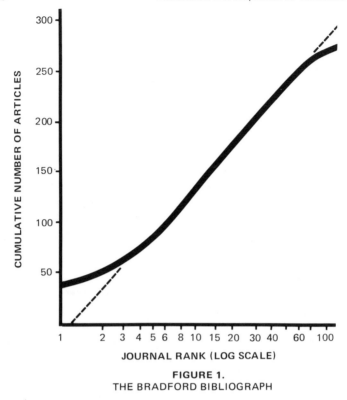

FIGURE 1.
THE BRADFORD BIBLIOGRAPH

ambiguity between Bradford's verbal and graphical formulations of his law of scattering. Vickery also showed that Bradford's law of scattering was applicable to any number of zones of equal yield, and not just for high-, medium-, and low-yielding zones as Bradford had proposed (52). Brookes derived the following expression for the "exact Bradford distribution function" (53):

$$R(n) = k \log n$$

where $R(n)$ is the cumulative total of relevant papers found in the first n journals when the journals are ranked in the order of decreasing productivity.

A number of subsequent studies have confirmed the Bradford distribution of journal literature in diverse subject areas. In 1958,

Kendall analyzed a bibliography on operations research and found that out of 1,763 references, 611 (or roughly one-third of the references) came from 5 journals. Fifty percent of the references occurred in 18 journals, and 75% in 67 journals. The remaining 25% of the references were scattered in 203 journals (54).

In a statistical sample study of the scientific and technical journals at the National Lending Library for Science and Technology (now the British Library Lending Division), Vickery found that 52% of the articles occurred in 74 journals or less than 7% of the titles sampled; 92% of the articles came from 370 titles or one-third of the sample. On the basis of this study, it was estimated that 90% of scientific and technical articles appear in about 8,000 journals. The National Lending Library had some 26,000 journal titles in 1965 when this study was made (55).

Frick and Ginski found that of the 5,860 papers published in the fiscal year 1967 by the grantees of the National Heart Institute, one-third appeared in 13 specialized cardiovascular journals (56). In a study of the frequency of citation in biomedical secondary journals, Windsor found that 22% of the references occurred in two primary journals, 35% in 5 journals, 52% in 17 journals, and 79% in 75 journals. The remaining 25% of the references came from 118 journals (57).

In 1973 Sen Gupta developed a ranked list of biochemical journals on the basis of citations in the *Annual Review of Biochemistry* to update a similar list made in 1938 by Henkle. It was found that 73% of the citations came from 18 core journals in biochemistry; the remaining 27% of the citations were scattered in 515 journals (58).

The pattern of dispersion observed by Bradford has been shown to be consistently valid for fairly large samples in a number of subjects including astronomy, geodesy, information science, marine biology, mast cells and schistosomiasis, petroleum, transplantation immunology, and agriculture (59-69).

Statistical patterns similar to Bradford's law of scattering have been observed in all the important phases of generation, recording, dissemination, and utilization of recorded knowledge. Lotka's law of scientific productivity, and Zipf's law in linguistics are other examples of such statistical regularities (70). Fairthorne has suggested that such empirically observable statistical relationships or "laws of scattering" are simply variant manifestations of a more general "empirical hyperbolic distribution" in which the product of fixed powers of the variables involved is a constant (71). The general equation for such distribution is:

$$x^n \bullet y = k$$

where x and y are the interacting variables; the values of the exponent n and the constant k depend on the variables involved and the nature of their interrelationship. Some specific variants of this general statistical relationship may be observed in situations in which a large number of independent *sources* (e.g., journals) contribute *items* (e.g., articles) randomly in a given field of activity. Other examples of *sources* and *items* which display a hyperbolic relationship are: (a) all book publishers in a country, and the number of books published by each of them in a given period of time; (b) all periodicals indexed in an indexing system such as MEDLARS, and the number of references indexed from each periodical; and (c) the number of books acquired by a library, and the number of times each book is borrowed by users (72). Naranan and, more recently, Derek Price have also attempted to view Bradford's law as the manifestation of a fundamental mathematical regularity (73-75). The effect of such generalized theories on the usefulness of Bradford's law is not yet clear.

METHODS OF CITATION ANALYSIS

The basic method of citation analysis consists of counting the number of times a document is cited in footnote references or bibliographies appended to journal articles, books, reviews, or in secondary journals (i.e., abstracting or indexing services). When such citation data are collected for a number of cited documents, the next step is to arrange the cited documents in the decreasing order of frequency of citation. If one were developing a core list of primary journals based on their frequency of citation in published articles in journals, then, the journal cited the most number of times would be ranked first on the core list, the journal receiving the next highest number of citations would be ranked second, and so on. The journal receiving the lowest number of citations would be the last item on the list. An additional column indicating the cumulative total of citations, R(n), may also be added to the core list, and a Bradford Bibliograph (as shown in Figure 1) may be obtained by plotting R(n) against the logarithm of the number of journals, n.

A core list of primary journals in computer science is shown in Table 1. The citation frequency for primary journals in this list was determined by adding (a) the number of source items reviewed from the journals in *Computing Reviews* during the years 1970 and 1971, and (b) the number of times the journals were cited in articles in the *IEEE Transactions on Computers* during the same years (76). Journals receiving fewer than 10 citations during the two years are not included in this list. The last column in Table 1 shows the cumulative percentage of citations received by the journals. The figures in this column are derived by dividing each number in the preceding column by the total number of citations (in this case 3,747), and multiplying by 100 to get a percentage.

Such a core list of journals, ranked by the frequency of citation and number of source items contributed by each title, would provide a simple tool for identifying the significant journals in a subject, if one assumes that frequency of citation of a journal is a valid measure of its significance. Scanning down the last column, one can now observe that nearly one-third of all the cited items come from the top two journals in the list, and slightly over one-half of citations are received by the top 7 journals. Similarly, the top 19 journals have received three-fourths of the total number of citations, and so on. As one goes down the list, the journals with lower ranks may be seen to have received fewer and fewer citations. When viewed from the standpoint of library management, these results indicate that while a library can cover about 80 to 85% of the material by subscribing to a relatively small number of journals, it becomes increasingly difficult to provide the last 15 to 20% of the material since these are scattered in a very large number of sources each of which contributes only one or two items.

TABLE 1.

CORE LIST OF JOURNALS IN COMPUTER SCIENCE

Rank (1)	Journal Title (2)	Number of Citations (3)	Cumulative Total Number of Citations (4)	Cumulative Percentage of Citations (5)
1	IEE Transactions on Computers	924	924	26.60
2	ACM Communications	238	1,162	33.45
3	ACM Journal	194	1,356	39.03
4	Numerische Mathematik	133	1,489	42.86
5	SIAM Journal on Numerical Analysis	106	1,595	45.91
6	Computer Journal	98	1,693	48.73
7.5	IBM Journal of Research and Development	94	1,787	51.44
7.5	IEE Transactions on Information Theory	94	1,881	54.14
9	Information and Control	92	1,973	56.79
10	IEEE Proceedings	89	2,062	59.35
11.5	Datamation	72	2,134	61.42
11.5	Simulation	72	2,206	63.50
13	BIT	66	2,272	65.40
14	Computers and Automation	63	2,335	67.21
15	Computer Bulletin	56	2,391	68.82
16	Journal of the American Society for Information Science	54	2,445	70.38
17	Bell System Technical Journal	53	2,498	71.90
18	Computing	48	2,546	73.29
19	Journal of Computer and System Science	46	2,592	74.61
20.5	Computers and Humanities	35	2,627	75.62
20.5	IEEE Transactions on Circuit Theory	35	2,662	76.63
22.5	Australian Computer Journal	33	2,695	77.58
22.5	Journal of Franklin Institute	33	2,728	78.53
24	IBM System Journal	32	2,760	79.45
25	IEEE Transaction on Audio and Electro-Acoustics	30	2,790	80.31
27	Journal of the Acoustical Society of America	26	2,816	81.06
27	Angewandte Informatik	26	2,842	81.81
27	Information Science	26	2,868	82.56
29.5	Computing Surveys	25	2,893	83.27
29.5	Journal of System Management	25	2,918	83.99
31	Information Storage and Retrieval	24	2,942	84.68
33.5	American Mathematics Monthly	23	2,965	85.35
33.5	Pattern Recognition	23	2,988	86.01

(continued)

TABLE 1 *(continued)*

Rank	Journal Title	Number of Citations	Cumulative Total Number of Citations	Cumulative Percentage of Citations
(1)	(2)	(3)	(4)	(5)
33.5	Data Processing	23	3,011	86.67
33.5	Educational Technology	23	3,034	87.33
36.55	IEEE Transactions on Systems Science and Cybernetics	22	3,056	87.97
36.5	IAG Journal	22	3,078	88.60
38	Electronics Letters	21	3,099	89.20
39	IEEE Transactions on Communications and Electronics	20	3,119	89.78
40.5	Journal of Computational Physics	18	3,137	90.29
40.5	Computer Decisions	18	3,155	90.82
42.5	Biomedical Computing	16	3,171	91.28
42.5	Computers and Biomedical Research	16	3,187	91.73
44.5	Canadian Surveyor	15	3,202	92.17
44.5	Jurimetrics	15	3,217	92.60
47	Computer Studies in Humanities and Verbal Behavior	14	3,231	93.00
47	Cybernetics	14	3,245	93.40
47	Simulation and Games	14	3,259	93.81
49.5	Mathematical Computation	13	3,272	94.18
49.5	Data Management	13	3,285	94.55
54	Annals of Mathematical Statistics	12	3,297	94.90
54	SIAM Review	12	3,309	95.25
54	Behavioral Science	12	3,321	95.59
54	Science	12	3,333	95.94
54	IEEE Computer Group News	12	3,345	96.29
54	Computing Techniques in Biochemistry	12	3,357	96.63
54	IEEE Spectrum	12	3,369	96.98
60	Management Science	11	3,380	97.29
60	Cambridge Philosophical Society Proceedings	11	3,391	97.61
60	IEE Proceedings (London)	11	3,402	97.93
60	Journal of Educational Data Processing	11	3,413	98.24
60	Machine Intelligence	11	3,424	98.56
65	SIAM Journal of Applied Mathematics	10	3,434	98.85
65	American Journal of Mathematics	10	3,444	99.13
65	Delta	10	3,454	99.42
65	Electronics	10	3,464	99.71
65	Revue Francaise d'Informatique et de Recherche Operationalle	10	3,474	100.00
	Total Number of References	3,474		

SOURCE: K. Subramanyam, "Core Journals in Computer Science." *IEEE Transactions on Professional Communication*, PC-19 (1976): 22-25.

Ranked lists of cited publications may be developed by collecting citation data from a variety of sources including primary journals, abstracting and indexing services, bibliographies, and review journals. The relative merits and disadvantages of these sources of citation data have been analyzed by Brittain and Line (77). Circulation and interlibrary loan records as well as direct observation of in-library use of materials can also be used for generating data for bibliometric analysis to assess the pattern of use of library materials and to identify frequently used materials.

ASSUMPTIONS AND LIMITATIONS

Citation and Significance
The use of citation frequency as an index of the significance of the cited document is based upon certain assumptions:
1. The subject content of the cited document is related to that of the citing document.
2. The number of times a document is cited is directly proportional to its value or intrinsic worth.
3. The primary or secondary publication used as the base for deriving citation data is representative of the entire subject field.
4. If more base publications than one are used, then all of them can be weighted equally.
5. All publications cited have actually been used by the citing author.
6. All publications used in preparation of the citing document have actually been cited.

Some of these assumptions were made explicit by Estelle Brodman in 1944 (78). More recently, Griffith and others have analyzed the basic assumptions underlying the use of citations in the study of scientific achievements and communication (79).

The frequency of citation of a journal is influenced by a number of factors such as its age, frequency of publication, number of citable source items in each issue, its coverage in secondary services, accessibility to users, language of publication, reputation of authors, and so on. A journal that has been in existence for 50 years is likely to receive more citations than one which is only 5 years old. A semi-monthly or monthly journal is likely to receive more citations than a quarterly or semi-annual journal. Factors such as exhaustive and rapid coverage of a journal in secondary services, publication of articles on controversial issues by reputed authors, and extensive reprint dissemination tend to increase the probability of citation of a journal. Other factors such as publication in a foreign language, and low accessibility because of geographical, political or other barriers may decrease the frequency with which a journal is cited.

A low frequency of citation of a journal does not necessarily reflect a low intrinsic quality of the journal. The journals most often cited by authors are likely to be those that are most readily accessible to them through personal subscription, library services, or reprint dissemination. Also, articles are sometimes cited for reasons other than their quality or relevance to the citing paper. A paper containing a factual or conceptual error published in a reputable journal is very likely to be cited many times in a flood of correspondence and short papers that usually follows in the wake of such a publication. Some classical articles such as Vannevar Bush's paper titled "As We May Think" (*Atlantic Monthly*, 1945), are likely to be cited innumerable times for "cosmetic" reasons. It is also suspected that authors may not cite all references used, or even use all references cited. As Griffith and others have pointed out, "a series of complex social, psychological, and bibliographical factors intervene between any intentions of the author to acknowledge precedent work or to recognize any form of similarity" (*80*).

Moreover, alerting services, "news" journals, technical and trade magazine, house organs, and similar publications serve primarily as current-awareness tools, and rarely contain the type of papers that are usually cited in published literature. Some examples of such current-awareness publications are: *Chemical Engineering*, *Chemical and Engineering News*, *Chemical Titles*, and *Chemical Week*. Such journals are very important, although they are not highly cited. Other types of literature such as textbooks, encyclopedias, handbooks, and other reference works, are heavily used but rarely cited. Citation analysis does not provide an effective means of identifying publications of these types so essential for developing a balanced and useful collection.

Sources of Citation Data

One may now examine the third and fourth assumptions mentioned above. As stated earlier, citation data may be derived from a variety of sources including primary and secondary journals, bibliographies, and reviews. References cited in primary journals are the most commonly used source of citation data. An advantage of this source is that data can be gathered from the *Science Citation Index* or *Journal Citation Reports*. Brittain and Line have concluded that if a large enough number of base journals are used for generating citation data, this method could yield very valuable information on literature use and key journals (*81*). Citation data derived from primary journals are also helpful in determining obsolescence patterns of the literature. However, the problems of selection of base journals and weighting of various base journals still remain. Thus far, in studies made using multiple base journals, the base journals have been given equal weight, although they were different in their scope and coverage characteristics. On the other hand, assigning relative weights to base journals tends to be arbitrary, and the effect of such weighting on the resultant ranked list of primary journals is not very clear.

Chemical Abstracts was used as the source of citations by Charles Brown for compiling a list of most frequently cited chemistry journals (*82*). More recently, Donald Hawkins developed a core list of electrochemistry journals using data obtained from an on-line search of the *Chemical Abstracts Condensates* data base (*83*). Citation data derived from indexing and abstracting services provide an overall general view of the literature of a subject and are helpful in obtaining distributions by type of publication, language, country of origin, and other similar attributes of literature. However, coverage of an item in a secondary service does not really reflect the significance of the source item indexed or abstracted, since each item is covered only once in a secondary service. The coverage of a secondary service is defined by its editorial policy, and is often subject to linguistic and geographic preferences and limitations. Also, the coverage of non-journal material such as technical reports, theses, monographs, and conference papers tends to be uneven in secondary services.

Citation data obtained from annual reviews were used by Sen Gupta for ranking primary journals in the medical sciences, biochemistry, and physiology (*84-86*). Since reviewers are likely to choose the more significant contributions for review, there is a built-in qualitative evaluation of references cited in reviews. Brittain and Line feel that reviews combine some of the advantages of both primary and secondary journals, and references in reviews are probably the best source for quality assessment of the documents reviewed. However, citation data derived from references in reviews are not completely free from the problems of inaccessibility of documents in time for the review, and the linguistic and other predilections of the reviewers.

Nearly all citation studies involve sampling techniques. Samples must be so designed as to eliminate linguistic, geographic, and other types of bias. Also, large volumes of citation data have to be collected and processed in order to obtain reliable and valid results.

RECENT DEVELOPMENTS IN CITATION ANALYSIS

Among the more recent developments in citation analysis, mention should be made of bibliographic coupling and co-citation. Bibliographic coupling, developed by Kessler, is the number of common references cited in two documents, and indicates the degree of similarity of contents of the citing papers (*87*). Two source documents containing a large number of common references are said to have a high "coupling strength," and are likely to be on the same topic The coupling strength of two source documents can be easily determined by comparing their lists of references. In a review of the theory of applications of bibliographic coupling, Bella Hass Weinberg has questioned on logical grounds the use of bibliographic coupling for automatic classification of documents (*88*). Bibliographic coupling is based on the assumption that papers citing the same references are likely to be on identical subjects. This does not seem to be always true since different citing papers may refer to different parts of the same cited paper.

The concept of co-citation was introduced by Henry Small in 1973 to generate clusters of related papers (*89*). The number of times two papers are cited together in subsequent literature determines the co-citation strength of the two cited papers. This concept has been used in studies on the structure of scientific literature by Small and Griffith and others (*90, 91*). Co-citation is a dynamic measure in that the co-citation strength of cited papers can be studied over a period of time as they continue to be cited together in subsequent literature. But a disadvantage of the co-citation technique is that it requires comprehensive citation data, preferably in machine-readable format.

In order to offset some of the limitations of citation analysis using raw citation data discussed in the preceding section, some modified measures have recently been suggested. The *impact factor* and *immediacy index* are two such measures (*92, 93*). Impact factor is the ratio of the number of times a journal is cited in a given time period to the total number of source items published in the journal during a specified period of time. Impact factor is a measure of the frequency with which the average cited article in a journal has been cited in a particular year. It offsets the effect of the age, size, and frequency of publication of a journal on the frequency of citation.

The immediacy index of a journal considers references made during the year in which the cited items were published. Thus, the 1979 immediacy index of a journal would be calculated by dividing the number of citations to items it published in 1979 by the total number of source items it published in 1979. Immediacy index is a measure of the rapidity with which the articles published in a journal are cited in subsequently published literature. It is influenced by the rapidity with which primary journals are covered in secondary services, and by the accessibility of the source articles themselves to users. There is a delay of at least six to twelve months between the publication of a given document and its use as a reference in a subsequent publication. This delay is likely to be much longer for foreign language materials. Cover-to-cover translations of foreign language journals appear with a time lag of at least six months after the publication of the original journal. Often this time lag is one year or even longer. Also, journals published weekly or monthly have a chance of being cited faster than those published less frequently. The low immediacy index likely to be received by foreign language journals, translated journals, and low-frequency journals may lead to an unjustified underestimation of the importance of such journals.

The availability of large volumes of citation data pertaining to the literature of science and technology in machine-readable form from the Institute for Scientific Information has facilitated citation analysis studies for a variety of purposes. *Journal Citation Reports* (JCR), a product of the *Science Citation Index* data base, is especially useful in identifying important journals in science. The JCR, now published annually as a part of the *Science Citation Index*, consists of lists of scientific and technical journals ranked according to various criteria including impact factor, immediacy index, total number of citations received, total number of source items published. Citation data from the JCR have been used by Hirst and Talent to identify core journals in computer science and by Cawkell to develop a core list of acoustics journals (*94, 95*).

Citation practices differ from one discipline to another, and therefore, the ranked lists of journals in the JCR should not be used to compare journals from different disciplines. For example, it would be absurd to say that the *Journal of Experimental Medicine*, which had an impact factor of 11.251 in the 1976 JCR, is a better journal than *Physical Review Letters* whose impact factor during the same year was 5.915. To overcome this problem, Hirst has suggested the use of "discipline impact factors" for determining the core journals in a discipline (*96*).

There are additional factors that have to be kept in view while using the JCR. The impact factor is an aggregate measure for the whole journal, and indicates the number of times a *journal title* is cited expressed as a fraction of the total number of citable source items contained in that journal during a given period of time. A journal may have published one or two extraordinary articles in a year, and these articles might have been cited much more frequently than the other articles in the same journal. The impact factor that such a journal would receive may result in a distorted evaluation of the journal.

Also, the coverage of journals printed in the non-Roman alphabet is admittedly uneven in the *Science Citation Index*, and this unevenness of coverage is reflected in the citation data presented in the JCR. These limitations are made clear in the introduction to the JCR, and users are urged to exercise caution in using the tool for journal evaluation.

APPLICATIONS OF CITATION ANALYSIS

Brittain and Line have categorized the various types of citation analysis and their possible applications (97). Analysis of bibliographic citations can be used in the following types of studies:
1. identification of key documents and creation of core lists of journals;
2. study of the coverage of primary journals and other material in secondary services;
3. clustering of documents according to common references and citations;
4. study of the attributes of literature including growth rate, obsolescence, citation practices (e.g., self-citation);
5. study of the structure of scientific literature according to language, country of origin, age, subject, form, authorship, or any combination of these attributes;
6. study of the historical and sociological aspects of scholarly communication in science and technology.

Almost all types of citation studies mentioned above, with the possible exception of the last type, are helpful in formulating policies for collection development and management in libraries and in library budgeting.

Serials Selection
Ranked lists of journals may be used as an aid in the development and management of journal collections. More specifically, citations studies can enable decision makers in libraries to answer the following types of questions:
1. What would be the cost of collecting all the journals relevant to a given subject?
2. What fraction of the total coverage would be available at any specified limit of cost?
3. What is the optimum distribution of journal collections as between a central reference point and satellite departmental or regional collections?

4. How can a given collection best be subdivided into collections of primary, secondary, and tertiary relevance or into stores requiring frequent, occasional, or only rare access? (98)

Citation data can be used to establish the need for expensive serials and monographic series. A couple of interesting (though fictionalized) case studies in which citation data could be used effectively to aid collection development decisions have been described by Jasper Schad and Norman Tanis (99). In one case ("It's Not As Simple As You Think"), the high-powered chairman of a geology department, with only two research-oriented faculty, requests subscription to expensive geology serials in German costing over $13,000. The newly appointed science bibliographer has a hard time convincing the assistant director for collection development that these serials are rarely used, and the large investment would be wasteful. An early study of references in American geology periodicals by Gross and Woodford in 1931 had shown that foreign publications (i.e., those published outside the United States and Canada) accounted for less than a third of all references, and that one-half of these foreign references were in German (100). The study also showed that mineralogical papers contained more foreign references than the more strictly geological periodicals. For instance, in the 1929 issues of the *Journal of Geology*, all the references to foreign literature occurred in 17 of the 50 papers. Only 12% of the references in the *Journal of Geology* during 1929-1930 were to serials published abroad. A more recent study of references in geology literature by Craig has shown that 87.3% of literature cited in American geological journals was in the English language (101). Of the 400 references studied, only 6 (i.e., 1.5%) were in the German language. These results could be used effectively to counter unreasonable demands for expensive and rarely used material, especially when the serials in question are available in several other nearby libraries.

In another case ("I'll See What I Can Do"), a newly appointed science librarian in an academic library is asked to evaluate the periodical holdings in the biological sciences, and to select a few of several new journal titles recommended by faculty. The *Journal*

Citation Reports could be used as an aid in identifying highly cited journals for selection. Also, biological journals with very low impact factor, already on the subscription list, could be considered as candidates for cancellation, and the funds thus saved diverted for subscribing to those with high impact factor.

Core Collection of Books

Most of the citation studies have been based on journal citation data, presumably because in any large sample of references a very large proportion of the items are likely to be references to journal literature. For reasons discussed in an earlier section on assumptions and limitations, books and other monographic literature are not cited very heavily though they are used extensively in libraries. It would therefore be logical to use circulation data, rather than citation data, to study the use pattern of books and to identify highly used books. In an analysis of book circulation data at the University of Pittsburgh Hillman Library, the pattern of book use was found to follow the Bradford-Zipf phenomenon (*102*). Such an analysis is useful in determining the core collection of books. Book use may be maximized by obtaining additional copies and shortening the loan periods for frequently circulated books.

In a study of medical monographs, a sample of 770 monographs published by 326 publishers and listed in the National Library of Medicine's *Current Catalog* under subject headings in the cardiovascular diseases category was examined by Dennis Worthen (*103*). The distribution of monographs by publishers was found to conform to Bradford's law of scattering. Studies of this type are helpful in identifying the most prolific publishers of medical books. This information could perhaps be used in placing standing orders for medical books, or for entering into approval plans with medical publishers.

Obsolescence of Literature

Citation measures have been used by Brookes, Buckland, Line, Morse and Elston, and others to study the rate of obsolescence of the

literature of science and technology (*104-110*). Studies on obsolescence of literature have generally indicated that the amount of use
made of scholarly scientific literature reaches a peak about two years
after publication, and then gradually tapers off with time. Some
authors have suggested a decay pattern based on "half life" of
periodicals (*111-113*). In a study of references made to articles in the
first number of *Physical Review* (1960), Line found that articles that
were cited heavily during the years immediately following their
publication continued to be cited frequently during the following 12
years; those receiving fewer citations in the early years received fewer
and fewer citations as time went by (*114*). In general, it may be said
that the amount of use made of scholarly literature is an inverse
function of age, but this function is not generalizable across disciplines because of wide variations in the patterns of use of literature
and citation practices in different disciplines. Citation studies can be
used only as general predictors of future use of literature. Such
predictions will be useful in developing back runs of serials, in
strengthening collections of materials that are expected to be used
heavily, and also in weeding, binding, and similar collection management operations.

SUMMARY AND CONCLUSIONS

Citing earlier literature is an established tradition in the scholarly
communication of scientific and technical information. Bibliographic
references in published literature may be considered as an "unobtrusive measure" of scholarly communication in science and technology.
In recent years, the use of frequency of citation as a bibliometric
measure has been advocated, upheld, and questioned. A number of
citation analysis studies have been made for a wide variety of
applications ranging from selection of significant documents for
collection development purposes to sociometric studies for the
assessment of scholarly productivity. In at least one case, citation
data have been used to challenge the faculty tenure decision in a
university (*115*). The National Science Foundation has been considering the use of citation data for post-grant evaluation and for the
study of interdisciplinary interaction (*116*).

By far the largest number of citation studies have concentrated on the identification of core journals in the various scientific and technical disciplines. Citation analysis is a very useful tool in the selection of journals and other types of documents. However, two important factors have to be kept in view while interpreting the results of citations analysis for collection development purposes.

First, all citation-based measures of significance have a common limitation: the use of journals is strongly influenced by their availability. Authors of papers cite those journals that become known and available to them through personal subscription, library, or reprint dissemination. An indeterminate quantity of journal literature pertinent to their work may remain unused by authors because of linguistic, geographical, cultural or other barriers. These limitations also apply to other types of publications.

Second, the importance of a journal to an individual user or group of users is subject to change with time because of changes in user interest or in journal scope and quality. Hence, regardless of the measure of significance used, ranked lists of journals have to be revised from time to time.

Citation studies on the significance and obsolescence of scientific and technical literature are especially helpful in developing and managing collections. Like any other evaluation tool, citation frequency should not be used in isolation. "Like one scale on a nomogram, it must be used along with other scales to obtain anything useful or meaningful, particularly if the object of the evaluation is in any way qualitative" (*117*).

REFERENCES

1. Melvin Weinstock, "Citation Indexes." *Encyclopedia of Library and Information Science* 5 (1971): 16-40.
2. Edwin B. Parker, William J. Paisley, and Roger Garrett, *Bibliographic Citations as Unobtrusive Measures of Scientific Communication.* (Stanford, Calif.: Stanford University, Institute of Communications Research, 1967.)
3. F.J. Cole and Nellie B. Eales, "The History of Comparative Anatomy. Part I. A Statistical Analysis of Literature." *Science Progress*, 11 (1917): 578-596.

4. Alan Pritchard, "Statistical Bibliography or Bibliometrics?" *Journal of Documentation* 25 (1969): 348-349.

5. E. Wyndham Hulme, *Statistical Bibliography in Relation to the Growth of Modern Civilization.* (London: Grafton, 1923.)

6. Pritchard, "Statistical Bibliography of Bibliometrics?"

7. Charles F. Gosnell, Obsolescence of Books in College Libraries." *College and Research Libraries* 5 (1944): 115-125.

8. L. Miles Raisig, "Statistical Bibliography in the Health Sciences." *Bulletin of the Medical Library Association* 50 (1962): 450-461.

9. Ibid., p. 450.

10. Gosnell, "Obsolescence of Books in College Libraries," pp. 115-116.

11. Pritchard, "Statistical Bibliography or Bibliometrics?" p. 348.

12. Ibid., p. 349.

13. P.L.K. Gross and E.M. Gross, "College Libraries and Chemical Education." *Science* 66 (1927): 384-389.

14. Estelle Brodman, "Choosing Physiology Journals." *Bulletin of the Medical Library Association* 32 (1944): 479-483.

15. Charles H. Brown, *Scientific Serials: Characteristics and Lists of Most Cited Publications in Mathematics, Physics, Chemistry, Geology, Physiology, Botany, Zoology, and Entomology.* ACRL Monograph No. 16 (Chicago: Association of College and Research Libraries, 1956).

16. Richard L. Barrett and Mildred A. Barrett, "Journals Most Cited by Chemists and Chemical Engineers." *Journal of Chemical Education* 34 (1956): 35-38.

17. Ching-Chih Chen, "The Use Pattern of Physics Journals in a Large Academic Library." *Journal of the American Society for Information Science* 23 (1972): 254-270.

18. I.N. Sen Gupta, "Physiology Periodicals." *International Library Review* 6 (1974): 147-165.

19. H.H. Henkle, "Periodical Literature of Biochemistry." *Bulletin of the Medical Library Association* 27 (1938): 139-147.

20. Joseph C. Donohue, "A Bibliometric Analysis of Certain Information Science Literature." *Journal of the American Society for Information Science* 23 (1972): 313-317.

21. E.J. Crane, "The Growth of Chemical Literature: Contributions of Certain Nations and the Effects of War." *Chemical and Engineering News* 22 (1944): 1478-1481.

22. Parker, Paisley, and Garrett, *Bibliometric Citations as Unobtrusive Measures.*

23. F. McMurtray and J.M. Ginski, "Citation Patterns of the Cardiovascular

Literature." *Journal of the American Society for Information Science* 23 (1972): 172-175.

24. Tefko Saracevic and Lawrence J. Perk, "Ascertaining Activities in a Subject Area through Bibliometric Analysis." *Journal of the American Society for Information Science* 24 (1973): 120-134.

25. T.T. Thompson, "Study of the Subject Relationship Between Citation and the Core Subject Matter of the Parent Article." (Master's thesis, Drexel University, School of Library Science, 1968.)

26. Herman H. Fussler, "Characteristics of the Research Literature Used by Chemists and Physicists in the United States." *Library Quarterly* 19 (1949): 19-35; 119-143.

27. Susan Crawford, "Communication Centrality and Performance." (The Information Conscious Society. Proceedings of the American Society for Information Science, 33rd Annual Meeting, Philadelphia, October 11-15, 1970), vol. 7, pp. 45-48.

28. Lissa Velke, "The Use of Citation Patterns in the Identification of 'Research Front' Authors and 'Classic' Papers." (The Information Conscious Society. Proceedings of the American Society for Information Science, 33rd Annual Meeting, Philadelphia, October 11-15, 1970), vol. 7, pp. 49-51.

29. John M. Davis, "The Transmission of Information in Psychiatry." (The Information Conscious Society. Proceedings of the American Society for Information Science, 33rd Annual Meeting, Philadelphia, October 11-15, 1970), vol. 7, pp. 53-56.

30. Derek J. de Solla Price, "Networks of Scientific Papers." *Science* 149 (1965): 510-515.

31. Eugene Garfield, "Citation Indexing for Studying Science." *Nature* 227 (1970): 669-671.

32. Nicholas Wade, "Send Not to Know for Whom the Nobel Tolls: It's Not for Thee." *Science* 202 (1978): 295-296.

33. H.R. Simon, "Why Analyze Bibliographies?" *Library Trends* 22 (1973): 3-8.

34. B.C. Brookes, "Numerical Methods of Bibliographic Analysis." *Library Trends* 22 (1973): 18-43.

35. R.T. Bottle, "Information Obtainable from Analyses of Scientific Bibliographies." *Library Trends* 22 (1973): 60-71.

36. Rolland E. Stevens, *Characteristics of Subject Literatures*, ACRL Monograph No. 6 (Chicago: Association of College and Research Libraries, 1953).

37. S.C. Bradford, "On the Scattering of Papers on Scientific Subjects in Scientific Periodicals." *Engineering* 137 (1934): 85-86.

38. S.C. Bradford, *Documentation*, 2nd ed. (London: Crosby Lockwood, 1953), p. 148.

39. Ibid., p. 154.

40. B.C. Vickery, "Bradford's Law of Scattering." *Journal of Documentation* 4 (1948): 198-203.

41. B.C. Brookes, "The Derivation and Application of the Bradford-Zipf Distribution." *Journal of Documentation* 24 (1968): 247-265.

42. B.C. Brookes, "Bradford's Law and the Bibliography of Science." *Nature* 224 (1969): 953-956.

43. P.F. Cole, "A New Look at Reference Scattering." *Journal of Documentation* 18 (1962): 58-64.

44. M.G. Kendall, "The Bibliography of Operations Research." *Operations Research Quarterly* 11 (1960): 31-36.

45. R.A. Fairthorne, "Empirical Hyperbolic Distribution (Bradford-Zipf-Mandelbrot) for Bibliometric Description and Prediction." *Journal of Documentation* 25 (1969): 319-343.

46. F.F. Leimkuhler, "The Bradford Distribution." *Journal of Documentation* 23 (1967): 197-207.

47. S. Naranan, "Bradford's Law of Bibliography of Science: An Interpretation." *Nature* 227 (1970): 631-632.

48. S. Naranan, "Power Law Relations in Science Bibliography—A Self-Consistent Interpretation." *Journal of Documentation* 27 (1971): 83-97.

49. W. Goffman and K.S. Warren, "Dispersion of Papers Among Journals Based on a Mathematical Analysis of Two Diverse Medical Literatures." *Nature* 221 (1969): 1205-1207.

50. E.A. Wilkinson, "The Ambiguity of Bradford's Law." *Journal of Documentation* 28 (1972): 122-130.

51. Peter Praunlich and Michael Kroll, "Bradford's Distribution: A New Formulation." *Journal of the American Society for Information Science* 29 (1978): 51-55.

52. Vickery, "Bradford's Law of Scattering."

53. Brookes, "Derivation and Application of the Bradford-Zipf Distribution."

54. Kendall, "Bibliography of Operations Research."

55. B.C. Vickery, "Statistics of Scientific and Technical Articles." *Journal of Documentation* 24 (1968): 192-196.

56. B.F. Frick and J.M. Ginski, "Cardiovascular Serial Literature: Characteristics, Productive Journals, and Abstracting/Indexing Coverage." *Journal of the American Society for Information Science* 21 (1970): 338-344.

57. Donald A. Windsor, "Rational Selection of Primary Journals for a Biomedical Research Library." *Special Libraries* 64 (1973): 446-451.

58. I.N. Sen Gupta, "Recent Growth of the Literature of Biochemistry and Changes in Ranking of Periodicals." *Journal of Documentation* 29 (1973): 192-211.

59. A.J. Meadows, "The Citation Characteristics of Astronomical Literature." *Journal of Documentation* 23 (1967): 28-33.

60. Ole V. Groos, "Citation Characteristics of Astronomical Literature." *Journal of Documentation* 25 (1969): 344-347.

61. Ole V. Groos, "Relative Advantages of Articles-Cites versus Titles-Cited Frequency Counts." *American Documentation* 19 (1968): 102-103.

62. Donohue, "Information Science Literature."

63. C. Freeman, "Citation Analysis and the Literature of Marine Biology." *Australian Library Journal* 23 (1974): 67-71.

64. C. Freeman, "Bradford Bibliographs and the Literature of Marine Science." *Australian Academic and Research Libraries* 5 (1974): 65-71.

65. Goffman and Warren, "Dispersion of Papers."

66. P.F. Cole, "Reference Scattering."

67. W. Goffman and Thomas G. Morris, "Bradford's Law and Library Acquisitions." *Nature* 226 (1970): 922-923.

68. S.M. Lawani, "Periodical Literature of Tropical and Subtropical Agriculture." *UNESCO Bulletin for Libraries* 26 (1972): 88-93.

69. S.M. Lawani, "Bradford's Law and the Literature of Agriculture." *International Library Review* 5 (1973): 341-350.

70. K. Subramanyam, "Scattering, Laws of." *Encyclopedia of Library and Information Science* 26 (1978), in press.

71. Fairthorne, "Empirical Hyperbolic Distribution."

72. B.C. Brookes, "The Complete Bradford-Zipf Bibliograph." *Journal of Documentation* 25 (1969): 58-60.

73. Naranan, "Bradford's Law of Bibliography of Science."

74. Naranan, "Power Law Relations."

75. Derek J. de Solla Price, "A General Theory of Bibliometric and Other Cumulative Advantage Processes." *Journal of the American Society for Information Science* 27 (1976): 292-306.

76. K. Subramanyam, "Core Journals in Computer Science." *IEEE Transactions on Professional Communication* PC-19 (1976): 22-25.

77. J. Michael Brittain and Maurice B. Line, "Sources of Citations and References for Analysis Purposes: A Comparative Assessment." *Journal of Documentation* 29 (1973): 72-80.

78. Brodman, "Choosing Physiology Journals."

79. Belver C. Griffith, M. Carl Drott, and Henry G. Small, "On the Use of Citations in Studying Scientific Achievements and Communication." *Society for Social Studies of Science Newsletter* 2 (Summer 1977): 9-13.

80. Ibid., p. 10.

81. Brittain and Line, "Sources of Citations and References."

82. Brown, *Scientific Serials.*

83. Donald T. Hawkins, "Electrochemistry Journals." *Journal of Chemical Information and Computer Sciences* 17 (1977): 41-45.

84. I.N. Sen Gupta, "Impact of Scientific Serials on the Advancement of Medical Knowledge: An Objective Method of Analysis." *International Library Review* 4 (1972): 169-195.

85. Sen Gupta, "Recent Growth of Literature of Biochemistry."

86. Sen Gupta, "Physiology Periodicals."

87. M.M. Kessler, "Bibliographic Coupling between Scientific Papers." *American Documentation* 14 (1963): 10-25.

88. Bella Hass Weinberg, "Bibliographic Coupling: A Review." *Information Storage and Retrieval* 10 (1974): 189-196.

89. Henry G. Small, "Co-Citation in the Scientific Literature: A New Measure of Relationship Between Two Documents." *Journal of the American Society for Information Science* 24 (1973): 265-269.

90. Henry G. Small and Belver C. Griffith, "The Structure of Scientific Literatures. I. Identifying and Graphing Specialties." *Science Studies* 4 (1974): 17-40.

91. Belver C. Griffith, Henry G. Small, Judith A. Stonehill, and Sandra Dey, "The Structure of Scientific Literature. II. Toward a Macro- and Micro-Structure for Science." *Science Studies* 4 (1974): 339-365.

92. Eugene Garfield, "Citation Analysis as a Tool in Journal Evaluation." *Science* 178 (1972): 471-478.

93. K. Subramanyam, "Criteria for Journal Selection." *Special Libraries* 66 (1975): 367-371.

94. Graeme Hirst and N. Talent, "Computer Science Journals: An Iterated Citation Analysis." *IEEE Transactions on Professional Communication* PC-20 (1977): 233-238.

95. A.E. Cawkell, "Evaluating Scientific Journals with *Journal Citation Reports.* A Case Study in Acoustics." *Journal of the American Society for Information Science* 29 (1978): 41-46.

96. Graeme Hirst, "Discipline Impact Factors: A Method for Determining Core Journal Lists." *Journal of the American Society for Information Science* 29 (1978): 171-172.

97. Brittain and Line, "Sources of Citations and References."

98. Brookes, "Derivation and Application of the Bradford-Zipf Distribution."

99. Jasper G. Schad and Norman E. Tanis, *Problems in Developing Academic Library Collections.* (New York: Bowker, 1974), pp. 9-25.

100. P.L.K. Gross and A.O. Woodford, "Serial Literature Used by American Geologists." *Science* 73 (1931): 660-664.

101. J.E.G. Craig, Jr., "Characteristics of the Use of Geology Literature." *College and Research Libraries* 30 (1969): 230-236.

102. Stephen Bulick, "Book Use as a Bradford-Zipf Phenomenon." *College and Research Libraries* 39 (1978): 215-219.

103. Dennis B. Worthen, "The Application of Bradford's Law to Monographs." *Journal of Documentation* 31 (1975): 19-25.

104. B.C. Brookes, "The Growth, Utility, and Obsolescence of Scientific Periodical Literature." *Journal of Documentation* 26 (1970): 283-294.

105. Michael K. Buckland, "Are Obsolescence and Scattering Related?" *Journal of Documentation* 28 (1972): 242-246.

106. M.B. Line, "Does Physics Literature Obsolesce? A Study of Variation of Citation Frequency with Time for Individual Journal Articles in Physics." *BLL Review* 2 (1974): 84-91.

107. M.B. Line, A. Sandison, and Jean Macgregor, *Patterns of Citations to Articles Within Journals: A Preliminary Test of Scatter, Concentration, and Obsolescence*, BATH/LIB/2 (Bath University Library, 1972).

108. Philip M. Morse and Caroline A. Elston, "A Probabilistic Model for Obsolescence." *Operations Research* 17 (1969): 36-47.

109. P.F. Cole, "Journal Usage versus Age of Journal." *Journal of Documentation* 19 (1965): 1-11.

110. I.K. Ravichandra Rao, "Obsolescence and Utility Factors of Periodical Publications: A Case Study." *Library Science with a Slant to Documentation* 10 (1973): 297-307.

111. R.E. Burton and R.W. Kebler, "The 'Half-Life' of Some Scientific and Technical Literatures." *American Documentation* 11 (1960): 18-22.

112. M.B. Line, "The 'Half-Life' of Periodical Literature: Apparent and Real Obsolescence." *Journal of Documentation* 26 (1970): 46-54.

113. Duncan MacRae, "Growth and Decay Curves in Scientific Citations." *American Sociological Review* 34 (1969): 631-635.

114. Line, "Does Physics Literature Obsolesce?"

115. Nicholas Wade, "Citation Analysis: A New Tool for Science Administrators." *Science* 188 (1975): 429-432.

116. O.W. Adams, "NSF and Citation Analysis." *Science* 189 (1975): 86.

117. Eugene Garfield, "Citation Frequency as a Measure of Research Activity and Performance." *Current Contents* 5 (January 31, 1973): 5-7. Reprinted in Eugene Garfield, *Essays of an Information Scientist* (Philadelphia: I.S.I. Press, 1977), vol. 1, pp. 406-408.

Circulation Studies and Collection Development:

Problems of Methodology, Theory and Typology for Research

William E. McGrath

CONTEXT AND PURPOSE

Collection development is usually undertaken independently of any understanding of how collections have been, are, or will be used. This chapter places the problems of collection development firmly in the context of collection use.

In statements of collection development policy, we frequently encounter the phrase "to preserve, store and make available for future use." These seemingly discrete functions listed together, can easily convey the impression of mutual exclusion. To preserve implies protection for all time, from mutilation, theft, and the elements. To store implies systematic and impartial treatment of each book, whatever its quality. If preservation and storage were indeed separate and distinct functions, we could preserve without storing, and store without preserving. We could certainly preserve and store without making available for use. But we could not make available for use without preserving and storing.

Future use is rarely defined, but seems to imply distant—i.e., at least a generation or two from now, perhaps the year 2001, or when conditions of culture and knowledge exist that we cannot imagine. If librarians spend any part of precious funds for materials which may or may not be used 25 years from now, and when we have difficulty in determining which books may or may not be used today, the policy of building for the future must seriously be questioned. Either the future must be specified—e.g., "we will need this book exactly 10 years from now, for the purpose of . . ." or, the idea of undefined future must be abandoned altogether. The future is as much this afternoon as it is the day after tomorrow, six months, a year or 100 years from now.

We know that immediate past use can help us to predict immediate future use, depending upon how immediate past and immediate future are defined. To be predictable, the future must be specified as a time period, say, the next academic semester, or the next fiscal year. Conditions for the immediate future—semester or academic year—such as enrollment, faculty count, and budget, are not only foreseeable, they are controllable to some extent. It is much more difficult to determine these things 10 years ahead of time. Budgets, frequently passed on enrollment counts, should be used to fill the needs of that enrollment. If some portion of student fees or tuition is allocated for library materials, this generation of enrolled students may rightfully question a policy which ignores their library needs for the unforeseeable needs of their descendants.

Figure 1 depicts the context of collection development—i.e., in the context of use, its analysis, and circulation policy. It is seen that the existence of a collection and its users are necessary conditions for use to take place. Of course, other conditions for use may well exist. Presumably, these would emerge in the analysis of use. Analysis would provide understanding, which would enable us to predict use. Ability to predict use would then help to shape collection develop-

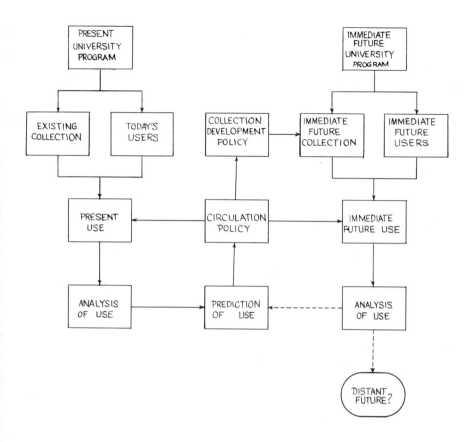

FIGURE 1.

The context of collection development.

ment policy. This policy would determine the nature of collection growth in the immediate future.

The nature of the collection being built might then help to anticipate immediate future use. This anticipation would in turn prepare us to modify circulation policy. And thus a continuing systematic monitoring takes place.

Use in the distant future, not being predictable, can have no practical affect on collection development. Most wisely then, we should collect and preserve and store for immediate future use. The distant future will require its own needs. The alternative is to preserve, store, and make available for nonuse—an acceptable and nonsensical policy. Present, or predictable future use, therefore, is the only acceptable rationale for building the collection.

Despite what classical collection builders would have us believe— that a great collection is its own argument for building a greater collection—the existing collection is neither a necessary nor sufficient condition for building a future collection. Lest this observation is taken as a lack of appreciation for great collections, let us repeat: anticipated use of the collection is the best argument for building a greater collection.

Throughout this paper, *use* generally refers to whether and how much a book or collection is used. It does not refer to the kind of use, unless so stated.

From almost the time libraries began to lend books, the most common measure of library use has been circulation. Librarians have long counted the total number of books circulated annually and even the total number within some classification, say, fiction, nonfiction, adult, children, Dewey class, or LC class. These were usually kept in gross form to monitor changes over time—most often by the year. But only within the last 10 or 15 years have circulation statistics been collected in more sophisticated ways for analytical purposes. Numerous studies have provided much insight into the behavior of collections, and only recently have these insights been systematically employed in collection development. Operations research, inferential and probabilistic techniques, simulation, modeling, systems analysis, econometrics, have all been brought to bear on fundamental and practical problems. These studies are most often performed by individuals having direct interest in or responsibilities for library management, usually teaching or research faculty, and sometimes the library manager, assistant director, circulation librarian, or in a very few libraries, the research librarian. The collection development librarian, expertly trained in book selection, with a wide knowledge of publishers and publishing, has little inclination to master complex analytical methods, though he or she may well recognize the need for them and will certainly be interested in results.

The purpose of this chapter than is to outline for the collection development librarian, and others, some of the ways in which circulation studies may be used in collection development, to discuss the goals of circulation research, and some problems of methodology, relationships, and the meaning of variables. It particularly emphasizes the need to specify precisely what is being studied or analyzed, i.e., the unit of analysis. It contains a good deal of commentary, or editorializing, on the interpretation of circulation research. It does not go into the mathematics of statistical methods. Texts abound which do this admirably. In the last section, a typology for circulation research at five levels of the unit of analysis is developed. And finally, the theoretical context of these levels is discussed.

Not discussed in this chapter is the importance of tying collection development to the college or university curriculum. Quite obviously materials reflecting specific teaching and research needs will have a bearing on circulation and circulation policy. The topic has been extensively explored in some of this author's previous work (1, 2). In the ensuing discussion, it is assumed that collection development policy includes provision for curriculum description.

REVIEWS

Many good reviews of circulation studies and collection development can be found in the literature. A few of the more recent ones will be briefly mentioned here. Throughout the chapter, reference will also be made to a few very recent or little-known studies. Otherwise, no general review will be made.

For background material the reader is referred to two books, both of which thoroughly review studies of the last decade or two on evaluating collections. Buckland (3) reviews research on circulation and collections from the point of view of availability. Lancaster (4) in a section of his book, *Measurement and Evaluation of Library Services*, reviews and summarizes work on evaluating the collection by its use. Much of the research upon which this discussion is based is documented in these two excellent texts. Both contain extensive bibliographies. Another good review by R.W. Burns (5) surveys libraries that use automated circulation in the evaluation of library performance.

It is a given these days that automated circulation systems provide unprecedented opportunity for analysis of circulation, results of which can then be fed back into collection building, inventory, and control. An excellent study of this sort, the findings of which were upsetting to some, is the Kent (6) study at the University of Pittsburgh. One finding from this study was that a very large portion of the collection is never used. This result, although wrongfully taken by some to imply criticism of book selection, does argue for critical analysis of collection building policy everywhere.

Schad (7) in a critique on allocation, including that of this author, concludes that a satisfactory method for building collections based on available kinds of data has not yet been devised. No method, he asserts, considers variability of publishing output in different subject areas.

Another study, less known to Americans perhaps, but with a thorough literature review, was done in Australia by Wainwright and Dean (8). Their review was part of a thorough and well-designed study to develop measures of adequacy for Australian college and university library collections. The review, equally thorough and well designed, organizes the world literature according to principles of collection development, quality and quantity, availability, cost, and methodology. The bibliography lists 743 references.

A second review by Burns (9) offers extensive rationale for studying use as a performance measure and for applying results of studies. He argues that circulation is the richest and easiest source of data about use and the user, and he lists a number of ways this source can be tapped for measures of user satisfaction. Burns also lists some of the "patterns beginning to emerge" from use studies. He also makes some interesting proposals about use studies, including methods for replication, creation of a computer package for processing user statistics, and creation of a center for the collection of user studies.

SOME PROBLEMS OF
METHODOLOGY IN RESEARCH

Definition

One of the most difficult aspects of research, particularly in the social sciences, is that of definition. As in many developing sciences, those in what Kuhn (*10*) calls the preparadigm state—or those in which much disagreement exists concerning theory, methodology, and what is known—the terms of circulation studies are ill-defined and carelessly applied.

Every investigator who has studied library circulation, including this writer, has at one time or another been challenged on use of the word *use*—particularly when one is counting circulation or books charged out. "How does one know the book has been used?" the question goes. Most authors sidestep the problem by inserting a qualifier, saying that either they do not really know whether a book was used, nor do they care, or that as far as they are concerned, a charge-out assumes use of some kind.

In the strictest sense, a use study would investigate the applications of information gained from reading books and periodicals. Traditionally, these uses—how to build a boat, understanding Shakespeare, laboratory exercises, and so on—have not been the concern of the librarian, except insofar as being pleased to have helped someone. Rather, the main concern, as has already been discussed, is to make books available for use.

In any case, if "charge-out" or "in-house reading," or "reserve checkout" are what the investigator means by use, then that must be so defined. The appropriate term for this genre then is *circulation study*, and the term for the reader's application of these activities would be *use study*.

A distinction is sometimes made between use study and user study. The first refers to *what* or *how*, the second to *who*. Zwei-zig (*11*) clarifies the distinction between use and users and adds a third distinction, uses. All three approaches have their place in the measurement of library use, he observes. The third approach measures the impact of the library on the community. Whether use, user, or uses, the investigator must indicate whether circulation or something else is being studied.

Careful distinction should be made between measure of collection use and measures of user satisfaction. Collection use refers to what users do. User satisfaction refers to what users feel. Feelings, of course, belong to the real of psychology. Similarly, frustration is a psychological reaction.

A study by Saracevic, Shaw, and Kantor (*12*) offers a model for measuring satisfaction and frustration using measures of acquisition and circulation. Although data was collected from individuals, the data was aggregated according to successful and unsuccessful requests. The study was therefore not about individual persons, but about aggregated requests. Accordingly, their study is more appropriately a sociological one of collection performance rather than a psychological study of frustration. Though much needs to be known about user satisfaction as well as user frustration, and though psychological research is rich in the study of these emotions, this chapter emphasizes the problems of collection performance and circulation patterns.

These problems may best be attacked at the sociological level, i.e., with aggregate data. The review and analysis of user satisfaction, i.e., the study of individual's reactions to library service, is best done at the personal or psychological level. Understanding these levels helps considerably when defining the unit of analysis (to be discussed later).

Unit of Analysis and Sampling Unit

Much of the confusion in library use studies lies not simply in failure to define but in failure to specify the unit of analysis. In a study of book use, what exactly is being studied? The user? Time unit? Loan period? The book itself? The library? The yearly total? The title? The subject? The department? These are the things that vary and thus the things that are analyzed or modeled. One famous, widely cited, study of a decade ago, which set the pattern for many later studies, drew conclusions from the results of a sophisticated statistical technique that defy interpretation. The reader does not know whether the study was done at the psychological or sociological level. Nor does one know whether the patterns discussed refer to individual titles, or to the classes of titles, such as all books on Shakespeare or all books in German. Another more recent study, hailed as one of the more important of its kind, makes the same failure. Conclusions are drawn, e.g., on the variability of periodical budgets in a large number of libraries, but the reader does not know whether the conclusions refer to price of materials, to budgets in general, or to differences in libraries.

Another well-known and much-criticized practice is the publication of national statistics on collection size (13, 14). These statistics are used to compare one library to others. The criticism always focuses on the question of just what is being counted. The difficulty can be traced to the failure to specify the sampling unit: volumes per library, titles per library, or items per library.

Mention of the unit of analysis in library research is rare. As already mentioned, Zweizig's paper on measuring library use is the only one found by this author that specifically addresses its role. The study of use, users, and uses, he points out, involves different units of analysis for each. In the study of use, the transaction is the unit of analysis. In the study of users, what a user is remains to be clarified but the user is the unit of analysis. In the study of uses, the unit of analysis shifts to the utilities or uses that interaction with the library has provided.

When analysis is done, the *unit* of analysis is inherent. The unit is what one samples, then measures by collecting data, and finally analyzes by comparing to other units. In a study of what makes individual books circulate, the book is what one measures—literally, its size, its language, the number of words in the title, the number of chapters, the number of index entries, numbers and type of illustrations, and so on. These are the variables, and the number of books are the number of units to be analyzed. The ns, or sample size, are the units about which inferences are made.

In a study of the user, the individual person is what one measures —his or her age, height, I.Q., grade-point average, the number of books he or she borrows, the length of time he or she keeps them, and so on. The person is the unit of analysis here. For example, for some mischievous reason, one might want to correlate I.Q. with personal overdue records. Analysis is done, inferences are made, and conclusions are then drawn about individuals with low or high I.Q., as the case may be, who return their books late. Clearly, this is not a study about I.Q., nor overdues—but about delinquent and punctual borrowers. And clearly, if the investigator did not report that he or she had collected data on 60 or 100, or whatever number of persons, the reader would be hard put to know that this was not a study of overdues, even though reduction of overdues might be the ultimate research goal.

A study of overdues would sample the population of overdue books, and then look for reasons (variables) that would account for the book's being overdue. In this case, the overdue book is the unit of analysis.

At another level, these units may become elements in a larger unit. For example, individual books may be aggregated into subject areas and persons may be aggregated into departments or majors. As another example, one may believe that subjects have something to do with overdues. Overdues in subject areas would then be the unit of analysis.

Another aspect of the sampling unit problem, one which often causes considerable frustration and conflict between doctoral students and their dissertation committees, is specification of the population to be sampled. A student may, for example, wish to determine the relationships between in-house use of periodicals and in-house use of books, with the discipline as the sampling unit. So the student chooses a large university with a large population of disciplines, a perfectly good research problem and acceptable procedure. In this case inference would be made from the sample of disciplines about that population of disciplines. But the student's research proposal is soon rejected because "unless the sample is taken from more than one university, conclusions would not be valid or generalizable." No criticism is more devastating or more unjustified. Not only does sampling two or more populations add enormously to the amount of work, it is unnecessary—unless, of course, it is the research question to compare universities instead of disciplines, in which case the university is the sampling unit. Further discussion on the unit of analysis and its role in generalization and theory in circulation studies and collection development appears later in this chapter.

Research Goals

Many of the problems of definition and specification could be avoided or resolved if the investigator offered a clear statement of the research goal—that is, the reasons for the research, and how the results might be applied. Such a statement helps to focus on the research and to put everything in context, and to exclude everything that does not directly bear on the problem. If, for example, the research is intended to determine the number of books a library should add to support an undergraduate course in cosmology, the questions become: Who will be using these books? Physics majors? Chemistry? Mathematics? Other majors? What level of books? Elementary? Advanced? Treatises? Surveys? Speculative? The research goal may then be stated: say, to determine the number and type of cosmology books needed by undergraduate physics majors and non-physics majors. With the problem well stated, the researcher knows that he or she must now define use, level of books, major, and even cosmology (or at least classify it). And that he or she must specify either the book, or the major, or both, depending on the analytical method, as the unit of analysis. The results may be applied not only to operations, i.e., to collection building, but to theory as well, since the research will presumably reveal relationships that are not generally known.

Relationships

Research is the study of relationships. It seeks, through definition, hypotheses, observation, and analysis to predict, explain, or otherwise describe the relationship between or among two or more things. Low-level library research, of which there is still much, rarely addresses or even has in mind all of these fundamental concepts. For example, an hypothesis is inherent in any question about relationships, but often an untrained researcher will deny that a hypothesis exists when he seeks to describe a simple phenomenon. Here are two observations made every year in nearly every library.

> Observation: The Library charged out 150,000 books in 1978 and 175,000 in 1977.
> Conclusion: Circulation is down this year.
> Observation: The Library added 25,000 volumes last year.
> Conclusion: The collection is larger this year.

The unspoken hypotheses are that circulation is down and that the collection is larger. Data was collected. The hypotheses were tested by analyzing the data to see which were larger. The conclusions are merely statements in support of the hypotheses.

It is absurd, perhaps, to treat such low-level observations as research. And yet it is almost universal concern with them that can lead to high-level research. Many hypotheses can be generated from the broad question: What are the relationships between the collection and circulation? It is meaningless to observe simply that the library has 500,000 volumes, and equally meaningless to observe that it circulates 150,000. A meaningful hypothesis, however, would be: a library containing 500,000 volumes will circulate 150,000. Then the researcher must gather data on circulation and collections from at least 100 universities in order to submit the hypothesis to a reliable test. The researcher should also probably collect enrollment data since the number of students should obviously have a significant effect on circulation (another hypothesis). Now the researcher is concerned with the relationships between circulation, collection, and enrollment (15).

Some administrators may not support this argument, saying "All I want to know is how many volumes we have. We don't need research to answer such a simple question." Nevertheless, there is an unspoken hypothesis in the administrator's statement that stems from the widespread assumption that it is good to grow larger, or that it is good to rank high in the number of volumes. The hypothesis is that the larger the collection, the better it serves its clientele. This hypothesis cries out for, and literally demands, testing (16).

Testing is the procedure for establishing the existence of, the nature of, and the extent of relationships between variables, and variables are the stuff of research.

Performance Measures, Criterion Variables, Dependent and Independent Variables

Library literature is replete with discussions of performance measures—the criteria by which we determine how well our libraries, and specifically our collections, meet the needs of their clientele, whether they are cost effective, efficient, and so on. Here the key word is *criteria*. For each determination (decision may be a better word), a criterion has to be identified, such as the percentage of times clientele succeed in obtaining the book they want (17). Since this percentage varies, it is called a variable, and the criterion, a criterion variable. In purely statistical terms it is called a dependent variable, since the criterion is dependent upon so many other influences. These other influences are the independent variables.

Techniques for determining and measuring relationships between variables are many. No enumeration will be attempted here. Excellent typologies can be found in the literature. In general, however, techniques can be divided into two categories: deterministic and probabilistic. Deterministic research attempts to make precise predictions and establish causal relationships. In modern research, determinism has mostly given way to probabilistic techniques.

The concept of variance, for example, is often computed within the context of multiple regression (MR), a technique for sorting out correlations and predictive coefficients that in turn are based on the properties of the normal distribution, a probability curve. These techniques are in common use and can readily be found in many good texts, such as that by Kerlinger and Pedhazur (18). MR, long a standard analytical technique in other disciplines, particularly in psychology, is encountered much more frequently in library studies now than even five years ago. Examples are the studies by Wainwright and Dean (8), Hodowanec (15), Harter and Fields (19), McInnis (20), Kim and Shim (21), McGrath (22, 23), and Pierce (24). MR quantifies the relationships between the independent variables and the dependent variables. It computes the ability of the independent variables to predict the dependent variable with coefficients that reflect how much weight each independent variable carries. And it explains the dependent variable by determining how much of its variance is accounted for by the dependent variables. It also determines the significance of these relationships, or the probability that the relationship is other than what the analysis shows.

There are many other techniques for quantifying relationships, but MR is especially powerful because of its ability to compute relationships among many variables in relatively complex designs. MR is really a whole family of techniques that include correlation and analysis of variance, or the study of means. The problems suggested in Table 1 could be attacked directly with stepwise MR, a method for testing, discarding, and retesting independent variables. MR, itself, is one of a larger family called canonical correlation (25).

Generalizing

A common remark, heard frequently in the corridors of a library conference, is "Well, the results of your research may hold in your library, but they certainly don't in mine. My library is unique." The remark, intended to dismiss the research as provincial, insignificant, and nongeneralizable, is itself provincial and presumptuous. It is equivalent to saying that the laws of physics may hold in your library but not in mine. It is presumptuous because the critic is claiming a degree of omniscience: he or she knows the results without every having conducted the research in his or her own library. It is provincial because the critic believes his or her library is unique. We could call it bibliocentric: everything revolves around his or her library. "The circumstances are just different," it is asserted. What circumstances? Both libraries serve undergraduate students, graduate students, and faculty. Both libraries have an extensive collection of books and periodicals, both have professional and nonprofessional librarians, both respond to the needs of a wide range of courses and departments, and both universities require teaching and research of their faculty. Wherein is the critic's library unique? The assertion seems to require that, if the research is to be generalizable, it discover constants, which would hold in every library. But research does not require that all analysis result in constants. It does require the discovery of relationships. If a significant relationship is found between two things, say, the number of books used in and out of the library, it behooves others to replicate the research or to test is generalizability, or to accept it. It cannot be rejected out of hand without counterevidence. A flaw in the tobacco industry's argument that smoking is not injurious to health is that the industry has produced no counterevidence whatsoever.

A significant relationship in one library is strong argument for hypothesizing a significant relationship in another library. The researcher must, of course, be careful about what is generalized. The mean number of books borrowed by undergraduates in one library may not be the same as in another, but if the difference between the mean number borrowed by undergraduates and that by graduates is significant in one library, then we are justified in postulating that the difference is significant in other libraries.

What the investigator cannot do is to generalize findings to some other hypothesis. Suppose, for example, that the difference between mean number of books borrowed by undergraduates and graduates is significant. It cannot therefore be concluded that the difference between number of periodicals read by undergraduates and graduates is also significant, even though our experience tells us that it is so.

In general it is instructive to compare findings of any investigation or analysis to findings of other investigations. Do the findings agree or disagree with what is known? Do they contradict findings of other investigators, and if so, why?

Collection builders, after conducting a study, may feel that, although they have learned much about collection use in their own library, they have uncovered nothing new in general and therefore their findings are not worth reporting. If their methodology is sound, the work systematic, and the results related to the literature, there is no reason why their findings should not be reported, even though conclusions might be identical to previous studies. Except for the many studies on the Bradford distribution, and to some extent, the work of Trueswell (26, 27), there is very little replication in library research. The reason may be that few problems have been well defined, and, therefore, good methodology is not identified.

The argument here is that any systematic description or analysis, whether or not the collection development librarian or other investigator chooses to call it research, may have something to offer other libraries—particularly if it has not been done before, and is novel or thorough, but most particularly if it specifically supports or contradicts previous work. In either case, results should have implications for theory building.

THEORY

Since quantitative research and analysis in library science is still in a relatively early stage—preparadigmatic, in Kuhnian terms—it is premature to proclaim the formulation of any scientific theory of collection development.

A good theory should explain phenomena in a satisfying way. It should enable us to predict. It should suggest hypotheses, results of which should contribute to the theory.

Scientists seek to predict and explain what they observe. The astronomer predicts the orbit of a planet, and explains why it orbits in terms of theory. He can predict a phenomenon without knowing why it occurs, i.e., without explaining. But if he can explain, he can predict. Thus explanation subsumes prediction. The better the explanation, the more accurate the prediction. When Ptolemy explained that all heavenly bodies rotated about the earth in concentric circles, predictions of orbital positions were not very accurate. Later when Copernicus theorizes that apparent motions of heavenly bodies could be explained by the earth's rotation about its axis as well as the sun, much more accurate prediction became possible.

In collection development research, our task is to predict which books will circulate and how often, which subjects will circulate, percentage of times a person or group obtains the book it seeks, the total number of books that will circulate in a given semester or year, what portion of collection will circulate, the number of copies needed to satisfy a given demand in a given period, and so on. These are the dependent variables. We want to predict from the things we can observe and measure—the number of students, faculty, or other clientele, number of credit hours, characteristics of the book or subject, sociological characteristics, demographic characteristics, and so on. The better these things explain circulation, the better our prediction, and the better we can predict, the better we can build our collections.

We express the success of explanation in terms of the percentage of variance in the dependent variable explained by the independent variables. Typically, in the early analysis of a research problem, only a small amount of variance is usually explained, and this is certainly so in collection development work. The challenge is to account for as much variance as possible. The more variance, the better the explanation. An excellent and readable discussion of the meaning and concept of prediction and explanation, using multiple regression, in the social sciences occurs in Kerlinger and Pedhazur (18).

Although collection development librarians may not construe their activities as theoretical, nor even consciously, think of theory, their activities nevertheless may be described in theoretical terms. Collection development officers should agree that libraries are social institutions. As professionals they should make an attempt to place their activities—results of research, collection building, or however we define them—in the larger context. The larger context is not just social, it is sociological.

A good theory of collection use, with consequent implications for collection development, should have deep sociological roots, particularly as developed by Robert Merton (28), Thomas Kuhn (10), and Donald T. Campbell (29).

Much insight into the patterns of information seeking or knowledge discovery can be found either in their writings or the studies inspired by their writings. Most such studies have been done by sociologists for sociologists. For example, there are many studies on the system of rewards and recognition for scholars and scientists who publish, i.e., those who, in our perspective, are responsible for creating the literature that we in turn collect. And there are many studies on how these scientists and scholars interact with each other through their publications. But there are few studies, in the sociological sense, on the role of libraries in this interaction.

One such study was Baughman's (30) "structural approach" in which he proposed that collection development is the "intertwining" of use (cluster of demands), knowledge (cluster of disciplines), and librarianship (cluster of subject literature relationships). Relationships between and among disciplines (the macro and micro levels) would be sought within the context of these clusters.

To show how much these studies may contribute to the theory of collection development is outside the scope of this chapter. Suffice it to say that concepts such as Kuhn's (10) paradigms in disciplines, the hardness and softness of disciplines, Merton's (28) concept of disciplines as bodies of practitioners on the one hand and practitioners on the other, his concept of measuring a paradigm by the degree to which it is codified, Campbell's (29) concept of the ethnocentricity of a discipline, the extent that disciplines are pure or applied, the ideas of the supportiveness of a discipline—the extent the materials of a discipline support other disciplines—ought to explain use of library collections in a satisfying way.

These, and who knows what other concepts, should, if the proper relationships can be demonstrated, enable us to predict general demand for library services, as well as for particular subjects.

It is probably misplaced emphasis to attempt to predict the need for individual titles. That is, it should be less the concern of the collection development librarian to determine the extent of demand for specific titles. That concern more appropriately belongs to the publisher of the book. He wants to know how many he can sell. We should be more interested in how many titles and how many copies we need to satisfy the demand for a particular subject.

When a satisfying theory of collection use is developed—one that encompasses and explains all the phenomena we observer—then the practice and policy of collection development may be so mature that even the sociologists may learn something from us.

Development of Policy

Policy should be a natural consequence of research. Research begins with policy, and policy should evolve from research, within the context of theory.

It may be policy for the library to extend its full services not only to its immediate clientele, but to all scholars in general. Research may show that this policy leads to inefficiencies in collection development. For example, if the policy requires representative coverage in all subjects, research may show significant lack of depth in subjects basic to the library's primary clientele. This may lead to changed policy.

The following are some familiar collection development policies that might be affected by circulation research:

1. Buy no more than one copy of any title in order to acquire as many titles as possible.
2. Build a minimal collection for nondegree programs, basic or study collection for undergraduate degree programs, research collection for master's and comprehensive collection for Ph.D. programs.
3. Take a slice-of-everything approach. Buy representative materials in all subject areas.
4. Select only those materials which meet severe critical criteria.
5. Buy only those materials requested by the library's clientele.
6. Collect only material which no other library in the region or network has acquired.
7. Collect only material which has proven value, i.e., only materials which other libraries have acquired.
8. Buy best-sellers only.
9. Buy only books which have redeeming value.

The following are some circulation policies which might be affected by collection development analysis:

1. Allow only graduate students and faculty into the closed stacks.
2. Allow the same loan period for all books regardless of subject.
3. Limit loan periods to one month for undergraduates, one semester for graduate students, an academic year for faculty.
4. Recall a loan automatically when someone else requests it.
5. Restrict certain subjects from general circulation except to faculty or adults.

6. Provide the name of anyone who has had a book on loan for more than two weeks to anyone who asks for it.
7. Do not allow children to borrow books from the adult collection.
8. Do not loan in-print books to other libraries.
9. Restrict certain types of materials, such as reference books and unbound periodicals, from circulation.

Burr *(31)* adds another proposition to the policy question: user behavior that remains constant while circulation policy may be variable. These constants should be considered when defining circulation policy. One of Burr's findings was that book returns tend to cluster around the due date, leading him to suggest that the due date be adjusted either to accommodate the borrower or to frustrate him. By accommodating, the library could reduce the costs of enforcing its overdue policy and collecting fines. By frustrating, the library could increase its revenue with more fines.

Burr's study is an excellent example of a well-thoughout problem, based on theoretical propositions and illustrated with good data, the analysis of which requires no special quantitative skills.

Three papers by Shaw *(32, 33, 34)* provide sharp contrast. Shaw simulated loan period distribution on a computer. Both Burr and Shaw observe that loan policy can have a significant affect on user behavior and ability to obtain a book—Burr in the context of theory, and Shaw by rigorous analysis of data.

Shaw used a stochastic model to predict book availability under both a variable semester loan policy and a fixed four-week loan policy *(33)*. He also showed that books are returned at a constant, predictable rate, which accelerates under the influence of the due date *(34)*.

According to Burr, the constants of circulation are determined more by the nature of the borrower and the material borrowed than by formal loan policy. Burr's proposition, what he calls the "cornerstone" of his theory, may be modified, however, by hypothesizing a cybernetic relationship: one affects the other.

Likewise, circulation and collection development should not be discussed independently of each other, i.e., the one is needed to define the other. The relationship is, or ought to be, cybernetic: a change in one brings about a change in the other, until a state of equilibrium, or optimal ability of the collection to serve its clientele, is attained. Few libraries can boast such equilibrium. More usual—in fact, the prevailing cybernetic relationship—is a lack of equilibrium: collections get bigger and bigger, while service gets worse and worse.

Just what the circulation/collection relationships may be, whether cybernetic or something else, will be borne out by rigorous empirical research within the context of theory. In the next section the levels at which this research may take place are discussed.

A Typology for Research in Circulation and Collection Development

In this part, some principles of the previous discussion are brought together in a more coherent fashion. The discussion focuses on the concept of the unit of analysis, how it differs from the concept of a variable, and how this difference may contribute to theory. This relationship is shown in Table 1. The table classifies levels of the unit of analysis in the following hierarchy:

> macrosociological
> microsociological
> psychological
> bibliographical
> bibliological

Macrosociological level refers to the things that vary from organization to organization, such as the number of groups or departments.

Microsociological level, or small groups, refers to the things that vary from group to group within an organization, such as number of persons in each group or department.

Psychological level refers to the things that vary from person to person, such as the number of books a person reads in a given period of time, the demographic variables (age, sex, status), and personality traits.

Bibliographical refers to the things that vary from book to book,

TABLE 1

THE UNIT OF ANALYSIS IN CIRCULATION AND COLLECTION DEVELOPMENT: A TYPOLOGY FOR RESEARCH

Level	Typical Units	Typical Variables
Macrosociological:		Total annual circulation per college* Ratio of circulation to volumes in library*
	Individual college or university	Number of FTE students Number of FTE faculty Numbers of academic departments
	Typical sample: 100 colleges	Number of academic courses Number of monographs in library Percent of faculty with Ph.D. Number of seats in library Prestige of university
Microsociological:		Number of books charged out per department* Number of books used in library*
	Individual disciplines or departments within a university	Number of students enrolled in department Number of faculty in department Number of credit hours offered Hard/soft index, scale value Pure/applied index scale value Prestige of discipline index
	Typical sample: 100 departments	Ethnocentric index Degree program (Ph.D., M.S., B.S.)
Psychological:		Number of books borrowed per person* Number of books kept overdue* Average time person keeps books overdue*
	Individual user, e.g., random selection of students, faculty, or adults	Age Sex I.Q. Rank, if professor Rank in other professions Personality traits:
	Typical sample: 100 users	dogmatism, aggressiveness, extroversion, assertiveness, motivation, creativity, etc.
	Individual child	Number of children's books borrowed* Number of adult books borrowed* Number and duration of overdues*
	Typical sample: 100 children	Same variables as above, if applicable Grade in school Number of brothers and sisters Grade point average Other scores: GRE, SATs, etc.

*Dependent Variable

Table 1 (continued)

Level	Typical Units	Typical Variables
Bibliographic:	Individual article, e.g., random selection from journal	Number of times cited*
		Number of references in article
		Number of pages
		Number of words in title
		Number of authors
		Age of article
	Typical sample: 100 articles	Number of illustrations
	Individual periodical, e.g., random selection from collection	Number of times cited*
		Number of issues per volume
		Average mo. of articles per vol.
		Average mo. of authors per art.
		Country of publication
		Whole names or initials
		Type:
	Typical sample: 100 periodicals	trade; scholarly; etc.
		Type of publisher:
		commercial; university press; association
		Bradford rank
	Individual book a. circulated, or b. overdue, or c. in the collection	Number of times circulated
		Number of times reviewed*
		Average length of loan*
		Number of pages
		Number of index entries
		Number of words in title
		Number of paragraphs
	Typical sample: 100 circulated books	Number of illustrations
		Number of chapters
		Ratio of any of above
		Language
		Country of publications
		Rank in best-seller list
		Edition (1st, 2nd, . . .)
Bibliologic:	Paragraph in a single book	Readability of each para. (judgment)*
		Number of words
		Number of sentences
	Typical sample: 100 paragraphs	Number of punctuation marks
		Number of nouns, verbs, etc.
		Average length of work
		Ratios of any of above
		First paragraph (yes or no)
		Last paragraph (yes or no)
	Illustration in a single book	Appeal of each illustration (judgment)*
		Color
		Black or white
		Graph, figure, etc.
	Typical sample: 100 illustrations	Length or width

*Dependent Variable

such as the number of paragraphs, number of pages, the title page, contents, and so on. That is, a book or article will have a fixed number of paragraphs, no more, no less. So that we would compare the number of paragraphs in one book to the number in another book, or in 100 or more books.

Bibliological refers to parts of a single book or article that vary within the book or article. A book contains many paragraphs, e.g., the elements of which will vary from paragraph to paragraph—the number of verbs, nouns, and so on—so that we would find a different number of verbs and nouns in each paragraph. Concordances and studies of literary style or content based on word frequencies would fall in this level.

Each level, macrosociological being the highest level of interest here, contains elements of the next lowest level, and each level may contain many different units of analysis depending upon the definition of the research problem.

At each level in the table some typical units of analysis are shown. The lowest level—the bibliologic—might include a sample from the population or paragraphs in a single book. Remembering that analysis starts with a hypothesis, one might pose the hypothesis that readability of a paragraph is dependent on such things as word length, sentence length, and so on (*35, 36*). This requires that paragraphs, or other portions of text, be sampled and analyzed.

At the next highest level, the bibliographic, typical units are the individual book, individual article, or individual periodical. Each of these may be specified more precisely depending on the research question. For example, to test a hypothesis concerning the average length of loan, a sample of books, say 100, would be taken from the circulation file. The typology also shows typical variables at each level for each unit. One of the variables that a researcher thinks might help account for length of loans is the number of paragraphs in a book (one way to measure book size). And therein is the essential lesson in Table 1: the unit of analysis at one level can become a variable at the next highest level. Thus, the hierarchy becomes that which is shown in Figure 2. The solid arrows represent the relationship between the unit of analysis and its variables within its respective level. The dotted lines signify a rule of correspondence from one level to the next.

FIGURE 2.

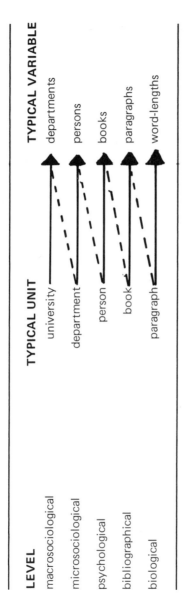

LEVEL	TYPICAL UNIT	TYPICAL VARIABLE
macrosociological	university	departments
microsociological	department	persons
psychological	person	books
bibliographical	book	paragraphs
biological	paragraph	word-lengths

TABLE 2

TYPICAL UNIT OF ANALYSIS AND VARIABLES
FOR THE BIBLIOLOGIC LEVEL; READABILITY HYPOTHESIS

Bibliologic Unit	Variables		
	Readability	Number of Nouns	Number of Verbs
First paragraph	5	30	21
Second paragraph	10	25	15
Third paragraph	3	35	26
.	.	.	.
.	.	.	.
.	.	.	.
One hundredth paragraph	8	20	13

TABLE 3

TYPICAL UNIT OF ANALYSIS AND VARIABLES
FOR THE BIBLIOGRAPHIC LEVEL; READABILITY HYPOTHESIS

Bibliographic Unit	Variables		
	Lenth of Loan in Days	Number of Paragraphs	Number of Illustrations
First book	30	356	16
Second book	25	323	15
Third book	40	415	45
.	.	.	.
.	.	.	.
.	.	.	.
One hundredth book	26	314	15

Each unit receives a score, a measurement, a count, or a classification for each variable. The data for the readability hypothesis might look like that in Table 2, and for the length-of-loan hypothesis like that in Table 3.

One property of the hierarchy is that, though we may learn much about the nature of a unit at its own level, information about its variability is lost when the unit becomes a variable at the next highest level. We may learn much about the nature or characteristics of books at the bibliographic level. But at the psychological level, we merely count the books, while learning much about persons. Similarly, psychological data about persons is not collected at the microsociological level, where we count persons instead. And so on up the hierarchy.

Dow (37) discusses this process in terms of metatheory—a theory which generates other theories. Metatheory can be expressed in three levels: casual, macroscopic, and microscopic. The casual is non-analytic, the macroscopic is analytic, and the microscopic is extremely analytic. A theory of information, Dow says, can and should be complete at any one of these levels, but can also be transformed, with appropriate rules, into any other. Dow's three levels are considerably more concise and economical than the five discussed in this chapter. Whereas his three levels are conceptual and methodological, the five can be called sociological sampling levels. Whether or not they are analogous, both authors note that the level is rarely explicitly identified in library and information studies. Dow concludes that "theorists must be careful not to inadvertently slip from one level to another, even if tempted by a more alluring explanation when their theory is weak at some point on one level. Theorists must also realize that the objects [units of analysis?] of the theories at these different levels are not the same."

Not only theorists, but readers should endeavor to determine the level of theory or analysis. Studies have been criticized for not investigating something the researcher never intended to investigate. If an investigator wishes to compare universities at the macrosociological level, he should not be criticized for failing to study departments when he merely wants to count them. Were such criticism justified, he could rightly be criticized for failing to count word lengths as a variable in a comparative analysis of universities. To collect data at two or more levels of the hierarchy in one study or analysis would add immeasurably to its complexity and cost, while contributing little to the hypothesis and consequent generalization. Thus, the level at which generalization can be addressed, and the theory to which generalization contributes, is a direct function of the unit of analysis.

In a good theory of circulation and collection development, postulates at the macrosociological level should not contradict, indeed they should contain and perhaps generate the postulates at the microsociological level. And so on down the hierarchy to the bibliological level. A metatheory, therefore, would embrace or contain, but not necessarily explain, the properties and behavior at all five levels.

Perhaps it is not too presumptuous to imagine that such an achievement might be analogous to Einstein's when he incorporated, in his theory of relativity, the discoveries of Gallileo, Kepler, Newton, Maxwell, Faraday, Lorentz, and so many others.

Since we are only imagining, we need not fear the presumption. While we are just now discovering methodology, we may be some time away from the kinds of discovery that we need for an integrated theory.

REFERENCES

1. William E. McGrath and Norma Durand, "Classifying Courses in the University Catalog." *College and Research Libraries* 30 (6): 533-539.

2. William E. McGrath, "A Pragmatic Book Allocation Formula for Academic and Public Libraries with a Test for Its Effectiveness." *Library Resources and Technical Services* 19 (1975): 356-369.

3. Michael K. Buckland, *Book Availability and the Library User*. (New York: Pergamon Press, 1975.)

4. F.W. Lancaster, *The Measurement and Evaluation of Library Services*. (Washington, D.C.: Information Resources Press, 1977.)

5. Robert W. Burns, Jr., *Library Performance Measures as Seen in the Descriptive Statistics Generated by a Computer Managed Circulation System*. (Fort Collins, Colo.: Colorado State University Libraries, 1975.)

6. Allen Kent, et al., *A Cost-Benefit Model of Some Critical Library Operations in Terms of Use of Materials.* (Pittsburgh, Pa.: University of Pittsburgh, 1978.)

7. Jasper Schad, "Allocating Materials Budgets in Institutions of Higher Education." *Journal of Academic Librarianship* 3 (1978): 328-332.

8. E.J. Wainwright and J.E. Dean, *Measures of Adequacy for Library Collections in Australian Colleges of Advanced Education. Report of a Research Project Conducted on Behalf of the Commission on Advanced Education*, 2 vols. (Perth: Western Australian Institute of Technology, 1976.)

9. Robert W. Burns, Jr., "Library Use as a Performance Measure: Its Background and Rationale."*Journal of Academic Librarianship* 4 (1978): 4-11.

10. Thomas Kuhn, *Structure of Scientific Revolutions*, 2nd ed. (Chicago: University of Chicago Press, 1970.)

11. Douglas L. Zweizig, "Measuring Library Use." *Drexel Library Quarterly* 13 (1977): 3-15.

12. T. Saracevic, W.M. Shaw, Jr., and P.B. Kantor, "Causes and Dynamics of User Frustration in an Academic Library." *College and University Libraries* 38 (1977): 7-18.

13. Eli Oboler, "The Accuracy of Federal Library Statistics." *College and Research Libraries* 25 (1964): 494-496.

14. George Piternick, "ARL Statistics—Handle with Care." *College and Research Libraries* 38 (1977): 419-423.

15. An example of such a study is George V. Hodowanec, "An Acquisition Rate Model for Academic Libraries." *College and Research Libraries* 39 (1978): 439-447.

16. Saracevic, Shaw, and Kantor in "User Frustration in an Academic Library" have, in fact, eliminated size of academic libraries as a significant factor affecting user satisfaction. Lancaster in *The Measurement and Evaluation of Library Services* reviews the literature on collection size as an indicator of utility.

17. Saracevic, Shaw, and Kantor in "User Frustration . . ." developed a simple and convenient model for determining the affect of acquisitions, circulation policy, library operations, and user performance on the users' success in obtaining their material.

18. F.N. Kerlinger and E.J. Pedhazur, *Multiple Regression in Behavioral Research.* (New York: Holt, Rinehart and Winston, 1973.)

19. Stephen P. Harter and Mary Alice Fields, "Circulation, Reference and the Evaluation of Public Library Service." *RQ* 18 (1978): 147-152.

20. R.M. McInnis, "The Formula Approach to Library Size: An Empirical Study of Its Efficiency in Evaluating Research Libraries." *College and Research Libraries* 33 (1972): 190-198.

21. Chai Kim and Eui Hang Shin, "Sociodemographic Correlates of Intercounty Variations in the Public Library Output." *Journal of the American Society for Information Science* 28 (1977): 359-365.

22. William E. McGrath, "Predicting Book Circulation by Subject in a University Library." *Collection Management* 1 (1976-1977): 7-26.

23. William E. McGrath, "Relationships Between Hard/Soft, Pure/Applied, and Life/Nonlife Disciplines and Subject Book Use in a University Library." *Information Processing and Management* 14 (1978): 17-28.

24. Thomas J. Pierce, "An Empirical Approach to the Allocation of the Book Budget." *Collection Management* 2 (1978): 39-58.

25. Francis J. Kelley, et al., *Multiple Regression Approach: Research Design for the Behavioral Sciences*. (Carbondale, Ill.: Southern Illinois University Press, 1969), p. 246.

26. R.W. Trueswell, "Some Behavioral Patterns of Library Users: The 80/20 Rule." *Wilson Library Bulletin* 43 (1969): 458-461.

27. R.W. Trueswell, "User Circulation Satisfaction vs. Size of Holdings of Three Academic Libraries." *College and Research Libraries* 30 (1969): 204-213.

28. Robert K. Merton, *The Sociology of Science: Theoretical and Empirical Investigations*, N.W. Storer, editor. (Chicago: University of Chicago, 1973.)

29. Donald T. Campbell, "Ethnocentrism of Disciplines and the Fish-Scale Model of Omniscience." In *Interdisciplinary Relationships in the Social Sciences*, Muzafer Sherif and Carolyn W. Sherif, eds. (Chicago: Aldine Publishing, 1969), pp. 328-348.

30. James C. Baughman, "Toward a Structural Approach to Collection Development." *College and Research Libraries* 38 (1977): 241-248.

31. Robert L. Burr, *Toward a General Theory of Circulation*, Occasional Paper No. 130. (Champaign, Ill.: University of Illinois, Graduate School of Library Science, 1977.)

32. W.M. Shaw, Jr., "Computer Simulation of the Circulation Subscription of a Library." *Journal of the American Society for Information Science* 26 (1975): 271-279.

33. W.M. Shaw, Jr., "Library—User Interface: A Simulation of the Circulation Subsystem." *Information Processing and Management* 12 (1976): 77-91.

34. W.M. Shaw, Jr., "Loan Period Distribution in Academic Libraries." *Information Processing and Management* 12 (1976): 157-159.

35. E.B. Coleman, *On Understanding Prose: Some Determiners of Its Complexity*. NSF Final Report GB-2604. (Washington, D.C.: National Science Foundation, 1965.) Coleman developed a "readability" formula consisting of the number of sentences and one-syllable words per 100 words of text.

36. Paul B. Mayes, "A Comparison of the Readability of Synopses and Original

Articles for Engineering Synopses." *Journal of the American Society for Information Science* 29 (1978): 312-313.

37. John T. Dow, "A Metatheory for the Development of a Science of Information." *Journal of the American Society for Information Science* 28 (1977): 323-331.

PART V

COLLECTION DEVELOPMENT BY FORMAT

Microforms as a Substitute for the Original in the Collection Development Process

Alice S. Clark

INTRODUCTION

When a library first decides to collect materials in microform as a substitute for the original, the decision requires a commitment to build a subset of the library that will be a microcosm of the whole—a library within a library. To add a collection of such materials means that special procedures will have to be developed from the placing of orders to the provision for use. It means that costs will have to be assumed for staff, equipment, and special processing. Before making this commitment, it is important that a careful analysis of the actual cost/benefits of a microform collection be assessed.

A great deal of the micrographics universe is not for libraries as such, but rather for the records of commercial and governmental agencies. The production, research, and published material on micro-forms, therefore, is not always geared to what is good for the library. The sizes of reduction, the forms, and equipment often reflect the needs of business and industry. Published articles on microforms appear in library periodicals such as *Library Resources and Technical Services*, *Special Libraries*, and *Microform Review* but some of the significant new research and development appears in journals aimed at the micrographics expert not the librarian. If the librarian decides not to subscribe for the few relevant articles, some important aspects that ought to be known will be missed.

A consideration of major importance in choosing microforms is their use for containing data versus their use for containing informa-tion. In commercial uses of microforms, data content usually sur-passes information content. Microforms, especially computer-output microfilm (COM) is extensively used for frequent updates of such items as parts inventories, accounting records, personnel lists, and payroll data. Since this kind of list is consulted frequently, but for short periods only, no consideration needs to be given to quality of image or comfortable use of equipment. In selecting microforms as a substitute for print the librarian is primarily using microforms for information. Commercial uses for information, such as filming out-dated correspondence, are primarily for materials consulted infre-quently and again little concern needs to be given to comfort. As a result of the heavier demands of business, government, and industry, there is a limited choice of film supplies and equipment that are designed to meet the library's need for long hours of use in examin-ing information. Libraries do benefit from the commercial uses when they use microform for data such as serials lists, in-process catalog records, on-order acquisitions lists and COM catalogs. For these purposes libraries reap the advantage from commercial uses in the variety of equipment designed for data record keeping.

DEFINITIONS

Before making the decision to purchase material in microform in-stead of the original hard-copy form, it makes good sense to learn something about the technical aspects of microphotography, and it is necessary to learn some of the terms used to describe microforms.

The term *micrographics* has been co-opted by the microphotography industry to mean the field of commercial microphotography rather than its original derivation from micrography, the study of microscopic objects. Micrographics is therefore defined here as the technology that produces microforms, and the equipment, supplies, and systems for their use. Because of its contribution to records management in business and government, the micrographics industry has expanded rapidly in recent years. Colleges and universities are beginning to offer courses in micrographics, and library schools and associations offer short courses and workshops.

Microform is the generic term for many different types of microphotographic reproduction. All microforms are photographs reduced many times in size that can be read or viewed only by the use of equipment to bring it back to a clear or legible size. The most common forms used for library materials are microfilm, microfiche, microcard, and microprint with variations such as aperture cards, ultrafiche, and microdot. A *reader* is the equipment which uses a lens to bring the film image back to normal size. A *reader/printer* will print the film image on paper in the same size as the original document.

Microfilm is a series of photographed pages reduced in size on a long strip of film. This film is usually rolled on a reel for viewing either to be threaded manually on some kind of reader equipment or to be placed in cassettes or cartridges for easier use. While 35 mm is the most common size in libraries, many materials are offered in 16 mm. Both sizes are usually reduced in size 18 to 24 times described as an 18x to 24x reduction. For some purposes several frames of microfilm may also be stored in flat strips in clear acetate or polyester jackets.

Microfiche is similar to microfilm except that the pages are in rows on a card-size piece of film and require a somewhat simpler type of reader to bring the image back to readable size. Microfiche is extensively used in business and commercial micrographics. The process of *computer-output microfilm* (COM) has been in use for 20 years but has become especially popular in the past 10 years for producing microfiche printouts of materials stored in computers. Using a high-speed camera, a COM recorder photographs the image on a cathode ray tube or CRT terminal. The resulting product is usually a film with dark characters on a light background. Some COM recorders are combined in one system with the developing processor and produce a finished product in one operation. Since the best form for viewing on a reader is the white on black (negative) form, the first generation of the COM film may be reproduced as a duplicate with negative polarity.

Microcard and *microprint* are opaque forms of microphotography, both are sometimes called *micro-opaques*. Microprint is a product of the Readex Microprint Corporation and is in the form of 6" X 9" cards with pages in rows—10 across and 10 down. Micarcard is a smaller version of opaque microphotography 3" X 5" holding 40 images. While microcards are no longer produced, many libraries still have large collections.

Ultrafiche is a high reduction form of microfiche which permits many more images on a single fiche. It is usually defined as at least a 90x reduction.

Microdot is the ultimate form of reduction of more use to a spy than to a librarian. Its high reduction permits the phenomenon used in World War II whereby secret messages were sent in the periods placed at the end of the sentences in innocent messages. As a gimmick, the Bible or Shakespeare's works have been produced on a dot the size of a pinhead.

The *aperture card* is a file card of punched card containing one or more microfilm images coordinated with data in printed or key-punched form.

The terms, *silver halide*, *diazo*, and *vesicular*, refer to types of film. Silver halide is the film used in the camera to make the original first generation microform, and may also be used to make the duplicate copies where archival quality is needed. Either negative (white on black) or positive (black on white) duplicates can be made. Diazo film uses ultraviolet light and ammonia to produce a negative copy, a duplicate of the negative master. Diazo film resists scratching but fades when exposed to constant light source. Vesicular film is produced by ultraviolet light and heat and produces a positive copy.

It stands up well under heavy use, but is destroyed by pressure. Librarians usually choose silver halide film for archival materials because it is made to standards set by the American National Standards Institute (ANSI), whereas no standards yet exist for the permanent qualities of dizao and vesicular film. Allen Veaner, editor of *Microform Review*, discussing diazo and vesicular film has warned that: "*MR* does not believe it proper to employ these materials for micropublications intended for the permanent collections of research libraries" (*1*). Committees of the Resources and Technical Services Division of the American Library Association have taken a similar stand, and the California State University and Colleges have specified that only silver halide be purchased for archival purposes. Carl M. Spaulding has raised many questions about the permanency of silver halide even though standards exist for this type of film. Spaulding recommends that: "Most libraries abandon the delusion that their microform collections are permanent" (*2*). However, the increasing use of the diazo or vesicular film by publishers, their cheaper cost, and relative permanency under careful storage conditions probably dictate their choice by many purchasers. Originally the Government Printing Office decided to send each regional depository both an archival silver halide and a duplicate diazo set of microfiche of its distributed government documents. Recently the Government Printing Office changed this practice and is distributing only the diazo copy while maintaining the archival silver halide to provide a duplicate when the library needs it. This seems to be an ideal way to use the types of film. Of course, protection from excess heat, light, and humidity is important for all types of film.

Generation refers to the distance a particular printing of a film varies from the first photograph of the original object. For example, the first positive copy made from the original negative would be a first generation positive while a second negative made from the original negative would be the second generation negative. The original film may be either a negative or a positive depending on the kind of processing used.

Polarity is a term often described more clearly in its two forms: negative image (white print on a black background) or positive image (black print on a white background). On most readers a negative is preferred in order to eliminate the glare of the screen. It is less tiring to look at the light while the glare of the screen is blacked out by the dark page. On most reader/printers this negative form will then print out as black print on a light background.

Reduction ratio relates the linear measure of the document to the linear measure of the image on the film. For example, if a page is 10 times the size of its film representation, the reduction would be 10:1 and expressed as 10x. Industrial uses of microfiche are often somewhere near the ultrafiche ratio of 90x, but library materials are often in the range of 18x to about 40x, limited by the need to use existing equipment purchased for older collections which were often in that range of reduction.

Resolution is a number ratio which describes the quality of the image. It is expressed as the number of lines per millimeter.

Title Area or *Eyeball Characters* is the printing on the top of the microfiche that contains index information and is legible by the naked eye.

GUIDELINES

There are several sets of guidelines which help to familiarize a librarian with microforms:

1. *Guidelines on Manuscripts and Archives.* Chicago: Association of College and Research Libraries, 1977. This item contains guidelines on the reproduction of manuscripts and archives by commercial firms.

2. Fleischer, Eugene B. *A Style Manual for Citing Microform and Nonprint Media.* Chicago: ALA, 1978.

3. La Hood, Charles G., Jr. "Film Stock—Some Considerations on the Purchase of Different Types for Library Use." *Library Technology Reports* (March 1975).

4. *Specifications for the Microfilming of Books and Pamphlets in the Library of Congress.* Washington, D.C.: Library of Congress, 1973.

5. *Specifications for the Microfilming of Newspapers in the Library of Congress.* Washington, D.C.: Library of Congress, 1972.

6. *User Evaluations of Microfilm Readers for Archival and Manuscript Materials.* Washington, D.C.: National Archives and Records Service, General Services Administration, 1973.
7. Veaner, Allen B. *The Evaluation of Micropublications: A Handbook for Librarians.* LTP Publications, No. 17. Chicago: ALA, Library Technology Program, 1971.

These basic guidelines form a basis for selection and in-house filming decisions and offer checklists of points for consideration. Such information can be updated by consulting recent books which give an overview of the whole field of micrographics. Such monographs as William Saffody's *Micrographics* (3) and S.J. Teague's *Microform Librarianship* (4) will help the selector of library materials be informed about the ramifications of microform purchasing.

COLLECTION DEVELOPMENT

The collection development considerations for selecting microforms as a substitute for original publishing are complex. The following checklist of advantages indicates some of the reasons for making the choice of this form.

1. *Purchase Cost.* Usually the microform will be less expensive than the original. Since each copy can be produced on demand, the publisher will not have to maintain a large stock. Publishing equipment and supplies take very little space when compared to the needs of printing. Film materials are less expensive than paper, and the cost of packaging and shipping is lower. Some of this saving in cost is passed on to the purchaser.
2. *Binding Cost.* Often purchasing in microform such materials as backfiles of periodicals may be less expensive than the costs of binding and storing the original.
3. *Storage Space.* Microforms will take up less space and may be stored in a variety of ways that could produce greater efficiency in the use of a small library facility. Microforms are especially desirable for collections which require a large amount of space but are little used. High school and elementary school libraries,

which are often short of space, can now keep larger collections of periodical backruns by using microforms.

4. *Ease of Access.* Microforms permit uniform storage and handling by creating one standard form out of many diverse types of material. Searching of such bulky items as bound newspapers is much simpler in the form of microfilm on a motorized reader. College catalogs and telephone book collections are easier to handle in microform.

5. *Rare and Out-of-Print Items.* The decision to purchase this type of material depends on many values not necessarily related to costs or efficiency. Certainly a rare book library cannot settle for anything less than the original edition. An elementary or secondary school selecting material for display and appreciation of the cultural past will be more interested in a facsimile of the Declaration of Independence or of a medieval book of hours. In many cases, a microfilmed copy may be the only way a library can obtain access to rare and out-of-print materials. One publisher maintains an extensive collection of this type of filmed material, and in its Books on Demand program will attempt to find and film any such book requested. The purpose for the purchase of out-of-print materials should govern the choice of microfilm as a substitute (5).

6. *Preservation.* Microfilming a fragile collection will protect it from further wear, and separate remote storage may insure that no natural calamity such as fire or flood will destroy the content.

7. *Dissemination.* The information in unique archival collections, rare books, and manuscripts can be disseminated to various locations and access can be offered to a greater number of scholars.

8. *Speed of Publication.* At present, this characteristic of microforms, especially production by computer, is primarily of benefit for updating data such as COM catalogs to replace the card catalog. In the future, however, speed of publication may result in much greater use of micropublications as the form for publishing reference books of all kinds. This could mean that these library tools would be updated more frequently.

9. *Duplication.* The lesser cost of microfilm permits libraries to

duplicate materials in heavy use. A library which circulates its bound periodicals might wish to keep a noncirculating duplicate on microfilm.

10. *Security.* At least until inexpensive portable microform readers catch the attention of users, microform collections will be used inside the library facility where equipment is available. As a result, the film collection is less vulnerable to theft and mutilation and more apt to be always available.

11. *Low-Use Materials.* Some collections are large and bulky to store but are used relatively infrequently. This type of collection can be purchased in microform and reproduced in a full-size copy only on demand. For example, a library maintaining a large collection of government report literature may choose to buy it in microform and produce a hardcopy on a reader/printer when an item is requested by a patron.

The disadvantages of selecting microforms instead of the original also have to be carefully considered.

1. *Equipment Costs.* A variety of readers and reader/printers may be required to use the microforms. The varieties of forms and reduction ratios will demand different types of equipment and a variety of lens sizes. The likes and dislikes of library patrons will also require that a choice of equipment be available to bring the image in the film back to normal print size. It will also be necessary to purchase special storage cabinets for large collections. Reader/printers may be required if library users demand a paper copy of the material.

2. *Space Requirements.* It is necessary to set aside space for the microform equipment. If cabinet storage is used, care must be taken that the floor will support the weight of the cabinets and their contents. Temperature and humidity should be controlled where the film is stored, and light may need to be controlled where reading equipment is used. Readers and reader/printers will require adequate wiring.

3. *Supply Costs.* Proper storage of microfilm and microfiche requires replacement of envelopes, boxes, and reels as they become damaged in use. An ongoing expense of no small concern is the

constant replacement of bulbs in readers and reader/printers. The lenses are subject to theft if not firmly secured to the readers, and lens replacement is extremely expensive. Since some microform equipment uses the same lenses as those on popular makes of cameras, thefts are a common occurrence in some libraries.

4. *Bibliographic Control.* Microforms are often difficult to index or catalog for easy retrieval. Large sets may be expensive to analyze and all too often will not be accompanied by any kind of publisher's index.

5. *Circulation Difficulties.* Since few individuals own reading equipment, the library which permits circulation of microforms may also have to circulate portable equipment. The small size of the items also makes loss more frequent and handling more difficult.

6. *Inspection Problems.* The size and form of micropublications makes them difficult to inspect as they are acquired, and as they are returned to storage after use. Sometimes missing items or damage is not discovered until the item is needed for use and when its loss seriously hampers the user. Competent staff must be trained to examine and film microforms accurately after use.

7. *Nonstandardization.* The use of microforms is seriously hampered by the lack of standardization in forms, types of film, equipment, reduction size, format, and means of retrieval.

8. *Staffing.* The staffing of microform services is more expensive than services on books or periodicals. Users need special instruction and help in locating them and in using the reading equipment. Large continuing collections in government documents and reports are expensive to file.

9. *User Resistance.* It is difficult to persuade library users that microforms are an adequate substitute for the original material. While there is less reluctance to use items such as newspapers whose originals are hard to handle, real resistance occurs when users have to read whole books at a reader. Microforms usually do not permit the variety of reading situations available for the use of the original.

COLLECTION DEVELOPMENT POLICIES

As in any collection development situation there is a need for a collection development policy. In most cases the microforms selected as a substitute for the original will fall under the same subject collection policies as the original material. Collection development policies are as often used to explain why a library does not purchase certain material as they are to justify why some types of material are selected. However, this may not be the case with collection development policies on microforms. In the case of microforms, their selection usually has to be justified. It may, therefore, be appropriate to have a collection development policy by form that will supplement the subject collection policies.

A microform collection development policy might be combined with a statement of certain procedures and include consideration of cost, availability of bibliographic control, and supporting services. Certain elements might be identified that would always justify the selection of a microform version rather than the original print edition, or depending upon the needs of the library, broad areas might be defined where microforms would be the usual choice. A school or small public library could decide that all backruns of periodicals would be in this form. Research libraries, either public or academic, might make a decision to use such criteria as: 1) items requiring extensive space but used infrequently, 2) items needed but too expensive to purchase in paper form, 3) items too technical for general interest, or 4) all indexed newspapers. Since many medium-sized libraries restrict their commitment to rare and special materials only to local interests, their policies might require microform for all works in history and literature older than a specific date.

Early use of microforms in the 1930s and 1940s was often for large collections such as the *Books for College Libraries* set offered by Microcard Editions. In recent years there is less demand for this kind of purchase. Selectors of materials resist the purchase of large sets preselected by others. Librarians prefer to make their own selections suited to their own clientele. The microform collection development policy might address the problems of acquiring large collections. For example, the policy might go so far as to forbid selection of any collections that did not have complete indexing.

One major decision may need to be made and at least recognized in a collection development policy for microforms. This is the decision on newspapers and periodicals: 1) when to discard the originals and buy microforms for retrospective use, 2) when to both bind and buy microforms as a duplicate, and 3) when to buy only microform. Each decision is going to require individual consideration, title by title, but some broad guidelines might be established. The first category might fit current newspapers. All or almost all originals could be discarded in favor of microforms. Question two might fit such items as frequently used scholarly journals. There are real advantages to having two copies of the *American Historical Review*, one bound original and one set in microform. The third category fits government publications selection in many libraries. Use might not justify the cost and space for hard copy but a microform subscription would be useful. Sometimes the decision will be a mixture of these applications. For example, for a collection of local nineteenth-century newspapers, a library might discard its incomplete collection, buy a whole backrun on film and keep some scattered issues as a sample of the physical form of the original publication.

Even in the smallest libraries, the preparation of a collection development policy would focus attention on the special nature of microforms as a form of information, and help to make the proper choice between the original and the microform copy.

FILMING UNIQUE MATERIALS

One kind of microfilm collection is sometimes almost forced upon the library. This is the decision to microfilm a collection of unique material that 1) may belong to the library, 2) may be available in the community but not accessible to the public, or 3) may be a joint project with other libraries.

Where a library owns a collection of manuscripts or archival records, the decision to duplicate it in microfilm may be based on the need to protect these unique items from excessive use and the damage that can result from many people handling fragile documents. Another consideration is the need to protect unique information in case the original is accidentally destroyed by fire, water, or other natural calamity. The costs of filming and purchase of materials can be considered in the same way that a similar decision is made to purchase a duplicate of any library material, or it can be thought of as another form of binding. Like the money spent on binding, this cost is also to preserve and make items more accessible. Estimates that archival quality film will last 500 years may not yet be totally accepted, but it does appear that film outlasts paper with a high acid content.

Another reason for a library to do its own microfilming is to provide greater accessibility. It may be important to have certain items available in more than one place. For example, there might be advantages to several locations on a campus if the student newspaper is filmed by the library and distributed. Greater accessibility is also provided to such a newspaper collection by the greater ease of handling and by locating an item in this more compact form.

Certainly a third factor to consider in local microfilming is the expense of storing the originals. Such things as business archives, newspapers and other records have not always been sought by libraries because of the high cost of storage. By their compact nature, microfilms are more acceptable and they encourage the collection of information that might otherwise be discarded and lost forever.

The decision to acquire a collection of locally produced microfilm should not be made lightly. If the goal is to produce library materials more legible, more accessible, and more permanent than the original, great care has to be taken for every step. Microfilming can be done by library staff with in-house equipment or done by a contractor who may work either in the library or by taking the material out for filming. Information in the form of automated records such as the library's new book list may be put in microfilm form rather than a paper printout. This process of computer-output microfilm (COM) is more often done by the city's or university's computer center than by the public or university library, or a commercial firm can provide this service.

If the decision is to do the microfilming of materials as a regular library function, careful standards must be set and maintained. The standards used at the Library of Congress may be the best choice to create material that will be useful to libraries nationwide.

A rotary camera can be used for many similar small items. This equipment will film catalog cards, letters, or items that are similar in nature and require the same resolution. For an archive of dissimilar items of cards, letters, broadsides, newspaper clippings, and other miscellaneous material, a planetary camera is used in order to provide a high degree of resolution for each item. A planetary camera is also necessary to film large items. Other equipment is needed to insure the results of the filming: a densitometer to assure the correct optical density for reproduction, a spectrophotometer for determining that the film is properly washed, and a microscope for examining the quality of the image.

Purchasing the camera, the lights, and the film itself to exact specification is only the beginning. To maintain the quality, periodic checks on film and lenses must also be made. The negative produced will sometimes provide an even better image than on the original through its removal of gray tones, and this original negative should be preserved in a controlled-environment vault for use only as a master copy. From it a second-generation negative or positive prints could be made to distribute copies to branches or other libraries.

Preparing material for filming is one of the most important steps. Staples and clips are removed, wrinkled sheets flattened, and miscellaneous items sorted for proper use. The film will protect an archive in its original order where that is important and keep a permanent record of how the archive was originally filed. A consistent form of insert should be used to create identifying title pages, omission sheets for missing pages, and additional notes. Placing a numbered card over the corner of each item can create a means whereby indexing would later be possible. Whether the filming is done in house or by a commercial firm, the whole process must be carefully monitored by library staff well trained to watch each part of the process and to certify the quality of the final product.

Some of the cost of such an in-house microfilming project may be offset by selling copies of the collections to other libraries at a price enough in excess of costs to gradually repay the total expense of filming. Occasionally a library may have an archive or rare book so much in demand by other libraries that it may pass on to the first purchaser the cost of preparing the library's own master and public user copy.

It is especially important that any such microfilm collection be reported in the *National Register of Microform Masters*, which is maintained by the Library of Congress.

ACQUISITIONS

Regardless of whether or not a library has a separate acquisitions department, the librarian choosing microforms as a substitute for original material should become aware of the ordering problems. Without this active involvement in the acquisitions process, it may be impossible to insure receipt of the proper material. A fine set of guidelines to help in acquisitions has been produced by the Book-dealer-Library Relations Committee of the Resources and Technical Services Division and published by the American Library Association in 1977 (6).

The selector of microforms often has no choice in finding a source for micropublications since microforms are usually sold directly by the publisher rather than through a vendor. Sometimes these are major publishers of microforms such as Bell and Howell or University Microfilms International. Sometimes the source will also be the publisher of the original material such as Pergamon Press, which offers its subscriptions simultaneously in print or microfiche and its out-of-print books in either microfilm or microfiche. Often, however, the sources will be a wide variety of small scholarly publishers such as Johnson Associates or Research Publications and may include a library that has filmed one of its own archival collections and is willing to sell copies.

When placing orders for microforms, the descriptive information will have to include more information than is required for ordering the original. Besides the normal requirements of number of copies, author, title, place of publication, publisher, date, edition, series, volumes, numbers, purchase order number and date, and price, it will be necessary to include such descriptive items as format—whether fiche or film, number of pieces of fiche or reels of film, whether positive or negative and what generation is desired. It will also be necessary to select the film type since some publishers offer a choice of silver halide, diazo or vesicular. This choice will be affected by both the purpose for acquiring the microform and the price. Certainly in cases where storage conditions are good, the cheapest type is a reasonable choice, but the amount and anticipated longevity of use would also have to be considered. Sometimes there is no difference in price, and silver halide would then probably be preferred.

Sometimes materials desired for purchase will be offered in different forms of microimage. Also, the library may be going to microfilm one of its special collections of archival material. In these cases a decision needs to be made as to which of the various forms of microimage is desired. Several things must be considered:
1. How will it be used?
2. What and how much equipment is required?
3. Where will it be stored?
4. How often will it be copied or printed?
5. How much will it be distributed?
6. What local technical capability is available?
7. What does the user prefer—black on white or white on black?

Upon receipt, the microforms and any accompanying materials should be examined promptly to insure that the shipment is complete, and spot checked for quality and accuracy of the content against the description on the boxes or envelopes. It should be assumed that errors may be discovered later after payment has been made. Purchasers of large quantities of microforms usually cannot afford to examine completely all microforms received just as they cannot examine every book to insure that no errors of arrangements occurred in its printing and binding. In general, check-in, inspection, and claims will not vary widely from the procedures set for all materials. On cancellations and returns it is best to contact the publisher by telephone before shipping. Because the publisher will produce the microform as a response to the order, a cancellation may not be possible once the copy has been made. Some publishers will not accept returns because an unethical purchaser might have made a copy. However, most reputable publishers will accept returns if they are made promptly, or if the delivered material was damaged, or not as ordered.

A word of warning about the acquisition of microforms is appropriate. There are microform bootleggers who sell to libraries a third- or fourth-generation copy of a film made by a reputable publisher. It is often as expensive as the first-rate film you could purchase elsewhere. Another area to enter cautiously is an agreement to give up bound copies for the equivalent film. Before entering into such a contract, a library should be sure it knows the sale value of the original and the list cost of the microform edition. The selector of materials also needs to look with caution on the free equipment offered with film purchases. It may be a good value, but it may be better to request an equivalent discount and look elsewhere for a more suitable brand of reader equipment. Another area where caution is advised is the request by a publisher to film material from the library collection. A library must look carefully at the advantages and disadvantages of lending the material—possible loss in shipment, damage in filming, and reasonable compensation for the inconvenience.

SELECTION TOOLS

The Guide to Microforms in Print (7), which since 1977 includes also *International Microforms in Print: A Guide to Microforms of Non-United States Micropublishers*, formerly published separately by Microcard Editions, is the basic bibliographic source for publishing information. Books are listed by author and journals and magazines by title and publisher; type of microform and price are given. Companion titles which supplement the information in the *Guide* are *Subject Guide to Microforms in Print* (8) and *Microform Market Place: An International Directory of Micropublishing* (9), a source of publisher and micrographics information. *The Micropublisher's Trade List Annual* (10), a microfiche publication, serves the same function as the *Publishers Trade List Annual* does for print materials. All of these bibliographic tools are now publications of *Microform Review*.

Other sources to use for selection are *Dissertation Abstracts International* (*11*), *Serials in Microform* (*12*), *Newspapers in Microform: Foreign Countries* (*13*), *Newspapers in Microform: United States 1948-72* (*14*), and *Newspapers in Microform: United States 1973-* (*15*). Suzanne Cates Dodson's book *Microform Research Collections: A Guide* (*16*) also serves as a source for purchase or borrowing.

STANDARDS

While a librarian usually does not actually want to become a micrographics technician, it is necessary that the purchaser of microform material or equipment be aware of some of the kinds of standards that should be applied to these products.

There are standards organizations that give some attention to the production of micrographic materials and equipment. The American National Standards Institute integrates the work of other bodies that are developing standards. ANSI sets procedures and has a committee that works with manufacturers, publishers, government agencies, and associations of dealers and users, including, of course, librarians working through their associations. The National Micrographics Association has put much of its emphasis on standards, and the American Library Association has committees working on guidelines. Such bodies as the U.S. National Bureau of Standards, the U.S. Department of Defense, and the International Standards Organization include micrographic standards in their work. The documents put out by the Library of Congress on filming standards are helpful to librarians.

Standardization of film format and equipment in the near future is unlikely and perhaps undesirable since competition may stimulate more technological progress. However, a small library may decide arbitrarily to purchase only material on fiche so that only fiche storage cabinets and readers are necessary. Even large libraries are abandoning micro-opaques whenever possible. The California State University and Colleges have stated their intent to buy micro-opaques only when no other form exists or where sets are being completed (*17*).

CATALOGING AND INDEXING

Robert Grey Cole has said "if adequate bibliographic control is lacking, patrons of libraries will not read microforms simply because they will never know what is in them" (18). This demand for proper indexing and/or cataloging is an important consideration if microforms are selected in place of the original.

There are several possibilities for obtaining bibliographic control of microform collections. Sometimes the micropublisher provides card sets that can be purchased with the collection. However, these sets are often very expensive and may require adding headings, stamping "microfiche" somewhere on the card, and filing expense considerations when the collection is large. It might also be possible to buy one catalog card from the publisher and then produce the set in the way the library handles other materials, for example by OCLC. Sometimes the publisher has printed indexes or reel guides to index the materials. The most expensive solution is to do original cataloging, but this may be appropriate for cataloging a collection as a set and using some other means for analyzing and indexing the contents. One of the least expensive methods is the use of published bibliographies by marking the entries with information about location. It is sometimes necessary to write the microform publisher for information about a published bibliography.

In the past, catalogers have differed in their approach to cataloging of microforms that substitute for an original. Some librarians have treated microforms as a new edition of the original material and added the fact of its form in a note. Other libraries treated this form as a unique item with the original recognized in a note. The second edition of the *Anglo-American Cataloging Rules* (19) has devoted a chapter to microform cataloging. These rules call for treating microforms as a unique item and putting in the note area a fairly complete physical description, detailed information about the original, and special reader equipment requirements.

MICROFORM SERVICES

Before the selector makes the choice between purchasing the original material or a microform copy, it is essential that all of the requirements for microform services be carefully examined.

A microform collection will usually require a dedicated space. There are advantages in centralizing such a service because of its special needs for light limitation, heat and humidity requirements, and trained staff. However, in many cases decentralization is required in order to bring essential subject materials together, e.g., science microforms to the science library. In a multilevel building, the basement level is often a suitable choice for the centralized collection because it is easier to protect the collection from extremes of humidity and heat in an area where there are no windows. Also, if an extensive collection of microforms is stored in microfilm and microfiche cabinets, it is essential that the floor be able to support the weight of full microfiche cabinets. Temperatures should not exceed seventy degrees, and humidity should be below 40%. In most cases lighting must also be controlled. Several new models of readers have protective shields over the screens so that the image is clear even in normal light, but many models require dimming of the room lights for comfortable reading of the screen. Some carrels especially designed for microforms can also allow regular lighting, but generally a light switch that permits varied degrees of light is helpful.

Many library buildings will need additional electric outlets for readers and reader/printers. If the number is limited, it may be possible to install a multi-outlet strip and arrange the readers on tables along one wall. For a large microform collection floor strips may be used with rows of tables on each side of them. In new construction such wiring can be built into the floor. Usually the equipment has three-prong plugs, but requires only 110-volt wiring. Wherever multiple pieces of equipment are grouped, an electrician should examine the load requirements to insure that no fire danger exists. The combination of a small single entrance microform room, inadequate wiring, and flammable materials is not the situation any library desires.

Other safety hazards should be recognized. If the drawers are not kept closed, running into them may tear clothes or skin. When shifting the contents of drawers, it is well to remember that opening several top drawers will tip the cabinet. It is also very important when installing vertical-drawer microfilm cabinets that they be bolted to the base cabinet, or they may be top-heavy and tip.

The storage of microforms depends primarily on the size and nature of the collection. As in any library decision, it is never possible to make simple rules that apply in all cases. In certain limited cases one decision may apply but in large collections several solutions may be necessary. At Central State University in Edmond, Oklahoma, a decision was made to use microfilm as a major part of the collection and "the rule not the exception" (20). In order to provide the same access for the film as for its paper issues, the film box is shelved as a book in a totally integrated collection (21). The same kind of decision might be made in any small library when a backrun of periodicals is purchased in microfiche. It will certainly encourage use to place such fiche in storage notebooks in the proper place on the shelf next to the bound copies. However, no such solution is appropriate for huge collections of ERIC microfiche or long backruns of newspapers in a large library. Large floor-model file cabinets for film or fiche, while costing well over $500, are the most satisfactory in such a situation. Motorized rotary files are available for fiche storage, but their high cost precludes their use in most libraries.

In small libraries, especially in school libraries, microfiche is often stored on shelves in binders holding frames that contain about 20 fiche per page. These frames may also be used in rotary stands or wall-mount stands for easy access. The binders and boxes that store on shelves permit convenient intershelving of microforms with book and nonbook materials. Microfilm may also be stored by arranging the boxes on shelves as books are stored, and microfiche can be put on shelves by using the covered or uncovered plastic filing trays that are commercially available. Small desk-top cabinets are available for both microfilm and microfiche in various combinations or in sections to provide for growth.

Equipment needed to use a microform collection may include readers for microfilm, both manual and motorized; microfiche readers; readers for opaque microforms; ultrafiche readers; reader/printers for microfilm, microfiche and opaque microforms; portable microfilm and microfiche readers for lending; microfiche duplicators and film splicers. Some libraries may also need a hand-held viewer and a reader which projects the image on a wall or screen for group viewing. Special tables or carrels to hold readers are not really necessary as long as some provision is made to permit note taking as material is read. It is more important that chairs and tables be comfortable and at a correct height for the library's clientele. Children should have furniture designed for their use and older people may prefer low tables so that they do not have to hold their heads in awkward positions to read vertical screens. This is especially important for users who wear bifocals and may be of great importance in libraries serving senior citizens, or in community college libraries having many evening courses for continuing education of adults.

Some good guidelines have been developed to help in choosing equipment, and such publications as *Microform Review* and *Library Technology Reports* provide data about various products.

In selecting readers there are many considerations for a librarian to examine. Will the general physical characteristics of the reader equipment fit the library's needs in regard to size, portability, general construction, screen size, and cooling blower?

Will the reading conditions of this piece of equipment include printed instructions, easy-to-use controls, interchangeable but secure lenses, variable lighting, a clear image of a reasonably large section of a page, good focus control, and a simple and steady film load and rotation mechanism? Comfort factors should be considered such as whether the screen requires a bad position for reading, whether it has a screen that causes glare, whether it is noisy to operate, or whether a special light is required.

Maintenance is an important factor and requires that the equipment have a good maintenance contract available from a local servicing agency, be easy to clean and to replace bulbs, and have parts and a service manual available.

One of the best sources for information on reader and reader/printer selection is the library's own log of experience with various

pieces of equipment. The library's records should include:
1. A list of all bulb sizes required, the inventory on hand, vendors, and prices.
2. A list of all normal supplies used, the source of supply and ordering information. This would include printer paper, fiche envelopes, boxes, reels, fiche separators and index dividers, fiche binders and insert frames, film cleaner, glass cleaner, dusting swabs and brushes, and film markers.
3. Repair record sheets for each piece of equipment (see Figure 1).
4. A file for maintenance contracts.
5. A file for service and instruction manuals.

Of primary importance to the success of a microform service area is the proper personnel. Because of the difficult management, bibliographic, and reference duties, an experienced librarian must be available at least part time. The technical knowledge, skill, and talent needed to handle the service and equipment requires a subprofessional at a fairly high level. Someone will have to read current information and seek continuing education on new developments. While some clerical assistance is desirable, school and academic libraries may be able to use well-trained student assistants for filing and daily machine maintenance.

EQUIPMENT REPAIR RECORD
Bell & Howell portable microfiche reader.   U.N.M. No. _____

DATE		REPAIR PROBLEM	REMARKS (Include Cost)
Reptd.	Reprd.		

FIGURE 1.

Maintaining the service area requires many duties often over-looked when microforms are being selected as a substitute for the original material. Filing microforms is more time consuming than shelving books since microforms require frequent cleaning, splicing of broken film, and frequent reversal of the film on reels that have been improperly used by patrons. If both boxes and films are not marked with call numbers, the content of the film may have to be checked before boxing. Boxes and reels need to be replaced fre-quently because of their fragile nature.

Readers and reader/printers need to have daily care. Besides external dusting, they require that lenses be cleaned and glass plates and screens be cleaned and examined for scratches or other damage. If static electricity is a problem, a little fabric softener and water in a spray bottle may be used in the area to keep down carpet dust. Replacement of glass plates and bulbs will be a continuing problem. Since bulbs differ widely in price and length of life, it is difficult to anticipate need so an inventory of all of the required types must be maintained.

Service to users of the collection is required during all hours the library is open. Because of the diverse ways in which microforms are cataloged and indexed, users of the material need help in learning what is available and where it is located. A guide to the local collections may be necessary (see Figure 2 for a sample page of such a guide). Users of microforms need instruction in how to use the equipment. Instruction sheets need to be available at each machine to remind those who have had instruction, but have forgotten some of the directions (see Figure 3). If a library has an on-going orienta-tion and instruction program, a special section on use of microforms should be included. Occasional special workshops on microform holdings can stimulate use. Special handouts should be prepared and a section on the microform collection should be put in the library's handbook or guide.

Much of the library literature reflects the negative feelings of users of microforms in libraries. Even if the only use in a library is to search for bits of data, those who are unfamiliar with the form and the equipment will be reluctant to use microforms. However, by providing adequate assistance and offering the added advantage of

URBAN TRANSPORTATION SYSTEM

Catalog entry: U.S. Historical Documents Institute
                  Urban transportation information system, 1921-1971

Periodical bibliography of the urban transportation portion of the U.S. Department of
    Transportation's files: Transportation masterfile, 1921-71; UNM has reels 131-140

Call number: z 7164 T8U5
Form: microfilm
Publisher: U.S. Historical Documents Institute
Review: *Microform Review*: 6 (1977) 235-8
Index: U.S. Historical Documents Institute
                  Subject guide to transportation masterfile, 1921-1971
          Washington, D.C., 1973
                  (Ref Z 7164 T8U52)
          U.S. Historical Documents Institute
                  Transportation periodicals directory, 1921-1971.
          Washington, D.C., 1973
                  (Ref Z 7164 T8U522)

FIGURE 2.

From: Lewis, Linda. *Guide to Microform Collections*.
University of New Mexico General Libraries, Spring 1978.

being able to scatter duplicate access points in many parts of the
library or school building, patron opposition can be overcome. If
acceptance of microforms for containing data can be developed, that
will help in teaching the use of microforms for information purposes.

When microforms are used in reading for information, user
acceptance is harder to create. Comfort is a major factor in getting
users to accept the form. This means that a quiet space should be
provided, lighting should be properly limited so that the screen is
protected from glare, the chairs should be comfortable, and tables
should be a proper height. The requirements for proper conditions
dictate a centralization space for machines used for reading and the
placing of materials and reader equipment in fairly close proximity.
There is a limit to how far the patron should travel in bringing

C.O.M. PACT II MICROFICHE READER

1. Turn on machine (1) and set at LAMP position.
2. Pull out bar below screen (2).
3. Lift upper glass. With other hand, insert microfiche *right side up* with title facing *toward* you. Lower the upper glass over microfiche.
4. Push carrier all the way back in.
5. Focus by adjusting Focus Dial (3) above carriage.
6. After using, remove fiche from the glass. Push carriage back in.
7. Turn machine off.

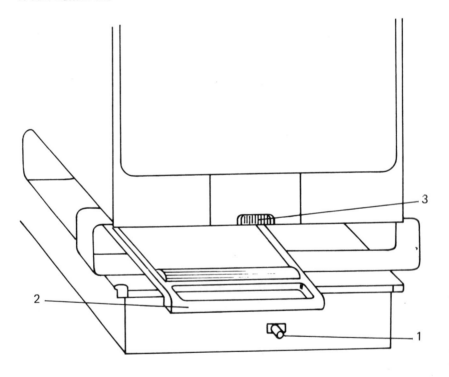

FIGURE 3.

432

together service and instruction, materials, and the reader equipment. A reader of print on paper has been used to the flexibility that permitted carrying the book to his favorite corner of the library, back to his office, or to the hammock under a tree in the back yard. In spite of the so-called brief case or lap readers, library patrons still demand the paper form when it is available. Welham R. Hawker summed it up when he said, "Had microform succeeded in its 'optical projection' mode, the reader/printer never would have been invented" (22). At least it certainly would not be as popular.

A hopeful development that will reduce user reluctance in the future is the increased use of microforms in school libraries. School librarians are introducing microforms with positive instruction programs. Nancy Deline in describing her program has said: "Any resource, particularly a new and unfamiliar one, requires promotion and every opportunity is used . . . to 'sell' the use of the microcollection" (23). Librarians in all kinds of libraries should be prepared to sell microforms as a valuable source of information.

REFERENCES

1. California State University and Colleges Library Microform Committee, "Revised Microform Procurement Standards," *Microform Review* 4 (1975): 99.
2. Carl M. Spaulding, "Kicking the Silver Habit: Confessions of a Former Addict," *American Libraries* 9 (1978): 665.
3. William Saffody, *Micrographics*. (Littleton, Colo.: Libraries Unlimited, 1978.)
4. Microform Librarianship. *(London: Butterworth, 1977.)*
5. *Guidelines for the Procurement of Out-of-Print Materials*, Acquisitions Guidelines, No. 4 (Chicago: American Library Association, Resources and Technical Services Division, Bookdealer-Library Relations Committee, 1976).
6. *Guidelines for Handling Library Orders for Microforms*, Acquisitions Guidelines, No. 3 (Chicago: American Library Association, Resources and Technical Services Division, Bookdealer-Library Relations Committee, 1976).
7. *Guide to Microforms in Print*. (Weston, Conn.: Microform Review, 1976-   .)
8. *Subject Guide to Microforms in Print*. (Weston, Conn.: Microform Review, 1976-   .)

9. *Microform Market Place: An International Directory of Micropublishing.* (Weston, Conn.: Microform Review, 1976- .)

10. *Micropublisher's Trade List Annual.* (Weston, Conn.: Microform Review, 1975- .)

11. *Dissertation Abstracts International.* (Ann Arbor, Mich.: University Microfilms International, 1969- .)

12. *Serials in Microform.* (Ann Arbor, Mich.: University Microfilms International, Annual.)

13. *Newspapers in Microform: Foreign Countries 1948-72.* (Washington, D.C.: Library of Congress, 1973.)

14. *Newspapers in Microform: United States, 1948-72.* (Washington, D.C.: Library of Congress, 1973.)

15. *Newspapers in Microform: United States, 1973- .* (Washington, D.C.: Library of Congress, 1973- .)

16. Suzanne Cates Dodson, *Microform Research Collections: A Guide.* (Westport, Conn.: Microform Review, 1978.)

17. Paul A. Napier, "Developments in Copying, Micrographics and Graphic Communications, 1975." *Library Resources and Technical Services* 20 (1976): 240.

18. Robert Grey Coles, "Bibliographic Control." *Illinois Libraries* 58 (1976): 211.

19. *Anglo-American Cataloging Rules*, 2nd ed. (Chicago: American Library Association, 1978), pp. 232-246.

20. *The Library at Central State University, Edmond, Oklahoma.* (Edmond, Okla.: The Library, n.d.), p. 5.

21. Ibid., p. 4.

22. Welham R. Hawken, "Making Big Ones Out of Little Ones: Current Trends in Micrographics." *Library Journal* 102 (1977): 2128.

23. Nancy E. Deline, "Microforms in the Secondary School." *Canadian Library Journal* 34 (1977): 177.

BIBLIOGRAPHY

American Library Association, Resources and Technical Services Division, Resources Section, Bookdealer-Library Relations Committee. *Guidelines for Handling Library Orders for Microforms.* Acquisitions Guidelines, No. 3. Chicago: American Library Association, 1976.

_____. *Guidelines for the Procurement of Out-of-Print Materials.* Acquisitions Guidelines, No. 4. Chicago: American Library Association, 1976.

California State University and Colleges Library Microform Committee. "Revised Microform Procurement Standards." *Microform Review* 4 (1975): 96-99.

Cluff, E. Dale. "Developments in Copying, Micrographics, and Graphic Communication, 1977." *Library Resources and Technical Services* 22 (1978): 263-293.

Cole, Robert Grey. "Bibliographic Control." *Illinois Libraries* 58 (1976): 211-216.

Costigan, Daniel M. *Micrographic Systems*. National Micrographic Association Reference Series, No. 16. Silver Springs, Md.: National Micrographic Association, 1975.

Deline, Nancy E. "Microforms in Secondary Schools." *Canadian Library Journal* 34 (1977): 175-179.

Dodson, Suzanne Cates. *Microform Research Collections: A Guide*. Westport, Conn.: Microform Review, 1978.

Hawken, Welham R. "Making Big Ones Out of Little Ones: Current Trends in Micrographics." *Library Journal* 102 (1977): 2127-2131.

Houser, Mary Ann. "Ohio Middle School Acquires Its Own Periodicals on Microfiche After Students Used Them Successfully in High School." Brochure. Wooster, Ohio: Bell and Howell Micro-Photo Division, n.d.

The Library at Central State University, Edmond, Oklahoma. Edmond, Okla.: The Library, n.d.

Lewis, Ralph W. "User's Reactions to Microfiche: A Preliminary Study." *College and Research Libraries* 31 (1970): 260-268.

Napier, Paul A. "Developments in Copying, Micrographics, and Graphic Communication, 1975." *Library Resources and Technical Services* 20 (1976): 236-258.

Saffody, William. *Micrographics*. Littleton, Colo.: Libraries Unlimited, Inc., 1978.

Spaulding, Carl M. "Kicking the Silver Habit: Confessions of a Former Addict." *American Libraries* 9 (1978): 653-656; 665.

Teague, S.J. *Microform Librarianship*. London: Butterworth, 1977.

Veaner, Allen. "Hurray for Meshed Mediums—Letters." *Library Journal* 103 (1978): 1449.

Veaner, Allen B., ed. *Studies in Micropublishing, 1853-1976: Documentary Sources. Microform Review*. Reader Series in Micrographics Management, No. 2. Westport, Conn.: Microform Review, 1976.

Developing the Government Publication Collection

Peter Hernon

INTRODUCTION

Library literature is replete with statements that collection development should reflect such factors as institutional mission, curriculum, publication quality, and user needs. For federal government publications one noted writer stated:

> The major research library will doubtless select all but a few of the series offered, but careless and indiscriminate over-selection is bad, both for the library in waste of time for handling and of space for storage, and for the public interest in waste of funds. Too limited selection, on the other hand, may jeopardize the value of the collection, in the unforeseen future, if not

at present. An intelligent selection requires a broad view of the possible needs and interests of all segments of the library's patronage and a general knowledge of the nature of the publications of all federal government agencies (1).

Another author maintained that selection is important for any type of material acquired by libraries. It is perhaps more important for government publications,

> . . . due to the multiplicity of material published and to the fact that, of the thousands of individual publications appearing each year, only a limited proportion can possibly be made currently available to users in libraries, even if all this material were of equal value, which it is not. The principles of book selection which apply to other classes of library material apply also to federal government publications (2).

In view of the general observations contained in library literature, some readers might conclude that depository libraries have practiced the controlled growth of documents collections for years. Such a conclusion might be questioned since many collections often include outdated, superseded, and seldom-used items. In certain cases, library documents collections have expanded and reached the space capacity allotted to them. Some libraries are now shifting lesser used and older documents to storage and are struggling with the problem of congestion. Increasing binery costs are also forcing them to rethink the policy of permanent retention of little-used material.

This chapter suggests that little is presently known about collection development for government publications, and that insights gained from studying collection development for other phases of library work have application to the documents field. The problem of making documents available when needed by library users may be different by an order of magnitude from providing other library materials, given the high rate of obsolescence for many documents and the ephemeral nature of a substantial proportion of the material. Still, collection development for government publications, as well as other library materials, embodies such factors as determining how much material to acquire and in how many copies, how long to retain it, and how to manage what is kept (3).

BACKGROUND INFORMATION

The *Guidelines for the Depository Library System* encourage depository libraries to maintain documents collections containing at least 25% of the available item numbers and certain recommended titles. In addition, libraries are advised to "select frequently and potentially useful materials appropriate to the objectives of the library," to "select materials responsive to the needs of the users in the Congressional district," and to "coordinate selections with other depositories in the district to insure adequate coverage within the area" (4). Such recommendations are consistent with federal legislation. For example, in 1922 libraries designated as depositories for the publications of the Government Printing Office were authorized to select those categories of publications most suitable to their needs and to reject unsolicited publications. The Depository Library Act of 1962 enabled selective depositories to dispose of documents after retention for at least 5 years.

The number of federal documents available for depository distribution by the Government Printing Office increases each year. During fiscal year 1975 the Superintendent of Documents distributed 12,998 individual publication titles to depository libraries, and by 1977 the total had increased to 21,033. Libraries often supplement the depository program with nondepository publications, print and nonprint, some of which are disseminated through the Educational Resources Information Center (ERIC) and the National Technical Information Service (NTIS).

The increasing volume and diversity of publications is not limited to the federal level of government. Other governmental units are also issuing information of value to the general public. In effect, there is a mounting flood of publications at all levels and in all branches of government. The tasks of storing, retrieving, and utilizing government produced information is becoming more difficult and expensive as the information explosion continues.

To compound difficulties, the receipt of numerous new sources impacts the amount of staff time available for activities other than processing. Other problems are that some users experience difficulty in negotiating separate documents collections arranged by specialized classification schemes, and that a major reason for infrequent use and nonuse of documents is that the amount of time expended in searching for them may be out of proportion to what is found (5).

USE STUDIES

Current Information

Only a few studies analyzing the utilization of documents collections have been reported in library literature. These concentrate primarily upon faculty members associated with academic institutions and indicate the role that depository documents collections play in meeting their information requirements. This chapter therefore reflects these findings. A qualification might be inserted at this point: the degree to which those faculty members surveyed are typical or atypical of all groups using government publications located in academic depository libraries merits investigation.

One study investigated social scientist use patterns at 17 different institutions, both public and private institutions with degree programs ranging from the baccalaureate to the doctorate. Faculty members in the disciplines of economics, history, political science, and sociology were investigated. It was found that interview subjects did not have uniform need for all types of federal publications.[2] In fact, they seemed to concentrate heavily on a few types. These were statistical data, primarily those of the Bureau of the Census, census reports, congressional hearings, congressional reports and committee prints, reports of investigations conducted by federal agencies and special commissions, annual reports, court cases, and foreign policy materials. More specifically the clustering of responses among a relatively few titles suggests that perhaps a core literature of government publications might be constructed for certain disciplines and across the social sciences. This literature might comprise titles such as the following:

Business Digest
Congression Record and Its Predecessors
Consumer Price Index
County and City Data Book

Current Population Reports
Economic Report of the President
Employment and Earning
Federal Reserve Bulletin
Foreign Broadcast Information Service (FBIS) Daily Reports
Foreign Relations of the United States
Historical Statistics of the United States: Colonial Times to
   1970
Monthly Labor Review
State Department Bulletin
Statistical Abstracts of the United States
Survey of Current Business
Treasury Bulletin

Other selected serial titles from the departments of labor and treasury might be added to this list. Undoubtedly interviewing social scientists in other disciplines and faculty members in the physical, medical, and behavioral sciences as well as those in the humanities would expand this core list (6)

The emphasis of most of these publications is on current information. They provide a means for certain economists, political scientists, and sociologists to update textbooks and monographic and periodical literature for their teaching. For example, if students found the theory behind deficit spending in textbooks but only dated supportive statistical data there, they could turn to government periodicals and other serials for current statistical data.

Even historians did not draw upon varied types of publications. They primarily consulted the depository collection for statistical data and census reports. This finding suggests that academic libraries may want to expand their collections of statistical data over time at the expense of acquiring certain other types of publications that are used less frequently. It seems that current information deserves greater emphasis in the documents collecting policies of academic depository libraries and that partial depositories might conceivably collect some types of government publications selectively or not at all.

Many of the social scientists interviewed who sought current information suggested that libraries either were not collecting all of the specific publications they relied upon or that the publications were too old to meet their needs by the time libraries placed them on the shelves. Social scientists drew heavily upon texts of speeches, press conferences, and news releases distributed by selected departments or agencies. Such ephemeral sources suggesting current policy positions, changes, and issues were often distributed by the State Department, Bureau of Labor Statistics, and Department of Energy.

Depository libraries do not have the storage space and facilities to acquire and retain, even for a short time, all available departmental news releases. Staff time for processing the releases would also be prohibitive. In addition, no one has ever identified all available public announcement newsletters. Still librarians might identify those newsletters most in demand and encourage faculty members to subscribe to appropriate one(s).

It seems on the basis of these findings that partial depositories ought to carefully determine those categories of topical publications that would be of greatest value to their clientele and to put less emphasis on those that are used infrequently or have been unused for years. Depositories, even those with a research mission and supporting doctoral studies, need not acquire a majority of the publications disseminated by the Government Printing Office and by other government agencies. They would be better advised to concentrate selection and retention on those government publications that receive the greatest amount of use and to rely on regional depositories to provide support in the form of lesser-used publications.

Publication Date

Section 9 of the 1962 Depository Library Act, which provides for discretionary disposal of government publications after retention for 5 years, is testimony to the perceived short life span of the average document. In the study mentioned in the preceding section, survey subjects were asked, as one questionnaire item, to specify how old the government publications were that they consulted most frequently (7).

Some 51% of the respondents consulted publications no more than 3 years old, whereas 13% used publications more than 10 years old, and some 30% had no discernible pattern. As might be expected, 88% of the users of older documents were historians. The age of the documents most frequently consulted were compared to the level of government producing the documents used. The purpose was to see if a pattern prevailed across levels of government. A total of 50% of the users of federal publications consulted documents less than 3 years old, whereas 13% of the social scientists wanted publications more than 6 years old, and 31% had no pattern to the publications sought.

At the state level, 49% of the respondents wanted publications less than 3 years old, while material more than 5 years old appealed to only 15% of the social scientists. However, 29% of the faculty members had no discernible pattern to their search for information. Current information appealed to 58% of the users of municipal publications. Only 9% of them sought publications more than 5 years old, while 24% had no discernible pattern to the publications sought.

The pattern for use of foreign government publications also reflected an emphasis on current (not more than 3 years) publications. Some 51% of the social scientists sought current publications, while 9% desired historical publications (more than 10 years old), and 37% had no discernible pattern to their search.

More than half of the users of the publications of the United Nations and international organizations also desired current documents (55%). The majority of the other users had no noticeable pattern for the age of the publications desired (36%). Social scientists seeking documents 4 or more years old comprised less than 10% of the users of the publications of international organizations.

During the interview phase, social scientists, who had marked on the questionnaire the category of no discernible pattern, explained that they drew mainly upon current material less than 3 years old. When they needed older information, it was primarily for statistical data. Additionally they sometimes consulted congressional hearings, court cases, or material in the serial set. Even some of the historians interviewed adhered to this pattern. For supplementary information they consulted research libraries in the vicinity or visited archives that had collections pertinent to their research interests. Historians seemed to realize that libraries could not hold all of the source material needed. As a minimum their libraries should have the "basic documents such as census publications."

Interview subjects who used municipal publications drew upon materials issued within the last 10 years; however, they generally wanted the most recent ones, if these were available. Given the irregular nature of bibliographic control for publications of this level of government, they were willing to take whatever source material was available.

The findings of this study suggest that perhaps the requirement that depositories retain documents for at least 5 years could be relaxed. It would seem that documents, regardless of the level of government issuing them, could be weeded from the collection on a discretionary basis after 3 years.

Citation Studies

Numerous citation studies in the social sciences have included government publications as one category for analysis, but there have been no reported studies dealing exclusively with government publications. According to one library educator who analyzed the citation studies, some of them drew their citations from monographic literature while others relied on subject journals as their population for investigation. "Those drawing data from books . . . found a higher percentage of citations to government publications than did studies of the same subject areas drawing data from journals." However, "whether this reflects a difference in type of research or in citation behavior of the authors of books as opposed to authors of journal articles, or if it is due to other factors, cannot be determined from the studies listed" (8).

The proportion of total citations to government publications in the reported studies ranged from 2% to 36% (9). Because of the variation, comparisons and conclusions are difficult to make. Additional research is needed to determine within and across disciplines the proportion of total references that are to government publications. The population ought to represent a composite of the major reference sources for that discipline, and not just the sources listed in one index or bibliography. Analysis should identify the types of materials cited most frequently and have implications for collection development.

And, finally, there have been few citation studies involving government publications outside the social sciences. From the limited research, "one might speculate that the sciences make some use, but the humanities make less use of government publications in their published literature" (10).

Levels of Government Collected

Two studies have reported percentages of faculty use across the publications of different levels of government. They found that the publications of the United States government received the most interest, followed by those of the United Nations, other interntional organizations, and state governments. The publications of foreign and municipal governments received considerably less support (11). It should be noted that these findings do not indicate the relative frequency per academic year with which respondents used the publications of a level of government.

One of these studies examined the hypothesis that "the academic library collects, or has access to, the publications from the different levels of government needed and used by its faculty." Certain items on the faculty questionnaire were compared to questionnaire responses of the documents librarian at that institution. It was found that only the publications of the federal level of government were systematically collected by all of the academic libraries under investigation (12).

Some 65% of the libraries systematically gathered state publications, but use of these publications was not confined to these institutions. A large number of faculty members from the remaining institutions, all private, made some use of state publications. Half of these users were associated with two doctorate-granting institutions, while the remaining users were situated at master's- and baccalaureate-level institutions.

About 68% of the users of municipal government publications taught at institutions in which the libraries did not systematically collect municipal publications. These libraries were predominantly associated with doctorate-granting and public master's-level institutions. The libraries of approximately 50% of the faculty members using foreign government publications did not systematically gather such documents. More than two-thirds of these users were associated with private, graduate-level institutions, but none of these libraries collected foreign documents. The remaining social science users clustered at private baccalaureate- and public master's-level institutions.

At least some of the faculty members from all of the institutions used publications of the United Nations and other international organizations. Yet, only 65% of the libraries collected these publications. The exceptions, all private institutions, had degree programs below the doctorate.

Termination of the analysis at this point might be misleading as libraries may supplement their holdings of government publications by participation in cooperative depositories or consortia. Therefore, use of the publications of a particular level of government was compared to whether or not the libraries were members of such arrangements. Faculty members associated with institutions in which the libraries belonged to cooperative arrangements presumably could request that needed government documents be borrowed. Therefore, the number of these individuals was deducted from the list of faculty members whose libraries did not systematically collect the publications of a particular level of government.

Only 13% of the faculty members using state publications could not draw upon the resources of their institutional libraries for such materials. Again, these libraries were all associated with private institutions having degree programs ranging from the baccalaureate to the doctorate.

It was found that over one-third of the faculty members utilizing municipal publications had institutional libraries not involved in pertinent collection-building activities. These institutions ranged from those offering the baccalaureate to those providing the doctorate.

One-fifth of the faculty members utilizing foreign publications could not rely upon the systematic collection-building of their institutional libraries. These people were predominantly associated with institutions offering graduate-degree programs. All users of publications produced by the United Nations and other international organizations were associated with institutions in which the library either gathered such publications or had access to them through cooperative arrangements.

Faculty members interviewed, even those at research institutions, appeared to accept the fact that their libraries could not collect all of the source material that they might need. To supplement their libraries' collections, they visited other libraries in the vicinity or, in some cases, saved their requests until they were in Washington, D.C., and could use the resources of the Library of Congress or National Archives. Some interview subjects desiring publications of the Government Printing Office were unaware that their institutional library could supplement its collection by borrowing documents on interlibrary loan. Apparently libraries need to explain their ability to supplement selective depository holdings by drawing upon the resources of nearby regional depositories.

In summary, the particular hypothesis under investigation could not be entirely accepted. The academic libraries did not all collect from, or have access to, the publications of the different levels of government needed and used by their constituency. Yet, this finding does not necessarily mean that all academic libraries should systematically collect from all of the levels of government. It was beyond the scope of this investigation to look at such factors as institutional mission statements, the number of faculty requests for sources held by consortia, proximity of supplementary collections, and budget allocations. Still, the number of faculty members using but not being able to tap their own institutional libraries for needed publications was not small. For example, at two graduate institutions a large number of faculty members surveyed used municipal publications—14—and publications of foreign governments—18. However, these libraries, for whatever reasons, did not systematically collect publications of these levels of government.

COLLECTION ANALYSIS

It may be that depository libraries possess the majority of publications requested by their clientele, but that these items are not always on the shelves at the time of immediate need. User satisfaction therefore is based on more variables than just the number of titles held. Librarians might examine their documents delivery capability; their ability to answer reference queries based on the immediate collection and to retrieve sources requested. In order to study delivery capability, they might generate a pool of citations from indexes, representative of the actual needs of library documents users. The sample could reflect different publication dates and comprise both depository and nondepository items.

Next, librarians would determine the exact percentage of citations held by the library. They would compare and evaluate the different options for accessing materials not held. They would also find out if those publications held by the library were kept on the immediate premises or in a storage site, microform room, or branch library. They would then determine how quickly the documents could be obtained and pinpoint problems users might encounter. In other words, they would determine whether or not the publications were on the shelf or had off-shelf status. On the basis of the findings, library staff members might discover problems in accessibility for materials supposedly held (13).

Another approach might be to have documents users record their search patterns in diaries and note sources that they could not find. They might mark the supposed location of missing sources on the shelf. The purpose of this exercise would be to monitor items in demand, determine how successful users are in locating desired information sources, indicate reasons for failure in finding sources, and suggest possible ways to improve document retrieval (14).

Additional insights could be obtained by having documents staff members record unanswered reference questions, subject areas in which the majority of reference questions fall, the specific areas of the documents department that receive the heaviest use, and even all reference questions asked during a given time period (15). They might even monitor circulation records to determine use patterns.

The data gathered constitute a rough indicator of traffic patterns, have value for collection evaluation and the assignment of staff members to reference desks, and suggest the more heavily requested titles for which additional copies might be needed. The recording of reference questions shows which signs and audiovisual aids might potentially reduce the number of directional questions and indicates the level of question difficulty.

LIBRARIES TAKING LESS THAN ONE-FOURTH OF DEPOSITORY ITEMS

As mentioned earlier in this chapter, the *Guidelines for the Depository Library System* encourage depository libraries to take no less than 25% of the items available to them. However, approximately 30% of the depositories take less than the recommended percentage. In fact, 11% of these libraries take less than 10%. More than half of the libraries taking less than 25% are academic. Some 17 of these are affiliated with institutions offering doctoral degrees. The majority however are undergraduate institutions with enrollments under 5,000 (*16*).

Because of the present limited understanding of collection development in the area of government publications, these facts can be interpreted in two different ways. On the one hand, it could be maintained that these libraries are not taking enough categories to justify depository status. Perhaps another library in the congressional district might make better use of the status. On the other hand, these libraries might have determined their needs more precisely than many other depositories. Conceivably a majority of partial depositories do not need much larger collections. More libraries might determine their needs more precisely if it were possible to drop certain depository categories without losing potentially valuable publications.

RESOURCE SHARING

Partial depository libraries faced with zero growth for documents collections need to emphasize weeding and selective acquisitions of documents in order to avoid congestion in processing and servicing and in storage space. They should regularly review their category distribution needs, balance user and space needs, and rely on networking to speed the sharing of little-used resources from the nearest holding center.

Such centers might, but need not, be regional depository libraries. For a fee, libraries can borrow research materials from the Center for Research Libraries (CRL), a nonprofit organization in Chicago. Since January 1952, the Center has collected as regularly and as comprehensively as possible, all state documents excluding session laws and compiled statutes; agricultural experiment station publications have been collected selectively. There is also a selective collection of pre-1952 state documents.

Resource sharing extends to the distribution of computerized and microform lists of holdings.[3] With such information, libraries can provide more informed referral. Referral is an important aspect of reference service. It necessitates knowledgeable insight into which organizations, agencies, libraries, etc. can best respond to user needs.

At present the extent of resource sharing varies greatly from state to state. Most regional depositories provide interlibrary loan on government documents to all libraries normally using the services of the parent library (17). Some regional libraries, however, neither loan nor photocopy documents extensively. Furthermore, many regionals do not possess the equipment necessary to make microform copies of requested items. If partial depositories are to concentrate collection development on the more frequently requested items, they must be assured that, whenever necessary, they can draw upon the resources of more complete collections. Conceivably, materials that are seldom used might be distributed in a microformat so that they need not be returned. At any rate, expanded service on the part of regional depositories requires larger staff sizes, more funds allocated to cooperative endeavors, and the purchasing of duplicating and copying equipment.

ACQUISITIONS

Depository Libraries

Librarians often want a broad awareness of what the federal government issues so that they can select from among the numerous titles those most germane to their needs. In addition to items received gratis through depository distribution, they also maintain prepaid deposit accounts with the Government Printing Office to cover sales publications not selected as part of the depository profile. Awareness of these additional items is based on a variety of approaches and reviewing sources. In fact, there is great variation in the reviewing sources depository libraries most frequently consult. The ones most frequently consulted, in order of preference, seem to be: *Booklist*, *Selected U.S. Government Publications*, *Reference Services Review*, *Choice*, the *Monthly Catalog of United States Government Publications*, and *RQ*. In addition, notices and publishers brochures constitute an important resource for awareness (*18*). Publishers brochures are the major means depository librarians utilize in selection of microform government publications (*19*). It may be that delays in the appearance of evaluative reviews in library-related periodicals cause documents librarians to place extensive reliance on publishers announcements.

In addition to the above-mentioned sources, librarians might consult *Documents to the People* (Chicago: ALA, Government Documents Round Table, 1972-), *Government Publications Review* (Elmsford, N.Y.: Pergamon Press, 1973-), and *Microform Review* (Westport, Conn.: 1972-). *Documents to the People* provides a means for keeping aware of current developments, especially those associated with the Government Documents Round Table. It also publicizes a few new titles of broad interest. *Government Publications Review* contains selection aids highlighting new, general interest publications. It is the only reviewing source with columns covering United States depository publications, non-GPO publications, federal audiovisuals, publications of state and municipal governments, and the publications of Britain, Canada, Australia, Western Europe and other countries, as well as the United Nations and international organizations. *Microform Review* at present is the only periodical

extensively reviewing microform collections of government publications. It might be noted that the entire September issue, both articles
and review, is devoted to government publications.

Depository libraries might also draw upon agency mailing lists and
catalogs,[4] the resources of congressional staffs,[5] government distributors such as NTIS and ERIC, the Documents Expediting Project
(Doc Ex), and commercial companies, including reprint and out-of-
print dealers and microform companies.[6] The Documents Expediting
Project, which is located within the Exchange and Gift Division of
the Library of Congress, is a centralized service for the acquisition of
publications not available for purchase through the Government
Printing Office or from issuing agencies. Participating libraries pay a
membership fee and are entitled to all publications distributed
through the service. In cases where the service obtains a limited
number of copies of a publication, those libraries paying the highest
rates receive priority selection. In addition to the distribution of
documents, Doc Ex performs a special request, searching service. It
will locate needed publications, whether they are current, retrospective, or out-of-print. Doc Ex will also place libraries on government agency mailing lists for specified serial publications.

The Government Printing Office is increasing the range of publications available for depository distribution and is therefore reducing
the population of source material that Doc Ex can supply. The value
of the distribution service might be decreasing now that Senate
executive documents and reports as well as committee prints are
becoming available for depository distribution. Furthermore, if
libraries center their hard-copy collections on heavily used items they
may not need such a service as that represented by Doc Ex. They
might instead expand microform holdings.

Microforms
The Congressional Joint Committee on Printing has authorized the
Government Printing Office to distribute only in microfiche certain
items not previously printed by GPO procurement plants. The Government Printing Office anticipates obtaining two copies of these
publications, converting them to microfiche, and making them avail-

able to depository libraries. It is estimated that as many as 6,000 non-GPO titles could be converted to microfiche during the first year alone. The Government Printing Office will also obtain some items which federal agencies produce only in microfiche and offer them to depository libraries only in the microformat.[7]

Librarians view microforms as a means for acquiring needed research material, filling in gaps in the collection, and replacing badly worn copies. At the same time microforms are a space saver. Libraries encountering space limitations for the documents collection can replace hard copy with microforms and use the extra space for new acquisitions. Another advantage of microforms is the reduced processing time. Libraries can expand their collections while at the same time freeing staff members for other activities. A cautionary note might be inserted: weeding and careful evaluation ought to extend to microform collections. As these collections grow, they will undoubtedly present space management problems.

Depository libraries frequently develop their microform collections of federal publications within certain areas: 1) Congress (hearings, committee prints, the serial set, and *Congressional Record* or its predecessors); 2) the executive branch (e.g., sources of the General Services Administration); 3) independent and regulatory agencies; and 4) judicial decisions. The third and fourth categories are acquired less often than the first two (*20*).

Microforms are available from the private sector. For example, Readex Microprint Corporation (New York) has offered all depository publications listed in the *Monthly Catalog* since 1956 and all nondepository items listed there since 1953. The project is a cooperative venture involving the Library Division of the Superintendent of Documents, the Documents Expediting Project, the Library of Congress Photoduplication Service, and Readex. The Library Division arranges all items in order in which they will appear in the *Monthly Catalog*, forwards them to the Library of Congress for filming at Readex's expense, and sends the resulting microform to Readex.

The Congressional Information Service (Washington, D.C.) has a different program. Libraries can purchase a microfiche collection of depository and/or nondepository statistical publications listed in the

American Statistics Index. There is even an on-demand service whereby libraries can quickly obtain congressional and statistical publications listed in the *CIS Index* and *American Statistics Index*, which they do not possess.

Carrollton Press (Washington, D.C.) has developed *Declassified Documents Quarterly Catalog* and a companion microform collection, which enable libraries to obtain material declassified as a result of the Freedom of Information Act of 1974.[8] Documents covered by this service primarily relate to foreign affairs and have never been included in the *Monthly Catalog*. More than 10,000 items are now available through the index. Without this service, the acquisition of individual items from executive departments and agencies would be exceedingly difficult and time consuming. As is evident, this service represents an opportunity to expand documents collections in another area, that of formerly sensitive material.

Data Bases

An increasing amount of data, statistical and bibliographical, collected and disseminated by government agencies is becoming available to the public in machine-readable form. Agencies such as the Bureau of the Census release only a portion of their data in hard copy; more is available in microform and data files. As has been shown in one study, faculty members using government produced machine-readable files cluster in institutions with graduate-degree programs. Those at baccalaureate institutions infrequently consult bibliographic data bases primarily because their institutional libraries seldom have the sources cited. It might be noted that data base users who were interviewed were largely unaware that interlibrary loan services extended to government publications (*21*).

It was found that social scientists at graduate-level institutions most frequently consulted search systems exploiting the ERIC files or the Census Tapes, U.S. Bureau of the Census. With the exception of the ERIC files, social scientists seem to rely most often on magnetic tapes purchased with departmental funds or from grants relating to sponsored research. These tapes are then stored in faculty offices, departmental laboratories, or campus institutes.

The question arises as to the role academic libraries should play in the acquisition and servicing of machine-readable data files. Many libraries lack the staff time and expertise to process files for public use. Therefore, if use centers on a small range of data files, libraries could selectively acquire or tie into them. Libraries acquiring data files produced by government agencies find the process extremely difficult. There is no single, comprehensive reference source covering all or even the majority of data files distributed by the federal government. There is also variation as to the quality of the files and their supporting documentation.[9]

And, finally, librarians might identify tapes held by the departments on campus and disseminate this information to faculty members, since these people are often unaware of the files retained by other departments and may be duplicating holdings. They might also identify those libraries within the state acquiring bibliographical and statistical data files and disseminate this information.

Nondepository Libraries

These libraries build functional collections of those government publications most frequently needed, primarily those distributed by the Government Printing Office and publicized in the *Monthly Catalog, Selected U.S. Government Publications*, and *Consumer Information*. Such indexes and catalogs identify new publications, editions, and revisions.

To help librarians negotiate the wealth of source material, numerous guides have been published in the last several years. For example, W. Philip Leidy's *A Popular Guide to Government Publications* (Columbia University Press, 1976) lists several thousand titles selected from items issued by federal agencies between 1967 and 1975. Walter L. Newsome's *New Guide to Popular Government Publications* (Libraries Unlimited, 1978) is comparable to the Leidy guide; it describes some 2,500 general interest publications and overviews acquisition procedures for federal information. *Government Reference Books, 1976/77* (Libraries Unlimited, 1978) and its predecessors are guides to bibliographies, directories, handbooks, etc. Nancy Patton Van Zant's *Selected U.S. Government Series* (ALA, 1978) discusses 600 series of potential value to small-to-medium-size public libraries and academic libraries with collections up to 300,000 volumes. Richard King's *Business Serial Publications of the U.S. Government* (ALA, 1978) highlights about 100 serials pertaining to industry and commerce. And, finally, Yuri Nakata's *From Press to People* (ALA, 1979) assists nondepository libraries in understanding and negotiating the complexity of federal government publishing. It discusses selection, acquisition, organization, and arrangement.

Briefly, in order to acquire needed publications, nondepository libraries can establish prepaid deposit accounts with the Government Printing Office (a minimum of $50), charge all purchases against the account, and deal with the GPO bookstore in closest proximity. In some instances, librarians might contact congressional representatives and request publications gratis or approach issuing agencies or congressional committees themselves. In order to lessen the amount of time and paper work involved in the acquisitions process, some of these libraries might rely on commercial dealers and jobbers that negotiate the wealth of Government Printing Office publishing and distribute source material requested by their clientele.[10]

STATE PUBLICATIONS

Major efforts are currently underway to improve bibliographic control for state publications and to make it easier for libraries and users to monitor state publishing and to select those items most beneficial to their needs. For example, 39 states have either partial or full depository systems. Of the 11 remaining states approximately half are developing depository legislation (22). Other efforts to improve bibliographic control involve the channeling of state publications into the OCLC system and producing state checklists from the tapes, microfiche distribution of many or all state depository items, the production of current awareness services that highlight major publications listed in the regular checklist, the development of specialized reference guides (e.g., those explaining source material for conducting legislative histories and those monitoring the statistical output of a state), and the active participation of commercial companies.[11] In

Utah, it might be noted, the State Library Commission in cooperation with the Division of Archives and the State University Library
has collected, indexed, and microfiched all state publications. The
publications are then entered into the Utah Publications Retrieval
System, a computerized index for retrieval by title, author, agency,
keyword subject, and geographical location.

Librarians frequently concentrate collection development on the
resources of their own state and perhaps the immediate region. They
base their selections on listings found in the Library of Congress'
Monthly Checklist of State Publications, checklists of the states in
question, patron requests, and duplicate exchange lists. Limited use
is made of acquisitions guides, perhaps because they are all so
dated (23).[1][2]

It ought to be questioned how extensively state publishing needs
to be identified and how broadly libraries need to collect from state
governments. Perhaps many libraries should center their collection
development on reference sources. Determination as to how comprehensive the collection and how recent obtained sources should be
depends on frequency of publication, user needs, curriculum, and
whether the library contains other sources with similar information.
Even within states having depository programs, many libraries can
gather state publications selectively. Only one library or agency in
the state needs to collect comprehensively. Other libraries can rely
on resource sharing for seldom requested publications.

MUNICIPAL PUBLICATIONS

With the growing volume and importance of municipal documents
relating to a wide range of social, economic, and political problems
common to urban affairs, there is a role for libraries to play in
developing and servicing local documents collections. Yet, many
libraries collect these publications selectively or not at all. They do
not even systematically collect and provide access to the publications
of their own municipality.

The problem is that bibliographic control for municipal publications is haphazard and varies from city to city. Materials are often

published irregularly, printed in small quantities, and distributed on a limited basis. To gather materials for one's own city, it is often necessary to visit city agencies periodically and to request copies of new publications. Even depository legislation does not guarantee that all source material will be forwarded.

Few libraries have extensive collections of publications for cities across the united States. Even the Library of Congress collects for its permanent holdings only the resources of 14 cities. It acquires and retains for the permanent collection publications of other cities only "when these publications are recommended for acquisition as containing important information on subjects of particular concern to Congress and to the federal government in general" (24). Other noted collections include those of the U.S. Department of Housing and Urban Development and U.S. Bureau of the Census.

Because of the problems associated with collection development, many libraries focus selection and retention on the resources of their own city. Such libraries may benefit from Yuri Nakata and Susan J. Smith's manual, *Starting and Maintaining a Local Government Documents Collection* (ALA, 1979), which advises small public libraries about the selection, acquisition, and organization of local publications.

The question arises as to how extensively the publishing record of a city needs to be acquired. Most libraries could be selective in what they acquire and retain, especially if the majority of reference requests conform to certain patterns. Perhaps one library in the city or even in the state could become the official repository for municipal publications. Other libraries could acquire and retain them selectively. They could send publications that are used infrequently or not used at all to the official repository.

Libraries desiring publications for other municipalities might rely on Greenwood Press' *Index to Current Urban Documents* and companion microfiche collection. The index lists publications for over 200 cities, and there are various purchase options for the microfiche collection.[13] Libraries therefore can devise a profile to match their particular needs. The microfiche service performs an important function since many cities do not send municipal publications on interlibrary loan.

A recent survey of reference publishing for major cities across the nation indicated that most cities do not have a wealth and diversity of reference publishing (25). In fact, many reference sources are ephemeral and rapidly becoming obsolete. Since general reports containing statistical data and specialized publications often fulfill a reference function, it takes someone knowledgeable with the publishing record of a particular city to suggest appropriate source material and to devise search strategies for uncovering information difficult to locate.

Dealing directly with libraries and agencies in other cities can be a time-consuming process. First, one must know which agency deals directly with the subject or which library is most likely to collect municipal documents and to disseminate information about their contents. Since this determination can be difficult, the following suggestions are offered. When searching for appropriate libraries, it might be helpful to check the following.

1. American Library Association. Government Documents Round Table. *Municipal Government Reference Sources: Publications and Collections*. (New York: Bowker, 1978.)
2. American Library Association. Government Documents Round Table. *1978 Directory of Government Document Collections and Libraries*. (Washington: Congressional Information Service, 1978.)

For cities in which these guides are not helpful, one should check the *American Library Directory* (New York: Bowker, 1923-   ) for mention of municipal reference libraries and urban observatories.[14]

And, finally, in establishing municipal documents collections libraries ought to consider such questions as the following.

1. Are other libraries in the immediate vicinity collecting these publications? If yes, how extensively? Can a coordinated collection-building policy be formulated? In what areas will collections be duplicative?
2. Will the collection focus entirely or primarily on the immediate municipality? Will other cities be included? On what basis will they be selected?
3. How extensively will the library collect? Will it collect comprehensively, by subject, or by key departments and agencies?

Perhaps the library might only collect high-interest publications that merit permanent retention.

4. Will the library purchase documents from Greenwood Press or explore other acquisition alternatives?

5. How much money and how many staff members will be budgeted to collection development and maintenance? What facilities will be needed?

6. How will the collection be arranged, classified, and accessed (e.g., through the main public card catalog or computer retrieval)?

UNITED NATIONS PUBLICATIONS

The United Nations publishes a wealth of material including proceedings, reports, treaties, periodicals, special studies, and reference books. In 1971 alone, the United Nations headquarters in New York distributed 558,000,000 pages of materials and the offices in Geneva produced an additional 234,000,000 pages. Moreover one-seventh of the United Nations budget, over $30 million, was spent on paper work (26). Researchers and students seeking statistical data produced by the United Nations frequently consult one or more of the many United Nations statistical yearbooks or periodicals. Commercial publishers issuing reference tools that give an overview of various countries and their economies often draw upon United Nations gathered statistical data. As might be expected, many libraries find United Nations source material an important information resource.

It seems that many libraries building small collections of United Nations Materials primarily collect reference sources and those materials needed by debating groups and social science classes (e.g., those participating in model United Nations exercises). They select their acquisitions from among categories of sales publications, periodicals, official records, and mimeographed documents. For supplementary material, they acquire microforms, tap data files, consult depository libraries, and participate in cooperative arrangements. The United Nations, as well as many specialized agencies such as the Food and Agriculture Organization, operate depository library systems.[15]

In order to acquire source material, libraries can consult Unipub, United Nations Publications, or UNIFO Publishers Ltd. Libraries planning to start collections should contact these distributors, compare standing order options, and tailor selections to match local needs. Publications of such specialized agencies as the International Monetary Fund are available through separate sales organizations.

And, finally, libraries building function collections will want to be aware of two guides: Brenda Brimmer's *A Guide to the Use of the United Nations Documents* (Oceana, 1962), and Peter I. Hajnal's *Guide to United Nations Organization, Documentation and Publishing for Students, Researchers, Librarians* (Oceana, 1978). These guides complement each other and discuss the use, acquisition, and servicing of this material. The one by Hajnal also presents specialized agencies and a selected list of their publications. Other pertinent reference sources include the following.

1. *International Bibliography, Information, Documentation* (Unipub, 1973-   ), which is a quarterly bibliography of current publications of the United Nations and other organizations;
2. *United Nations Publications in Print: Check List English* (United Nations Publications, 1978), which covers sales publications and is comparable to *Books in Print* (Bowker, 1948-   );
3. *U.N. Sales Publications, 1972-1977* (United Nations Publications, 1978), which is useful for bibliographic control, selection, and the history of the organization;
4. *United Nations Official Records, 1962-1970* (United Nations, 1971) and *Supplement, 1970-1972* (1973), which are catalogs of the different series;
5. *United Nations Documents and Publications: A Research Guide* by Mary K. Fetzer (New Brunswick, N.J.: Rutgers University, Graduate School of Library Service, April 1978), which is a brief guide to the major sources and problems encountered in using United Nations materials;
6. "Documentation Activities of the United Nations Library at Geneva," by Heinz A. Waldner (*Information Processing and Management* 14 [1978] : 135-140), which analyzes the acquisition and bibliographic control of United Nations, Geneva, material;
7. *Documents of International Organisations: A Bibliographical*

Handbook by T.D. Dimitrov (ALA, 1973), which lists current catalogs and indexes as well as works on the structure and activities of the United Nations and other international government organizations (the directory of organizations at the end of the handbook provides addresses from which to obtain publications);

8. *Publications of the United Nations System: A Reference Guide* by Harry N.M. Winton (Bowker, 1972), which has useful ordering information and a list of current catalogs and indexes. It also has an annotated bibliography of important publications and a list of periodicals issued by the agencies.

TOPICS FOR FURTHER RESEARCH

Government publications represent an area fertile for research. Many of the current practices in the documents field are based upon supposition and opinion dating back at least to the 1930s. The research presented in this essay has been exploratory and has often had an insufficient basis upon which to predict the expected direction that findings would take. This essay has emphasized that little is currently known about collection development for documents and has suggested research on such topics as the following:

1. the identification of the core literature of government publications for individual disciplines and across disciplines;
2. types of government publications used most frequently and the rate of obsolescence for documents;
3. interlibrary loan practices for government publications and the use of resource sharing;
4. identification of core agency and legislative mailing lists;
5. comparison of present research findings on academic social scientists in the disciplines of economics, history, political science, and sociology with use patterns for faculty members in other disciplines. Research should also extend to other user groups and to other types of libraries.

CONCLUSION

Many libraries, including those supporting research collections, are discovering that their budgets for buying books and periodicals have lost much of their purchasing power. As a result, they are trying to determine how well their collections are meeting the information needs of their clientele "so that the limited funds for new materials can be allocated where they are most needed" (27). Library administrators face hard decisions about the reallocation of funding for library materials and personnel brought on by spiraling costs. Although government publications housed in depository libraries have not compiled an impressive record of past use, their rising and potential value to a wide range of clientele deserve reassessment. Since the informational content of government publications supplement library holdings of other genre, the application of collection management principles to documents collections may lessen the impact of stable or declining budgets. After all, many documents are received gratis as part of depository arrangements on the stipulation that they are made available to the public. As one library educator so aptly explained:

> Library administrators need to consider government publications collections as an information resource on an equal basis with books and serials, to the extent that they are integrated in information services, whether shelved as separate collections as in many major research libraries. The relationship between the documents collection and other library collections should be that of a single resource in meeting user needs. To restate: the key to a good government documents collection is integration into the mainstream of library information service (28).

"The wide diversity of practice among the different governmental units in the printing, distribution, and announcement," the same educator maintained, "constitutes a special challenge to librarians in the selection, acquisition, and servicing of collections matching the potential needs of their clientele." Basic to a resolution of the problem is consideration of government publications more as informational matter than as archival records, and the improvement of document delivery (29). At the same time, elimination of ephemeral, trivial, superseded, and duplicative publications from documents collections ought to better serve user needs. Partial depositories as well as nondepositories should identify and acquire high-interest publications and rely on resource sharing for material that is seldom or never used, much of which could be supplied as microform in a nonarchival format.

REFERENCES

1. Ellen P. Jackson, *The Administration of the Government Documents Collection*, ACRL Monographs No. 5 (Chicago: Publications Committee of the Association of College and Reference Libraries, 1953), p. 2.

2. Anne Morris Boyd and Rae Elizabeth Rips, *United States Government Publications*. (New York: H.W. Wilson, 1949), p. 555.

3. Michael K. Buckland, *Book Availability and the Library User*. (Elmsford, N.Y.: Pergamon Press, 1975), p. 3.

4. U.S. Government Printing Office, *Guidelines for the Depository Library System*, as adopted by the Depository Library Council to the Public Printer, October 18, 1977, p. 4.

5. Peter Hernon, "Use and Non-Use of Government Publications by Social Scientists in Selected Academic Institutions," (Ph.D. Dissertation, Indiana University, 1978), pp. 59 and 62.

6. Ibid., pp. 153-154.

7. Ibid., pp. 93-98.

8. Terry L. Weech, "The Use of Government Publications: A Selected Review of the Literature." *Government Publications Review* 5 (1978): 179.

9. Ibid.; James C. Baughman, "A Structural Analysis of the Literature of Sociology," *The Library Quarterly* 44 (October 1974): 295-296; June L. Stewart, "The Literature of Politics: A Citation Analysis," *International Library Review* 2 (1970): 329-353; and Robert Goehlert, "A Citation Analysis of International Organization: The Use of Government Documents," *Government Publications Review*, forthcoming.

10. Weech, "Use of Government Publications," p. 180.

11. Wilfred D. Danielson, "United Nations Documents at Northwestern University," *Illinois Libraries* 55 (March 1973): 139-146; and Hernon, "Use and Non-Use of Government Publications," p. 186.

12. Hernon, "Use and Non-Use of Government Publications," pp. 121-125.

13. Peter Hernon, "An Approach to Teaching Documents Courses," *Government Publications Review*, Ablex Press, 1979.

14. A detailed examination could be patterned after: J.A. Urquhart and J.L. Schofield, "Measuring Readers' Failure at the Shelf," *Journal of Documentation* 27 (1971): 273-276; and J.A. Urquhart and J.L. Schofield, "Measuring Readers' Failure at the Shelf in Three University Libraries," *Journal of Documentation* 28 (1972): 233-241.

15. Peter Hernon, "State 'Documents to the People'," *Government Publications Review* 3 (1976): 260, 265-266.

16. George W. Whitbeck, Peter Hernon, and John Richardson, Jr., "The Federal Depository Library System: A Descriptive Analysis." *Government Publications Review* 5 (1978): 263.

17. LeRoy C. Schwartzkopf, "Regional Depository Libraries for U.S. Government Publications." *Government Publications Review* 2 (1975): 97.

18. George W. Whitbeck and Peter Hernon, "The Attitudes of Librarians Toward the Servicing and Use of Government Publications." *Government Publications Review* 4 (1977): 185.

19. Peter Hernon and George W. Whitbeck, "Government Publications and Commercial Microform Publishers: A Survey of Federal Depository Libraries." *Microform Review* 6 (September 1977): 276.

20. Ibid.

21. Hernon, "Use and Non-Use of Government Publications," pp. 149-151.

22. Robert F. Gaines, "Recent Developments in Depository Systems for State Government Documents." *Documents to the People* 6 (November 1978): 229.

23. Whitbeck and Hernon, "Attitudes of Librarians . . . " pp. 185-186.

24. Peter Hernon, et al., *Municipal Government Reference Sources: Publications and Collections.* (New York: Bowker, 1978), pp. 1-2.

25. Ibid.

26. *The New York Times*, May 28, 1972, p. 4.

27. "Research Libraries' Collections Hit Hard by Inflation," *The Chronicle of Higher Education* 17 (January 22, 1979): 18.

28. Bernard M. Fry, "Government Publications and the Library: Implications for Change." *Government Publications Review* 4 (1977): 115.

29. Ibid., p. 112.

NOTES

1. Part of this essay is drawn from Peter Hernon, *Use of Government Publications by Social Scientists* (Ablex Publishing, 1979).

2. It should be noted that a mail questionnaire was the main data collec-

tion instrument. Interviews were carried out at a subsample of institutions and with a subsample of faculty members. The investigator did not circulate a list of titles among interview subjects. Titles reported emerged during the interviews. Social scientists repeatedly suggested that they subscribed to or gathered information from these titles on a regular basis.

3. By the fall of 1979, the Government Printing Office plans to have operational a computerized list of current item numbers selected by depository libraries. With such information libraries can better gauge, the collection-building interests of other libraries in the vicinity.

4. Issuing agencies frequently have a stock of items which must be ordered directly through them. These items are specially marked in the *Monthly Catalog*.

5. Some publications may be obtained gratis from members of Congress. Libraries placed on mailing lists of members of Congress can receive additional items.

6. For information on federal mapping and charting activities see: Jane Grant-Mackay, *The Acquisition of Maps and Charts Published by the United States Government* (Urbana: University of Illinois, Graduate School of Library Science, Occasional Papers No. 125, 1976). This source covers such topics as selection tools and federal agencies distributing and publishing maps.

The National Audiovisual Center, National Archives and Records Service, General Services Administration, serves as a central information source on federal audiovisual materials. Established in 1969, it provides government agencies and the general public with central information and with loan, sales, and rental service for audiovisual sources.

Libraries in other countries wanting federal publications should be aware of: J.A. Downey, *U.S. Federal Government Publications* (Brighton: University of Sussex, Institute of Development Studies, Library, 1975).

7. The General Accounting GC Legislative History Files are now being offered as part of the GPO microform program. It is "estimated that 40,000 microfiche would be issued over a period of two years" and that "the two year file would require 38 linear feet of storage space, and would weigh 334 pounds." LeRoy Schwartzkopf, "News from GPO," *Documents to the People* 7 (January 1979): 11. This news note also stated that "if a depository received a copy of every diazo fiche issued to date under the GPO Microform Program it would have received approximately 27 linear feet of microfiche weighing 112 pounds" (p. 12).

8. This act provides for the release of individual items but not for their widespread public distribution as part of the depository program.

9. For a discussion of collection development problems see: Judith S. Rowe, "Machine-Readable Data Files of Government Publications," *Government Publications Review* 5 (1978): 195-197.

10. For suggestions where to find a list of documents dealers and jobbers see: Joe Morehead, *Introduction to United States Public Documents*, 2nd ed. (Littleton, Colo.: Libraries Unlimited, 1978), p. 49.

11. Research Publications, for example, is microfilming and selling the publications of selected states. It is even offering certain items which were not available for depository distribution. Information Handling Services is producing a quarterly, consolidated checklist for publications of all states, U.S. commonwealths and possessions. For more information on the checklist see: "Information Handling Services' Checklist of State Publications and State Publications Microfiche Program: Two Viewpoints—A User's Viewpoint [and] The Publisher Responds," *Documents to the People* 6 (November 1978): 234-235+.

12. The guides are: David Paris, *State Government Reference Publications* (Littleton, Colo.: Libraries Unlimited, 1974); Council of State Government, *State Blue Books and Reference Publications* (Lexington, Ky.: The Council, 1974); and Peter Hernon, "State Publications," *Library Journal* 99 (1974): 2810-2819.

13. The index includes the following types of publications: reports of departments and agencies; budgets; special reports; proceedings of boards, commissions, and councils; special issues of periodicals containing budgets, etc.; court reports; publications of urban observatories; publications of special districts and regional organizations; publications of such civic organizations as the League of Women Voters; charters, codes, ordinances, regulations, and reference sources; and state publications pertaining to the municipality. Excluded from the microfiche collection are: copyrighted materials, periodicals other than special issues, preliminary reports (unless they are final), fugitive materials including brochures, news releases, and maps. Greenwood Press, "Documents for the Index to Current Urban Documents," August 1978.

14. Urban observatories are funded by the U.S. Department of Housing and Urban Development and participating local institutions. Their purpose is to encourage cities to apply the expertise of the academic community to their major problems and to further understanding with academia of the problems and issues confronting the cities.

15. A full explanation of partial and complete depository arrangements for United Nations publications can be found in *Instructions for Depository Libraries Receiving United Nations Material* (ST/LIB/13/Rev. 3, March 31, 1977).

Selection of Media

Margaret E. Chisholm

INTRODUCTION

To address the topic of media collection development is both intriguing and challenging. Development of media collections must be viewed somewhat as a paradox as there is no question that media can be selected by persons with little experience or knowledge and the task can be performed in a most unsophisticated manner. By contrast, the process can be performed by using complex models based on theory and research and thoughtful use of sophisticated selection, evaluation and assessment tools. The paradox becomes compounded since possibly the only valid criteria on which to judge the total process is to be able to determine whether the item of media selected eventually fulfills the complex needs of the user.

The purpose of this chapter is to examine a variety of factors relating to the selection of media. Ultimately it is expected that an examination of these factors will result in achieving the goal of selecting media that will most appropriately fulfill the needs of the users.

First there must be a common base of understanding so definitions are reviewed. In the field of media there can be great diversity in defining terms but the definitions as presented here are to help in clarifying the concepts discussed in this chapter.

The second section describes and analyzes the diversity of approaches to the development of media collections. The viewpoints presented range from the selection practices typically utilized in libraries to the models presented by instructional designers and educational technologists.

An historical review is presented in the third section to provide an understanding of the current status of media selection.

The fourth section is a composite of statements relating to current theory and practices as described by experts in the field, including persons practicing selection, those teaching media selection, those involved in evaluating media, and those utilizing media.

The fifth section includes caveats and recommendations as presented by experts in the field. Their comments relate primarily to current financial cutbacks, attitudes relating to the use of media, and current selection practices.

Finally, there will be a consideration of future developments which will inevitably have a dramatic impact on the selection of media.

DEFINITION OF TERMS

Even the dictionary has difficulty with the term *media*. It is such a strange word that the dictionary claims that *media* is the plural of *medium*—but that under some circumstances it can be used in the singular. In this chapter media will usually be regarded as plural.

In the general definition of the term *media* is usually interpreted as "a means for communicating information, including all printed materials." For our considerations we are concerned with materials such as audio tapes, slides, films, photographs, videotapes, drawings, filmstrips, programmed texts, television, audio discs, mock-ups, computer display equipment and computer software, models, dioramas, and real objects. Several terms have emerged through popular usage and through the literature to designate these materials, including *nonprint media*, *nonbook media*, and *audiovisual media*. The terms *nonprint* and *nonbook* are nonambiguous, but both are rather negative in that the interpretation depends on the idea of "all that is not." Audiovisual media is preferred by some, but excludes certain categories of media such as objects, dioramas and machine readable data formats. Educators often use the modifier *instructional* media or *educational* media. As the alternative terms and meanings have been discussed, it is simpler for the purpose of this chapter to use the term *media* to mean all the products, software, or materials which have been identified in the preceeding description.

A CONTINUUM OF VIEWPOINTS

A definition alone is not adequate to provide the setting for a consideration of media selection. There must also be a context within which the utilization of media is considered. When we consider the user of media services we usually are referring to the learner or user in formal educational settings in elementary schools, secondary schools, and post-secondary institutions. Users can also be found in nonformal programs which are usually attached to an institution but do not necessarily need to be. Users would include patrons who seek the services of a public library. The learner or user is the focal point of any media program because the learner is the person who will be most directly affected. If a teacher or librarian is involved in the process, he or she will serve as a mediator or facilitator for the learner. The selection and utilization of media are performed for the purpose of affecting the behavior of the learner and to assist the learner in achieving cognitive, affective, or psychomotor objectives, sometimes referred to as behavioral objectives.

It is also important to consider a number of points of view. The following comparisons are unfortunately based on generalizations and that is always dangerous, as there undoubtedly are many exceptions and deviations. However, for purposes of our considerations the following interpretations and reference points could be helpful.

Historically, libraries have acquired, stored, and disseminated print material. As technology developed, information began to be stored in a great number of formats and librarians began to consider it their professional responsibility to acquire and disseminate information regardless of the format. Prior to 1960, a number of libraries had provided recordings, maps, and art prints, and a few progressive libraries had provided film collections for their users. At this same time the program of audiovisual education was developing rapidly. The major thrust of the audiovisual movement was to provide a variety of media to learners and to assist them in appropriate utilization. During the decade of 1955 to 1965 the growth of the audiovisual field, both technologically and from the viewpoint of utilization in education, reached a peak of development. This, in turn, had the greatest impact on school libraries and they moved toward integrating both print and nonprint materials or media to become learning resource centers or media centers. Public libraries, also, were affected by these developments and expanded their collections to include films, filmstrips, slides, and audio tapes. Special libraries had been forerunners in providing collections of maps, slides, and music recordings, and microforms.

The audiovisual movement in education was the precursor of the approach identified as educational technology, which evolved from the perceived need to develop a comprehensive design for instruction. Educational technology is defined as a field involved in the facilitation of human learning through the systematic identification, development, organization, and utilization of a full range of learning resources, and through the management of these processes. It includes, but is not limited to, the development of instructional systems, the identification of existing resources, the delivery of resources to learners, and the management of these processes and the people who perform them (1).

CONDITIONS AFFECTING MEDIA SELECTION

There is a reason for establishing these differentiations in the contexts in which varieties of media are used. In each of these settings, whether it is a library, resource center, or instructional design center, there are certain traditional or established philosophies relating to the selection of media.

First, media selection in public libraries would normally be done by the librarian for a user group that in most cases would be broad and heterogeneous. The utilization might serve an individual but could also serve a very large group. Therefore, the goals of the user would necessarily have to be stated in broad, general terms and be quite subjective. Concomitantly the techniques to assess user needs would also have to focus on general needs. The selection strategies would most likely follow the pattern established in the library profession, primarily of using selection tools in the form of bibliographies and evaluative review.

Special libraries would refine selection somewhat, in that their clientele would, in most cases, be a narrow one, much more homogenous, and individuals would have somewhat similar needs and expectations. For example, an art library would most normally be expected to have media including prints, slides, and photographs, while a special library serving an airplane manufacturing company would expect to have mock-ups, models, blueprints, microforms and computer print-outs. Selection would normally be done through using a set of selection tools with a narrower range, and through a much greater focus on the special needs of the users.

School libraries, K through 12, would select media for their learning resource center program mainly through relating the selection to the curriculum. In most cases, selection of media has not taken on a high level of sophistication, however, there are some very comprehensive learning resource centers which have made impressive progress in selection techniques. Still, in most cases, selection would be related very closely to the curriculum, and only in limited cases would the needs of the individual student be analyzed.

The area in which most of the sophisticated techniques of selection have emerged and which has generated the greatest body of literature is in the field of educational technology. The selection process has taken on such complexity that a great number of models have emerged to attempt to solve the complex problem of selection if the educational technologist is to meet the objectives of a particular learning task, with a specific set of learners in a particular learning environment. The challenge is to provide the best means of instruction for individual students. These models will be described in a later segment dealing with selection strategies.

As these fields have evolved another paradox has emerged. The field of librarianship, in which there is, in most cases, less of an opportunity to focus on the individual, has provided the most impetus for developing selection tools such as media indexes and review sources, which focus on the item. At the same time educational technology, which focuses on the learning process, has given much more attention to the individual learner and has made relatively little significant contribution toward developing selection tools. The great need which has been apparent to leaders in both these fields is that until there is a coordinated and unified action to coalesce these efforts, both fields will be handicapped in making desperately needed progress in media selection.

STRATEGIES OF SELECTION

The term *strategy* will be used to indicate an overall plan, which would include a consideration of many factors, in some cases a model or a complex technique usually used by educational technologists or by instructional designers. What is meant by instructional design? Authorities in the field of educational psychology, learning theory, educational technology and instructional development all have come forth with definitions. For example, from Kemp . . .

> a realistic plan for designing improved instruction that may be applicable today by instructional staffs in any school. It can build on the old, making use of familiar language. It can draw from valuable experience in such areas as programmed instruction (objectives specification, small-step subject-matter presentation, and continual evaluation of student learning), and audiovisual materials, production techniques (primarily production

planning for motion pictures and television), and it can incorporate important elements from the systems model (2).

From AECT . . .

The part of the instructional development process that is analogous to the Design Function of the Domain of Educational Technology model; i.e., the generation of specifications for Learning Resources/Instructional Systems Components. (Not synonymous with, though often confused with, instructional development and instructional product development.) (3)

From Diamond et al., . . .

(1)   project generation and selection,
(2)   basic design inputs,
(3)   preliminary component outline, and
(4)   operational sequence (4).

From Davis et al., . . .

the word *design* is used when referring to learning systems, in precisely the same sense as it is used when one speaks of *designing* an information processing system. Good system design implies the careful specification of requirements and objectives, the systematic analysis of these objectives to specify alternative approaches to achieving them, the development of a system to meet the objectives, and the evaluation of its performance (5).

From Gustafson . . .

specifying all instructional strategies and leads to arranging and sequencing both human and nonhuman resources (6).

From Banathy who asks . . .

(1)   What has to be done to enable the learner to master the task?
(2)   Who or what has the capability of doing whatever has to be done?
(3)   Who or what will do exactly what?
(4)   When and where will they do it (7)?

From Merrill and Tennyson . . .

> means selecting and arranging instructional materials in a way which helps
> students learn more efficiently and effectively than they would from a
> natural situation. It also means selecting and arranging special materials
> which allow you as a teacher, or the students as learners, to find out
> whether they have learned what you intended (8).

As one can see from the above definitions, all have consistent
concepts which include a systematic arrangement of a variety of
materials, messages, methods, and personnel. The most succinct
definition which includes all elements is the following: "Instructional
design is the process of selecting, planning and using instructional
strategies and media based on instructional objectives" (9).

It seems appropriate to discuss these more complex strategies
taken from institutional design first and then move to the less
complex techniques. As through the review of the strategies, attention will be focused on the various elements and factors considered
in different selection models and then, by contrast, one will be able
to see how simpler techniques omit, condense, or ignore some of the
factors identified in these models.

Dr. Howard Levie of Indiana University has stated that the "search
for the ideal medium to convey maximum instruction with maximum impact to the broadest possible audience has often resembled
the fruitless search for the fountain of youth. There have been those
who argued that one single format for all media will increase utilization of what presently exists, as well as remove anxiety of decision-
making for producers and training for consumers" (10).

In giving balance and perspective to the interpretation of the following models for media selection, it is well to consider Gagnés'
argument.

> Most media of communication can readily perform most instructional
> functions. They can be performed by pictures, by printed language, by
> auditory language, or by a combination of media. So far as learning is
> concerned, the medium is not the message. No single medium possesses
> properties which are uniquely adopted to perform one or a combination of
> instructional functions. Instead they all perform some of these functions
> well, and some not so well (11).

It is also important to note that as educational technologists and instructional designers develop models for media selection they tend to emphasize different aspects of the total process. Some models are developed to be theoretical in approach and relate closely to relevant research. Others, by contrast, focus on pragmatic elements such as cost, equipment, and distribution options. A number of models emphasize learner differences or are related particularly to subject matter areas. Models also differ markedly in the manner in which they handle the broad concept of media. In some cases media attributes such as sound, color, motion are identified and analyzed. Other models categorize media according to the presentation hardware such as projectors, computers, or teaching machines. Others specify media by generic classes such as film, videotape, audio tape.

In addition, the models vary greatly in their level of sophistication and in complexity. They are presented in a great variety of formats from simply posing questions, or through questions and answers, flow charts, matrixes, and sequential step procedures.

Gerlach and Ely have articulated one commonality among model developers and that is the relationship between the medium and the task. They state the "Media Selection Rule: that a medium of instruction must be selected on the basis of its potential for implementing a stated objective" (12).

Most persons in the field of educational technology also hold the view that the behavioral objectives or learning tasks must be identified and then the medium of instruction should be selected which will most appropriately meet the needs of the individual student to accomplish the identified behavioral objective. In theory, this is an ideal approach, however, the production of instructional materials almost always takes place without close integration with the learning task. This is especially true of films which are usually made by creative persons who are intrigued by the subject of the film, rather than on the learning tasks it might fulfill.

Table 1 identifies authors and instructional developers who have introduced models relating to media selection. It is presented for several purposes. First, it provides the names of authors or instructional developers who have written in this field so that if the reader wishes to pursue this aspect of media selection these authors would provide meaningful information. Second, the point has been made

TABLE 1

Author or Instructional Developer	Date	Characteristics of Model
Allen (13)	1967	Simple model which identifies six different types of learning (such as factual information) and identifies 10 types of media to facilitate each type of learning and rates them as high, medium or low in facilitating each type of learning.
Tosti & Ball (14)	1969	The model is based on the concept of presentation form, which is the structure by which the information is carried, such as programmed instruction. Presentation forms are defined by stimulus factors, responsive factors and management factors. Stress is placed on entering behavior, technical behavior, and human intervention, or the management factor.
Van Moufrans & Houser (15)	1970	This model is offered in teaching concepts. The key stages are: (1) to describe the attributes of the concept, (2) describe the capability of the media, (3) identify the media which present sensory information required to convey the concept.
Goodman (16)	1971	The model outlines a selection development procedure consisting of 12 tasks. In summary, these are: analyze the behavioral objectives, determine student characteristics, list the equipment and methods, identify local resources, describe materials which could be locally produced, rank the alternatives according to instructional and cost effectiveness, select the most effective media combination, obtain or produce, then try to evaluate, recycle.
Kemp (17)	1971	A flow chart is used to present this model. The first branch requires a selection among large groups, class size, small groups and individuals. The second branch divides into options of verbal abstractions, concrete experiences, vicarious sensory experiences. For each option media possibilities are suggested. Further branching can be extended to reflect individual circumstances.
Nunney & Hill (18)	1972	Learner characteristics are the definitive factor in the model. Developed at Oakland Community College in Michigan, this model is based on diagnostic testing and the production of a cognitive map for each student. Factors considered are sensory aptitude, quantitative and verbal abilities, and social skills. Instructional modes and media are prescribed for each student.
Lonigro & Eschenbrenner (19)	1973	This model is based on Allen's matrix. Eight media types are rated as having high, partial, or low proficiency in facilitating the attainment of five types of learning. Production costs are calculated and cost is balanced against learning proficiency. A graph depicts the trade-offs.

Table 1 (*continued*)

Author or Instructional Developer	Date	Characteristics of the Model
Holden (*20*)	1975	A matrix provides seven media types rated according to seven decision factors. The critical factor is the degree to which the learners' responses should be controlled, such as high control would be appropriate learning to pilot an aircraft. Each media type is rated as high, medium, or low in this respect, production cost, flexibility, adaptability. An additional matrix is provided to deal with hardware considerations that may help in the final choice.
Levie (*21*)	1975	Levie attempts to make maximum use of research in media selection. Research demonstrates differential effectiveness between media attributes, such as sign-vehicle characteristics (words vs. pictures), realism cues (color, motion, still), and sensory modalities control characteristics (fixed vs. flexible pace or sequence) and response. Levie's model suggests that an analysis be made of the task though learner and the environment to determine what media attributes are required.
Wagner (*22*)	1975	This model is based on Edgar Dales' "Cone of Experience," which ranks various media and teaching techniques from abstract (verbal symbols) to most concrete (direct purposeful experiences). Wager proposes that the effectiveness of media in changing attitudes is related to the abstractness of the media used and the learner's age. Abstract media for adults tend to compress learning time, but for changing attitudes concrete media may be more effective.

that from the perspective of educational technologists and instructional developers the selection of media becomes a complex task. Granted, the term *selection* is used in a variety of interpretations. The instructional developer is focusing on *selection* as the identification of media for use with a particular student to accomplish an explicit learning task. In this case the emphasis is not primarily on where or how the medium was acquired or produced. However, in order for that medium to be available for the instructional developer to consider for use, it had to be acquired or produced by someone through some identification and selection process. Therefore, these models do indicate the complex factors that have been identified in the total concept of selection.

In summary, it could be pointed out that these models would vary in usefulness according to the context and individual instructional developers would wish to use different models in different situations. Some models present a perspective of the different characteristics of media resources, others provide assistance in decision making. Some models focus primarily on teachers while others would be of greater assistance to students. The models also provide procedures that facilitate sequential decision making. Most of these models could be modified and adapted to suit a number of specific situations and resources. Levie cautions that it is not reasonable to expect that media selection can ever become an automated process, but that considerable artistry and subjectivity are required. Holden states that "subjective judgment is more acceptable once the illogical choices have been eliminated" (23).

To emphasize the complexity of the selection process for instructional developers or educational technologists, the following are a number of factors identified as those that could determine or affect selection: Type of learning, behavioral objective or objectives, presentation form, management factors, characteristics of the media, attributes of the concept to be learned, student characteristics, equipment, teaching methods, local production capability and resources, size of the group, sensory impact of the medium, sensory aptitudes, quantitative and verbal abilities, social skills of students, cost, control of responses, flexibility, adaptability, media attributes such as sign vehicle characteristics, realism cues, sensory modalities, abstractness, and concreteness.

This list of factors is presented to emphasize the contrast between the complexity of factors considered by instructional developers and the relatively unsophisticated selection process in which the media resource center director looks in a producer's catalog to find a filmstrip which can be purchased with the minimal amount of money left in the budget.

To sum up and provide the framework for further considerations it can be said that media selection is a continuum in which many modes of selection activity take place—from the most unsophisticated to the most complex. Indeed, there can even be combinations of these levels of sophistication occurring in a single program. For example, the media resource center director might have a sophisticated selection system based on faculty recommendations, evaluative reviews and previews, while the instructor might decide to use a film because its length coincides with the time he has available in his class schedule.

The preceeding sections have laid the groundwork for this summary by describing various strategies and conditions in which media selection takes place. The following examples describe situations which would have an impact on the process of media selection:

1. a university where selection is done by a traditional librarian;
2. a community college which places major emphasis on selecting media for remedial purposes;
3. a four-year college which requires utilization of media by faculty members;
4. a university which employs an instructional developer, with an extensive staff;
5. an institution where selection is performed by personnel who have no professional background;
6. a college just opening a Media Resources Center.

Each of these conditions brings with it perspectives and constraints that affect the selection strategy or process. The examples are chosen to exaggerate the conditions, so an in-depth analysis is probably not necessary. However, there are additional factors which inevitably influence selection. These are budgets, the goals and objectives of the institution, the type of students, and the attitude of administrators and faculty toward media and the utilization of media.

HISTORICAL PERSPECTIVE AND ANALYSIS

Traditionally, the field of librarianship has developed thorough and comprehensive bibliographic information about all books published. Through a variety of reference tools it is possible to obtain complete information with which to order books, such as cost, place of publication, publisher, date, series, and author or editors. Similarly, a vast array of sources is available for the review and evaluation of books.

In the media field these identification and review tools have not been developed to the level of sophistication as that of books. There are a number of reasons for this, partly because media forms, such as films, are often produced by individuals, not companies, and are therefore difficult to track and to identify all descriptive information. In addition, the field is so diverse that to identify and provide total information to the user is a formidable task. Another problem is that this process was not started early when media products were relatively limited in number. Now, to provide retrospective coverage is virtually impossible and probably not absolutely necessary, nor reasonable to expect.

Historically, a number of types of reference sources for identifying and selecting media have evolved, some of which provide lists of indexes of media and others which provide more extensive bibliographic information. In addition, there are those which provide descriptions or evaluative reviews of the medium.

Each of these types of sources can be used effectively for gathering different types of information. If comprehensive bibliographic reference tools for media had been adequately developed, it would not be quite as necessary to rely on such a diversity of types of index and review publications.

As was stated previously, there is the desperate need for bibliographic organization and coverage in the media field. There have been some commendable attempts to compile comprehensive indexes including all types of media. This first serious attempt to accomplish this objective was the *Educational Media Index*. This index was intended to identify in one source the wealth of audiovisual materials available for educational use on a particular subject with the appropriate grade level indicated. This publication of 14 volumes indicated about 30,000 listings of media items arranged by subject with title indexes. Most of the listings were for films and filmstrips, however, also included were records, audio-types, charts, maps, models, mockups, pictures, slides and programmed instructional materials. Even though the intent of this publication was commendable, many problem areas appeared relating to the identification of types of materials, confusing format and type that was not easily read, titles were omitted, subject headings were misleading and cross-referencing was lacking. As a result, this publication did not live up to expectations.

The NICEM *Indexes* were next in the evolution of media indexes. The NICEM *Indexes* have since superseded the *Educational Media Index*. In 1958, the University of Southern California began experimenting with computer-stored data as a source for printing media catalogs. The result of this project was a data bank of information about 16 mm film and 35 mm filmstrips, formatted on machine-readable tape. In 1967, the National Information Center for Educational Media was established; it published the first *Index to 16 mm Educational Films* using the information which had been gathered, following shortly with the *Index to 35 mm Educational Filmstrips*. Since that time, the data base has been expanded to include overhead transparencies, 8 mm cartridges, slides, phonodiscs, prerecorded audio tapes, and videotapes and subject area specializations. These developments will be discussed later in this chapter.

When the publication began, in each volume the entries were arranged by title. There was a subject index to the titles and a separately cross-referenced guide to the subject headings themselves. A directory of producers and distributors was also included.

Citations were fairly complete, lacking only purchase/rental costs. The Library of Congress order number for catalog cards was indicated when available. Annotations were brief, one to three sentences in length and descriptive only. These were summaries of information supplied by the producers.

As with the *Educational Media Index*, the print was somewhat difficult to read. It was quite small in size, and almost entirely in capital letters. However, on the whole, the volumes were well bound and attractive.

Of all the indexes available, the NICEM indexes claim to have the largest data base, the best authenticated information, and the most easy-to-read format. For evaluative purposes, however, neither the *Educational Media Index* nor the NICEM *Indexes* offered more than a brief description of the content of the item.

In 1970 Westinghouse Learning Corporation published what they described as a "revolutionary" index, as it was the first major index combining print and nonprint material. It contained over 600,000 entries under 225,000 specific topics, claiming to provide convenient access to 205,000 indexed items. It addressed an audience level from preschool to college and intended to cover all material which had "intrinsically" educational and vocational training applications. The index was compiled from the current offerings of approximately 900 publishers, producers, professional groups, industrial firms, and government agencies. This index was compiled to have ease of use as its first objective so listings for all media that covered the same topic at the same audience level appeared together. Both print and non-print items were indexed together to make it easy to assemble sets of books and audiovisual materials on any subject. Data on prices were included and information about materials for loan and rental was provided.

All items whether they were films, games, specimens, textbooks, videotape or programmed material were grouped under the actual topic, such as "Gettysburg Address" or "Marijuana." This permitted the user to compare the features of each medium, the sources, and prices to help decide what materials were best suited to a certain instructional purpose. Each item could be listed as many as nine times, because it was listed under every word that seemed appropriate to indexers. Cross-referencing was not used, but the listing of the item and complete information listed included medium, title, color, sound, size, date, price, source, and reference notes.

A Source Index was included in Volume I which provided names and addresses of publishers, producers, and distributors whose products were mentioned. Also provided were the full titles and contents summary of each catalog which had materials included.

Some criticisms of the *Learning Directory* were that the Source Index appeared only in Volume I and not separately. Another criticism was that there was lack of standardization in indexing term usage that was the by-product of the keyword indexing process employed. For example, some items were listed under "black," some under "Negro," and some under "Afro-American," but all items were not repeated under all headings. The publishers acknowledged this lack of completeness as a fault directly attributable to the depth of specificity produced by keyword indexing.

Inclusion appeared to be inconsistent as there was no stated policy on reference books and some reference books were included, but many were not. Access to materials was by topic only as there were no author or title indexes; also authors' names were not included under subject entries unless they are the subjects.

Even though this was a significant publication, it must be considered a first step, as it was an index only, with no annotations or descriptions. For complete information the user had to refer to the producer's catalogs. For evaluative reviews the user had to refer to evaluative review sources such as those in this publication. Users still needed the *Books in Print* series and *Paperbound Books in Print* for the book coverage because the *Learning Directory* was intended to include only those books "intrinsically educational" and not comprehensive.

This effort was laudable in that it was a major effort to meet a need in the selection of media. It was not successful and that publication has been discontinued, but its strengths and weaknesses should be noted as other selection tools evolve.

The first attempt to publish a comprehensive index of media reviews came in 1970 with the publication of the *Multi-Media Reviews Index* by the Pierian Press. The index citations are gathered on a cooperative indexing basis by professional audiovisual personnel and librarians from every geographical location in the United States. The index includes references to reviews of films, filmstrips, nonclassical records and tapes, slides, transparencies, globes, charts, media kits, and other miscellaneous media forms appearing in 70 periodicals and services. Citations contain review ratings assigned to indicate the general nature of the evaluation made by the reviewer: + means good to excellent; + – means positive and negative attributes; – means fair to poor; * means descriptive. Citations are listed alphabetically by title under type of media. Supplements to the first annual volume have appeared in the October, November, and December 1971 and January 1972 issues of *Audiovisual Instruction* and were continued for some time. C. Edward Wall, Head Librarian of the University of Michigan at Dearborn is the editor and compiler.

The citations are extremely brief and contain no annotations or excerpts from the reviews. There is also no listing of grade level or subject identification. This was an extremely promising beginning, and will undoubtedly expand in content and coverage (24).

Historically these are landmark publications. An analysis was made of their strengths, weaknesses, and omissions to provide a base for judging selection and evaluation tools currently being developed. For a more thorough analysis refer to the publication *Media Indexes and Review Sources* by Margaret Chisholm. The original publications are available for locating media and are of historical interest. They are also of value because they provide evidence of which publications served the needs of users and, therefore, continued, and of those which had so many problems that they did not survive. The development of the computer, compilation of comprehensive data bases, and development of computer printing capability have aided these publications from the technological aspects. In addition, evaluative reviews are now much more widely accepted, much research has been done on individual learning needs, and concurrently, research has been done on the effectiveness of the evolving media types according to attribute and management. All of these factors have had an impact on the success or failure of a publication related to the selection and evaluation of media.

THEORY AND PRACTICE

In the preceeding sections the major focus of attention has been given to a presentation and analysis of theories and models related to media selection. However, pragmatic issues must be addressed and the following questions must be asked: What are the actual practices being used today, and what are the recommendations of the experts in the field? The media field is so extensive and the viewpoints on selection are so diverse that it seemed appropriate to contact a number of experts in the field, representing those practicing selection, those teaching media selection, those involved in evaluation, and those utilizing media. Rather than refer to any literature of the field, the opinions and comments of these experts was sought to determine what practices were currently being used. In addition, they were asked to comment on their assessment of the current practices and future directions, which will be summarized in the following sections.

It is needless to point out that there is a great gap between theory and practice, but there should never be one without the other. It is imperative to develop theory as the searchlight that illuminates the directions ahead, even if progress is slow and implementation difficult.

The following is a summary of practices which are employed, and that are recommended by these successful selectors and utilizers of media. There was amazing consensus, both within the country and internationally. There was unanimous agreement that virtually all selection must take place by working closely with the faculty. If work is not done directly with the faculty, then decisions must be based on curriculum areas being taught. Most persons selecting media recommended making appointments with individual faculty members, and holding discussions about each specific course, the objectives of the course, and, if possible, obtaining a written copy of these objectives, the course outline, and copies of the examination. The director of the media center must be knowledgeable about all formats of media available, new products that are available or in production and be sensitive to the teaching style of the professor and the needs of the students. The media director must structure the environment so that the faculty members will be receptive to the concept of utilizing media and will also be alert to new products emerging in their disciplines. Many media directors recommended "bombarding" the faculty with constant information about media and media utilization. Such vehicles would include newsletters about new products, calendars listing acquisitions and future previews, flyers, demonstrations, and current previews.

Previews were deemed essential by everyone. All media directors agreed that previews served multiple purposes. When materials were to be considered for purchase, they should be ordered to be previewed both by the director and by any professors considering their use. An important point brought up by a number of persons interviewed was the recommendation that students be encouraged to preview materials. After all, the student is the consumer and should have a responsibility in the decision to purchase and to use. Along with the idea of the necessity of the preview, stress was placed on the provision of easily accessible preview facilities. The space made available for previews should be consistently available. It must be convenient as far as location, adequate in size, viewing and listening ease, and available an optimum number of hours.

Another mechanism to encourage faculty involvement is a simple order form distributed to faculty to encourage them to order appropriate materials. Faculty must be assisted in trying to provide accurate and complete order information.

Additional suggestions for encouraging faculty involvement were innovations committees, teaching improvement committees and media utilization demonstrations. The success of all of these depend partly on the enthusiasm and support of the administration, the dedication and involvement of the media center director, and the philosophy and practice of the institution. It is important to note that they are used with great effectiveness in many places. Of course, to go back to the introduction and the emphasis on instruction design, the optimum way to approach the involvement of faculty is to have a fully implemented, administratively supported, institution-wide instructional design program. Anything less is only an attempt to move in that direction.

Most directors agreed that there was no one source of information or evaluations for ordering. Of the reference tools identified, most were criticized in general as not being up to date, limited in scope, not covering all disciplines, and not containing adequate purchase and rental information. The most frequently used practice is for the media director to be thoroughly familiar with producer's catalogs. The fundamental stressed is that the director must be familiar with the firm or the producer. There must be an effort made to have a comprehensive collection of producers' catalogs, be familiar with them, and have a very workable retrieval system for utilizing the catalogs. Other reference tools were referred to as aids, but none, in actual practice, took the place of the catalogs.

Evaluation of materials was heavily stressed. Most requested faculty members to fill out a simple evaluation form assessing the content and technical aspects of the product. In most cases the evaluations were on file so that other faculty members could review them.

Maintaining a "want list" of items for future purchase was noted by several professionals. Tight budgets do not permit purchasing every recommended item. Once materials have been previewed, evaluated, and approved, they should be placed in an active file until funds for purchasing are made available.

A number of the experts noted that there is no one medium that can be identified as being the only alternative to meet a learning objective, therefore, any collection must be marked by diversity of resources so they will be able to meet the unique requirements of individual learners through an optimum number of options.

One current aspect of great concern is that of the cutback in financial support, or the reduction of the budget available for purchase of media. There seemed to be consensus of a number of points, such as: great care must be taken to allocate funds where they will do the most good for the greatest number of students, and it is essential to assess the cost benefit before purchasing. Another aspect stressed was to purchase materials that would provide optimum flexibility. For example, one director recommended the practice of purchasing sets, but making individual items available to the user for maximum use of all items. There was an apparent diversity of opinion about the quality of the media. A number of directors noted with great emphasis that both students and faculty expect quality; for example, poorly produced black and white videotapes are just not the standard expected. By contrast, some suggested that possibly in these times of financial cutback, the users could use something less technically beautiful, but that fulfilled their learning needs. However, there was consensus that no matter how fine the technical quality or how renowned the producer, the final test of adequacy is always how relevant the medium is to the user's needs. A suggestion for flexibility is to make films into sets of slides or slide/tape packages. This combined flexibility with lowering the cost and making materials available to greater numbers. Another practice cited was to use slides or filmstrips, which were acceptable for their pictures, but redo the audio to suit the needs of a particular curriculum.

A suggestion for extending the value for the dollar invested is to develop consortium arrangements among institutions in which sharing arrangements can be established. Of course, this would not work in all areas, but among community colleges that were contiguous geographically and could identify materials appropriate for sharing, such contracts or agreements could be developed.

Several years ago some noteworthy efforts were made to integrate all nonprint materials and merge them with the print materials for shelving and access purposes. Some directors are now abandoning this plan, because the costs of packaging is an additional expense. Other directors have reverted to unprecedented creativity in developing their own packaging format at very low costs to continue this integrated plan. However, in all cases, there appears to be a dearth of funds to use to adapt formats for access purposes.

Another problem arises from the current copyright regulations. Selection practices have had to be adapted, based on the restrictions placed on duplicating.

Trends in selection seem to indicate that media are being selected as the basic mode of instruction, but not necessarily as much for supplementary purposes as in the past. Materials are also selected which can be used for a number of purposes. Also positive consideration is given to those items which can stand by themselves without needing auxiliary materials.

The most popular format currently appears to be video cassette and audio cassette because of their longer life span (e.g., they are less susceptible to damage than disc or reel format) and because of their ease of use.

A strange sense of resignation and acceptance appeared to pervade the discussions of the experts as they evaluated selection and evaluation tools. They agreed that a plethora of publications were on the market, some of which held out new hope and some of which appeared to be repeating the failures of the tools of the past. The following are some of the purposes that these tools are expected to fulfill: selectors and users of media need bibliographic or "mediagraphic" tools which will provide purchase information; assistance in locating items; annotations or reviews; evaluative reviews; assistance in identifying out-of-production items; listing by producer, author, subject, and disciplines; indexing of contents; and serve as a checklist for a comprehensive collection.

Although a vast number of new publications are flooding the market, they each need to be scrutinized to determine how well they fulfill their stated purposes. Each tool needs to be evaluated according to the qualifications of the author and/or editor, the scope and coverage, the arrangement, the ease of use, the physical attractiveness and sturdiness, the special features, the bibliographic information included, and finally, the cost.

Some of the newer or more thoroughly developed tools especially noted by the experts are: *Time Life Multimedia Video and Film Catalog* 1978/79, Dorothy Dunbar, editor. (New York: Time Life Films, Inc., 1978, 171 pp. Address: Time Life Building, New York, New York 10020.) This is a listing of 16 mm and video programs in 3/4" U-Matic and Betamax format video cassettes for rental or purchase. The catalog includes Nova Series and BBC productions listed under curriculum headings. Titles and descriptive annotations are listed. This publication was identified as very useful because of the current interest in film and video productions.

A source of information that appears to hold promise is *International Master File of AV Programme Catalogues*. (London and New York Videofilm Centre, 1978. Address: 14 Broadway, London SW1HOBH.) The director, W. A. Douglas, makes the following statement in his introduction:

> This is the first print-out of 6500 AV programme title listings from the first fifteen producers to have their catalogues entered into our microfiche master file service.
>
> All titles have been organized by the subject headings used by the individual producers within their catalogues. Therein lies a problem because no two producers agree on their subject designations (though we may well try one day to get them to do so!). Therefore, in the beginning we advise a careful scan of all the subject headings given at the beginning of the index for the areas likely to cover what you want.

This is an unusual publication as the format is a looseleaf plastic covered notebook containing pockets in which to insert the microfiche print-outs. Examples of catalogs on microfiche which are currently available are British Universities Film Counsel, BBC Enterprises, BFA Educational Media, Paramount Oxford Films, Harvard Business School (16 mm films for management training), Great Plains National Instruction Television Library, and Eye Gate Media.

Another reference source with rather comprehensive coverage is: *Index to Instructional Media Catalogs: A Multi-Indexed Director of Materials Equipment for Use in Instructional Programs*. (New York, New York, Bowker Company, 1974, 272 pp.)

The editor, Olga S. Weber, states:

> What we are attempting to achieve in *Index to Instructional Media Catalogs* is a simple guide to the catalogs of the suppliers of specific instructional materials. It is a reference tool which makes it possible for you to sort swiftly and accurately through the range of materials, media and producers; and match these with the subjects, grade levels and methodologies in your school system's curriculum.

The volume has been separated into three sections: A Subject/Media Index, Product and Services Index, and a Director of Companies Section.

The publications which have been published consistently for a number of years and have been developed from an ever-expanding data base are the NICEM Indexes which can be purchased from National Information Center for Educational Media, University of Southern California, University Park. (Los Angeles, California 90007.)

In the *NICEM Update of Non-Book Media* the following statement is made:

> Since 1964 NICEM has provided indices, non-print book catalogs and on-line search information from its computerized data banks at the University of Southern California to over 15,000 institutions, individuals and agencies involved in the process of education.

The *NICEM Update* is a quarterly subscription service for the year 1978-1979, which updates the following NICEM Indexes:

Index to 16 mm. Educational Films, 6th ed. (4 volumes)

Index to 35 mm. Filmstrip, 6th ed. (3 volumes)

Index to 8 mm. Motion Cartridges, 5th ed.

Index to Educational Overhead Transparencies, 5th ed. (2 volumes)

Index to Educational Audio Tapes, 4th ed.

Index to Educational Video Tapes, 4th ed.
Index to Educational Records, 4th ed.
Index to Educational Slides, 3rd ed.
Index to Producers and Distributors, 4th ed.
Index to Health and Safety Educational-Multimedia, 3rd ed.
Index to Vocational and Technical Education-Multimedia, 3rd ed.
Index to Environmental Studies—Multimedia
Index to Free Educational Materials—Multimedia
Index to Psychology-Multimedia, 3rd ed.

The publication states that until other more sophisticated means of information dissemination become economically viable NICEM will provide its users a complete update of its indexes alternating with completely new editions of Indexes. For example, complete new Indexes will be available in 1979-1980 with four updates again available in 1981. The three principle sections included are: 1) Subject Guide to nonbook media, 2) Alphabetical Guide to nonbook media, and 3) Directory of producers and distributors.

These tools are only examples of the great number and variety of indexes, listings, and guides which are being published or produced. Users must assess their own selection needs and find ways to combine the information provided.

CAVEATS AND RECOMMENDATIONS

The consensus of all the experts was that "Media is here to stay," but all recognized that serious obstacles exist. Restricting factors such as lean budgets, copyright, and limited and sporadic faculty interest all must be dealt with in a positive and creative manner. Basic to all progress appears to be the enthusiasm and knowledge of the directors of the programs. It is critical for the directors to involve faculty, provide hands-on experience and confidence in utilizing both software and hardware.

Dr. Diana Spirt of the Palmer Graduate Library School of Long Island University, C.W. Post Center, stated:

I consider that the fundamental problem in selection of media relates to its use. Therefore the attitude of those who provide access to media remains the foremost criteria for use. Ideas in all subjects must be made available in all formats and be made readily accessible; and individual and societal attitudes must change to make this possible. Collections of all sizes must contain media in all formats and be made available to users. Until this goal is accomplished we will not see sensible movement in education and entertainment toward effective selection and utilization of media.

Much needs to be done to change the attitudes of those allocating budgets and of those establishing priorities for purchasing and in working with middle management to facilitate dissemination and utilization.

FUTURE DIRECTIONS

It is virtually inevitable in predicting future direction to avoid being idealistic and indulging in wishful thinking. Therefore, one of the first predictions would be that those persons involved with research on utilization of media would develop their research findings with such success that meeting the needs of the user would become a scientific and predictable process.

Second, with the rapid development of computer technology and data basis it should be possible to develop comprehensive selection and evaluation tools to provide all information needed by the selector of media.

Third, we must acknowledge that individual learners and users vary greatly, are unique in their individual needs, and that instructors have innumerable distinctive teaching styles. For these reasons it is logical to predict that in order to answer which medium, for which objectives, for which type of learner or user, the answer may well be that nothing exists, so it will be produced locally. In other words, there will be a greater trend toward local production of media to satisfy individual needs.

Fourth, technological advances are taking place so rapidly that dramatic changes in media formats and utilization can certainly be expected. Rapid improvements and extensive utilization in the video cassette and video disc will certainly revolutionize the use of visual media. Miniaturization of computer technology and the lowering of costs will affect interactive data base accessibility. Computer-aided instruction and games will undoubtedly become more commonplace. Hard copy computer print-outs will be much lower in cost and interactive telephone/television systems will develop as the field of fiber optics evolves. Satellite transmission will enhance the effectiveness and availability of television, and utilization of cable will also have a dramatic effect.

As has always been the case, it appears that technology develops at a rapid pace, but the understanding of the human being and knowledge of the learning process has forever lagged behind. Therefore it becomes a challenge to focus on the understanding of the learning process and on the production and identification of materials which will enhance this effort.

REFERENCES

1. Donald P. Ely, ed., "The Field of Educational Technology: A Statement of Definition." *Audiovisual Instruction*, 17 (October 1972): 36-43.
2. Jerrold E. Kemp, *Instructional Design—A Plan for Unit and Course Development*. (Belmont, Calif.: Fearon Publishers, 1977.)
3. Association of Educational Communications and Technology Task Force on Definition and Terminology, *Educational Technology: Definition and Glossary of Terms Volume 1*. (Washington, D.C.: Association for Educational Communications and Technology, 1977.)
4. Robert M. Diamond et al., *Instructional Development for Individualized Learning in Higher Education*. (Englewood Cliffs, N.J.: Educational Technology Publications, 1975.)
5. Robert H. Davis et al., *Learning System Design—An Approach to the Improvement of Instruction*. (New York: McGraw-Hill, 1974.)
6. Kent L. Gustafson, "Toward a Definition of Instructional Development: A System Approach." In *Toward a Definition of Instructional Development— A.E.C.T. Occasional Papers*, Ivor K. Davies and Thomas M. Schwen, eds. (Philadelphia: Instructional Development Division of the Association for Educational Communications and Technology, March 1971.)
7. Bela H. Banathy, *Instructional Systems*. (Belmont, Calif.: Fearon Publishers, 1968.)
8. M. David Merrill and Robert D. Tennyson, *Teaching Concepts: An Instructional Design Guide*. (Englewood Cliffs, N.J.: Educational Technology Publications, 1977.)

9. Margaret Chisholm and Donald P. Ely, *Focus on Trends and Issues: Instructional Design and the Library Media Specialist.* (Chicago: American Library Association [in press].)

10. W. Howard Levie, "Models for Media Selection." *Journal NSPI*, 16 (September 1977): pp. 4-7.

11. R.M. Gagné, "Learning Theory, Educational Media and Individualized Instruction," Mimeo. (Paper presented at Bucknell University, 1970.)

12. Vernon S. Gerluch and Donald P. Ely, *Teaching and Media: A Systematic Approach.* (Englewood Cliffs, N.J.: Prentice Hall, 1977.)

13. W.H. Allen, "Media Stimulus and Types of Learning." *Audiovisual Instruction*, January 1967, pp. 27-31.

14. D.T. Tosti and J.R. Ball, "A Behavioral Approach to Instructional Design and Media Selection." *Audiovisual Communication Review* 17 (1969): 5-25.

15. A.P. Van Mondfrans and R.L. Houser, "Selecting Media to Present Basic Concepts." *Educational Technology*, December 1970, pp. 40-43.

16. R.Z. Goodman, "Systematic Selection." *Audiovisual Instruction* 16 (December 1971): 37-38.

17. J.E. Kemp, "Which Medium?" *Audiovisual Instruction* 16 (December 1971): 32-36.

18. D.N. Nunney and J.E. Hill, "Personalized Educational Program." *Audiovisual Instruction* 17 (February 1972): 10-15.

19. J.K. Lonigro, Jr., and A.J. Eschenbrenner, Jr., "A Model for Selecting Media in Technical/Vocational Education," *Audiovisual Instruction* 18 (November 1973): 27-32.

20. E.J. Holden, "Selection of Instructional Media Systems." *Programmed Learning and Educational Technology* (1974): 287-298.

21. W.H. Levie, "How to Understand Instructional Media Viewpoints." *Bulletin School Education* (Indiana University) 51 (1975): 25-42.

22. W. Wager, "Media Selection in Affective Domain: A Further Interpretation of Dale's Cone of Experience for Cognitive Learning." *Educational Technology* 15 (July 1975): 9-13.

23. E.J. Holden, "Selection of Instructional Media Systems," pp. 287-298.

24. Margaret E. Chisholm, *Media Indexes and Review Sources.* (University of Maryland: School of Library and Information Services, 1972.)

Developing the Serials Collection

Siegfried Feller

INTRODUCTION

Most librarians who are directly charged with the responsibility for selecting, budgeting, processing, maintaining, and/or servicing serials don't really understand them. The unknown ancient who first incised the Sumarian equivalent of "Volume 1, number 1" in cuneiform on the first series of clay tablets has received many derogatory remarks. Yet serials are an indispensible part of every library's collection. However, their definition and use remains a mystery.

Join in any discussion of serials with three other veteran librarians, and within half an hour the group will have produced at least five variant definitions for each of such terms as *serial*, *periodical*, *standing order*, and others. Small wonder, then, that the uninitiated listener feels excommunicated, and wanders off to seek less strenuous conversation or instruction.

SOME DEFINITIONS

A number of different kinds of publications fall under the general ruberic of serials and, therefore, it is important to try to define those various publications before a full discussion can ensue about this role in the collection development process.

Serial itself is a generic term for any publication issued at intervals in sequentially numbered or dated parts, and intended to continue publishing.

Periodical. A type of species of serial, issued at more or less regular intervals in sequential parts at least twice a year, usually containing several separate writings by different authors, and most often paid for in advance at a fixed rate for a specified period, usually not less than one year. It should be stated that this definition does not coincide exactly with the official ALA definition.

Newspaper. A kind of periodical usually issued at least once a week on newsprint paper in folded format, primarily devoted to reporting very recent events of interest to the readership, and often including feature articles, commercial advertisements, local announcements, and miscellaneous information.

Magazine. A periodical that is issued at regular intervals but is not a newspaper, and which is offered at a fixed rate, normally paid in advance, for a specified subscription period.

Journal. Often employed as a synonym for any of the three preceding terms, as well as to describe a sequential record of events, private or public, serial or not. Since it can be confusing when used without qualification, the term will not be used in this chapter.

Subscription. A type of order or mode of payment for all parts of a magazine or periodical issued during the period specified, and typically renewed on an annual basis.

Serial. A type of serial, other than a periodical, which is typically issued either (a) at regular intervals less often than twice a year, whether or not payment is made in advance at a fixed rate; or (b) at irregular intervals, no matter what the frequency, usually with an individual invoice for each shipment of one part or more. Not included in this category are publications such as the annually reissued (but only microcosmically revised/improved) *Encyclopedia Unbritannica*, and the biennially reissued (with chapter sequence altered and a new two-page introduction by the author's new spouse) *Introductory Urdu Grammar*, and the bicentennially reissued *Logbook of the "Bonhomme Richard"*.

Series. Often used more or less interchangeably with *serial*, but a more restructed use can be made to denote a type of serial whose parts can be treated as separate works. They can be cataloged primarily under author/main entry, with each work classified individually, but probably represented in the public card catalog with an added entry for the series title, and showing library holdings in numerical sequence. Alternatively, when the subject focus of a series is specific enough, the title can be used as main entry, with all parts classified and shelved together in numerical sequence, but probably also represented in the public card catalog by *analytics*, filed under the individual authors/titles. For many institutions, needs can be satisfied by acquiring only those parts of the series that seem most important for their programs.

Some other frequent uses of *series* that will be avoided in this context include: (a) a publisher's subject grouping without numbered parts; (b) a publisher's numbered series grouped primarily by size, format, or price range, and usually subject focus; and (c) to differentiate between segments or time periods in the publishing history of a serial, e.g., "*Nuovo Cimento*, series 9, volumes 1-12, 1943-54; series 10, volume 1, 1955+."

Loose-Leaf Service. A type of serial, usually in ring-binder format, containing a body of data or information subject to frequent changes or additions in details, so that corrigenda and addenda are published at appropriate intervals for insertion in the binder, supplanting or supplementing earlier pages.

Standing Order. A commitment to accept and pay for all parts of a serial, as issued, until the buyer specifically cancels the order or the publication ceases. This term is also used to describe the purchase of a multivolume work issued in numbered parts, but not necessarily in sequence, over a period of time, and scheduled to be completed in a specific number of volumes at some time in the foreseeable future. Such publications are not here considered to be serials, and will not be referred to in this chapter without the qualifying adjective, *terminal*.

Serial Commitments. Will be used generically, to include ongoing *subscriptions* and *standing orders*, as described.

OTHER KINDS OF
STANDING COMMITMENTS

Although attention here is focused on serials, many libraries have other types of self-perpetuating purchase programs, and these must be considered along with serial commitments in budget preparation and planning. Those categories, not technically serials, may pose similar problems because they are often ordered and processed by the same members of the library staff. They are covered in greater detail in other chapters of this volume, but briefly include the following.

Standing Commitment. Includes ongoing purchase plans and agreements that are meant to continue indefinitely, unless specifically stopped, i.e., the commitment stands until it is cancelled by one of the parties involved, or it dissolves on its own accord.

Membership Payment. Usually paid in advance at an annual fixed rate, like a subscription, to an organization offering benefits wanted by the library and available only to members. The most common reason for joining is to obtain the organization's publications, either free or at an advantageous price. Some nonprofit organizations simply offer only the serial, so that the only difference between the transaction and a subscription is semantic. Sometimes libraries are permitted to share benefits in memberships actually held by other agencies within the same institution. In an academic context, especially, librarians should explore the possibilities of free subscriptions and special discounts available through departmental memberships.

Blanket Order. A commitment to purchase, usually directly, all future publications of a publisher/agency, as issued, whether they are serial or not. A purchaser may exclude from the agreement certain categories such as pamphlets, or require that prior consent be obtained before shipping items priced over a fixed limit, but if too many exceptions must be made, some other mode of ordering might be more efficient. It is not unusual for the relationship between a library and a large, prolific organization to involve a combination of virtually every type of standing commitment so far described.

Blanket Approval Plan. A standing commitment to accept automatic shipments from a specific vendor of a broad range of newly published material, based on a detailed outline that specifies the institutional coverage wanted for each subject, and taking into account stipulated exclusions and limitations, e.g., level of treatment, price, language, country of origin. Periodicals are usually excluded, but serials are often supplied through such a plan. A common feature permits the library to return for credit any items that reviewers feel do not meet the specified criteria.

Terminal Standing Order. Already defined above; often called a *continuation*, but a term not consistently applied.

PLANNING PROBLEMS AND
PROCESSING PECULIARITIES

Many characteristics of serials may require special study and attention. Even the tamest of subscriptions or standing orders is an ongoing transaction that is likely to provide complications. The subscription becomes an ongoing financial burden until stopped. It is one of the library's many standing commitments, all of which must be taken into account when budget allocations are planned. The logistics of processing are also much more involved for an ongoing serial. Assuming that the periodical in question has already been cataloged in a normal manner, ownership and identifying marks are then applied to each piece, which is then sent to its destination in the library. If all goes well, this procedure must be repeated for each subsequent issue, on a regular schedule. Often, though, an issue will

not arrive on time, or at all; if a staff member notices the delinquen-
cy, the missing piece is claimed, usually on a form which has already
been prepared for this purpose. As one delay is coupled onto the
next, costlier correspondence develops.

In time, one may wonder why a periodical described as a quarterly
has produced only three issues in its first year. Then, halfway
through this second year, the library is presented with an additional
billing, not allowed for in budgeting, of 50% over the amount already
paid. An inquiry reveals that the surcharge is intended to cover costs
of a double issue to be released in September, plus a special Christ-
mas supplement in October for gift shoppers. When the last issue
finally arrives—three months late—one finds that without prior warning the title has been changed with the most recent issue labeled
volume 2, number 7.

MAINTENANCE AND PRESERVATION

At the end of a year or another designated interval, the separate parts
of a periodical may be ready to bind into one physical volume.
Perhaps it will be necessary first to replace a missing issue, or several
pages; the staff time in searching, plus payment for replacements add
substantially to the costs. When serials are removed from the shelves
for binding, records must be created and maintained, for patrons as
well as for processing and public services staff. The binding contractor must be instructed regarding types and colors of binding; the
style, size, color, and wording of the lettering on the spine and
elsewhere; and other details.

Serials are often subject to depredation, especially in libraries
where current issues are not permitted to circulate outside the building, and/or in cases where contents, particularly illustrations, are in
high demand. Preservation and replacement of materials are increasing problems in nearly all libraries, and close supervision and detailed
inspection after each use are virtually impossible. Installation of electronic detection systems has reduced the unauthorized removal of
bound volumes from libraries, but it is possible that their use has
increased the rate of mutilation of certain materials. In any case,

unbound issues of most periodicals are thin enough for a determined devotee to conceal beneath an outer garment.

There is no wholly satisfactory solution, but several measures have been introduced to alleviate patron and staff distress. It is helpful if photocopying facilities are readily and inexpensively available. Heavily abused periodicals may be backed up with another subscription, perhaps with only controlled access permitted. In some libraries, these are called *bindery subscriptions*, and may be held in one of the closed work areas but available for supervised use when the public copy is known to be missing or drawn. If only the single subscription is maintained, current issues can be placed in an area that is more closely supervised than the normal location; in an academic library, such titles may be sent to closed reserve.

When already commercially available, microforms can be purchased to back up endangered serials. It is edifying to observe in the 1979 catalogs of some leading producers that fewer and fewer publishers insist that only subscribers to their paper issues may purchase microform. This makes it possible to consider substituting microform for paper, instead of buying both when both are not really needed. One major company has been actively promoting the notion of purchasing microfilm instead of binding periodicals, arguing that this is the cheaper solution in the long run for the institution. This practice might be preferred in some but not all circumstances.

Several university libraries have refined this process. For instance, the University of Massachusetts identifies the most heavily depredated magazines in the collection by tallying recorded incidences of missing issues and pages. This led to the cancellation of a few titles of marginal value. In addition, orders were placed for the last volume (and, selectively, for partial backfiles) of some titles that are available in microform. On a title-by-title basis, decisions have been made, either to (a) discard paper issues as soon as microform can be substituted, or (b) bind remaining parts "as is," with a label affixed to advise readers that missing/damaged pages are available in the Microform Room. Patron response to this last practice has been favorable, because everyone prefers to read the originals, and photocopying is simpler than printing from microcopy. Wear and tear on the film is also thereby reduced. The most economical binding is used for the incomplete volumes, and the relatively small cost is more than offset by other advantages.

Backup in either paper or film reduces reader frustration, as well as the work loads of interlibrary loan personnel. Staff costs of finding replacement parts and effecting repairs, coupled with required payments for missing issues and/or photocopies usually exceed the costs of either a bindery subscription or microform by a significant margin. Since most serials that are heavily abused are also heavily used, the additional expense is probably warranted anyhow. For the more expensive titles, acquisitions budgets may not permit duplication, so that restricted/supervised access may be the best feasible protective measure.

THE IMPORTANCE OF SERIALS
IN THE COLLECTION

Depending on the size and type of institution, serials can meet a variety of needs better than any other categories of library material. Some of their vital functions are already evident from their descriptors and definitions.

Newspapers, for example, rapidly report information and data to a depth not possible by the still swifter electronic media, and in a format that permits us to refer back to the information later, in libraries. They are an important communications link between potential customers and the merchants and service agencies in the locality. Distant communities and societies can be studied by reading their newspapers, both recent issues and historical files.

Loose-leaf publications are able to provide very recent data or information on many subjects, e.g., on laws and governmental regulations affecting business and industry, various professionals, and/or private individuals. Their utilization requires sophisticated experience, and even the people for whom they are intended can benefit from the advice of a competent reference librarian. Unfortunately, the competition between rival publishers offering the same data has not kept costs down, so by now many smaller libraries can no longer afford to maintain even the most vital titles.

Among "serials," serials are the most difficult to characterize. In physical appearance and in frequency of issue, the individual parts are often indistinguishable from ordinary books; many are processed in exactly the same way, especially volumes in a series. A useful feature is that the numbering/dating permits patrons and staff to determine quickly whether the latest parts have arrived, and whether the run is complete or has gaps. Assuming that the supplier is efficient, each new part will arrive automatically and promptly, without the necessity of selecting and ordering successive pieces.

Periodical issues also arrive automatically on subscription, and usually with the convenience of a single payment for the volume. The frequent appearance of the parts ensures that the contents reach their audience quickly, regularly, and in a format that is durable and easy to use and reuse. For an enormous number, the contents are widely indexed and/or abstracted in many ways, so that interested readers can find needed information readily. These features make periodicals especially vital to scientific researchers. In many instances, advertising fees defray a significant proportion of production/distribution costs, so that subscribers receive more for their money. Rising costs have long since led quite a few publishers of scholarly periodicals to require payment of their authors whose research may have been subsidized.

WHO NEEDS SERIALS?

Apart from questions about the merits of individual serial titles, their relative importance ranges from "trivial" to "indispensable," depending on the audience and the subject. Interruption in the service of a favorite children's magazine or a popular pictorial monthly would surely disappoint many regular readers in the school or public library. Reference serials, dealing with regulations, educational opportunities, demographic statistics, etc., contain a great deal of data useful to many members of the community. Scholarly magazines provide an efficient means for sharing the results of research conducted nationally and internationally, this helping to forestall needless duplication of effort, and keeping readers informed of recent advances in subjects of interest.

On the concept of indispenability, there are many strong adherents, especially in academic circles. Probably *Chemical Abstracts* fulfills a more vital function in our society than does *Shakespeare Quarterly*, by several orders of magnitude, this differential also being reflected in their rates for 1979: $4,200 to $12.50. Relative costliness of a serial is a possible indicator of its importance within a specific subject discipline, even though not needed by all workers in the department. Another gauge might be the number of copies currently active within a library or system.

It is evident that in all types of libraries, nearly all classes of readers will find at least some serials to be useful and desirable. As a category, serials are probably most important to research scientists. They may be nearly as important to some lawyers, businessmen, and some other professions, but a little less so in the social and behavioral sciences, and least important in the humanities and recreational pursuits, where the sense of urgency is diminished, or nonexistent. But the perceptions of individual patrons may well defy the general pattern; and since these observations are relative, even the lesser urgency felt in some areas will never eliminate the need for a goodly range of subscriptions and standing orders.

ESTABLISHING PARAMETERS FOR SELECTING SERIALS

One must begin assessing a serials collection by assuming or at least hoping that there has been an orderly development, and that the status quo represents a sensible apportionment of institutional resources. No matter what the size, shape or type, a collection development policy for serials cannot be devised to put into effect without considering fully the total library situation, including acquisitions, personnel, and equipment budgets. Planners must begin by matching library objectives as much as possible to the needs of the community their libraries intend to serve.

In a public library, staff may be assisted in their deliberations by municipal officers, trustees, and/or interested citizens. A common approach is for administrators to allocate acquisitions funds in various ways or combinations, such as (a) by category of material (e.g., books, serials, films, recordings, art prints, etc.); and (b) by department or subject (e.g., children's department, adult fiction, business, reference, etc.). In larger systems, existing branch locations or mobile units must be included in the calculations. The selection of serial titles to be added may be left to staff within each department; a committee may be asked to review and act upon recommendations submitted by other staff or patrons. These activities must take place within existing policy guidelines, written or oral, and within budgetary limitations.

Public school governing authorities frequently function in much the same way, providing broad guidelines, and leaving it to school administrators to subdivide library acquisitions funds in a suitable manner. Librarians and teachers are given responsibility for choosing individual titles, within established parameters.

In many academic libraries, allocations of acquisitions funds are made to teaching departments so that authority for selection of serials and books is in the hands of faculty members, with library acquisitions staff acting as comptrollers and processors. Where allocations to departments are the norm, a faculty library committee often shares responsibility with library administrative offers for initial distribution of funds, and for the redistribution of unencumbered amounts, usually at the beginning of the last quarter of the fiscal period. At this level, not much is said about how much of its allocation a department may spend on serials commitments, as long as budgetary limits are not exceeded. In some institutions, serial renewals are paid from a central pool, in which case the faculty library committee may participate in establishing ground rules to ensure equitable distribution of serial funds among competing departments.

Special libraries exist in any of a variety of environments—within a university, a business firm, a government agency, an art museum, a hospital, and many others. Collecting policies may be quite specific, reflecting the often narrow subject interests of the clientele they serve. If the sponsoring organization's objective does not include pure research, serials are likely to be selected exclusively for their immediate utility for ongoing activities and production projects. Actual choices may be made either by the principal users, or by experienced library staff, capable of anticipating needs of their clientele. It is not uncommon in project-oriented organizations to find relatively fewer titles on the active list, but multiple copies of the most intensely used serials.

The question as to what proportion of a library's acquisitions funds should be allocated for serial commitments has been asked ever more frequently as costs have risen and budgets have lagged. There can be no definitive answer, even for a given type and size of library. A small college library located at a great distance from other institutions of higher education might need to own many titles that would not be needed if accessible in nearby collections. In a medium-size public library, the proportion of serials might be relatively low, with larger amounts for books and audiovisual materials. In highly specialized scientific research facilities where even the reference works are mostly serials, it is conceivable that the expenditure on serials is 90% or more.

Some respectable amounts must be available in an academic context for books, microforms, and other materials. The desired proportions will fluctuate from one department to another, and with the amounts of money available. Where acquisitions funding has been erratic, the recent history of percentage expenditures for serial commitments will vary even more radically, and an analysis of patterns in one institution may have little meaning for another. But everywhere, the trend is upward, with serials payments sustained at the expense of books and other purchase categories. It will remain so until the institution's standing commitments are pruned.

THE ZERO-BASE COLLECTION

If one were charged with the task of creating a serials collection from point zero, one might approach the situation by assuming that budget amounts have been assigned in three categories:
1. an annual allocation for serial commitments to start selected subscriptions, with the expectation that moderate increase will be granted to keep up with normal inflation;
2. a substantial sum to be renewed at the same level in each of the several succeeding years, for purchase of selected backfiles;

3. an annual percentage allocation of the first amount, to begin in the second year, to be used for binding, replacements, and preservation of the growing serials collection.

It should also be assumed that the goals and objectives of the organization are clearly understood and that, in consultation with appropriate colleagues and constituents, agreement has been reached on how the funds in each category are to be allotted by subject and/or department.

USEFUL PUBLISHED SOURCES

Every library needs a variety of reference works, both general and specific, and many of these are serials: national bibliographies, statistical compilations, business directories, etc. For the selection process, at least one comprehensive bibliography that is arranged by subject and which offers informed evaluations and descriptions of the titles included is needed. An excellent example is the (Winchell) *Guide to Reference Books*, compiled by E.P. Sheehy; the latest edition at this writing being the ninth, published by the American Library Association, Chicago, 1976. Despite possible implications of the word *books* in the title, serials are also included. Another is *Guide to Reference Material*, A.J. Walford, editor, currently in its third edition, published in London by the Library Association, 1973-1977. For libraries with more specialized interest, the three-volume format can be extremely helpful.

Each of those foregoing guides concentrates on reference material, including important works in all subjects, and new editions appear at reasonable intervals to update the contents. The scope of coverage of both is international, but with understandable emphasis on materials in the English language. The listings include serials that have ceased publication and these should be considered along with other potential backfile purchases when one reaches that category. However, some of the older publications may not be available in microfilm or reprint editions, in which case they will probably be costly and difficult to find. Some of the currently published serials are as great a problem to obtain as the rarer deceased titles.

Unless the hypothetical library is lavishly endowed and universal in its span of interests, either of these guides will contain many more reference serials than one would normally order. Moreover, it is likely that many other serials that are not included in either work will be needed and therefore other sources should be consulted. Whatever the library's objectives, guides that are general in their coverage, plus some more specialized sources that fit institutional requirements will probably need to be consulted. One such general guide is Bill Katz's *Magazines for Libraries*, published by R.R. Bowker; it is now in its third edition, 1978. Titles are grouped by subject, and all 6,500 have been carefully chosen. It contains descriptive/evaluative comments and other information useful in the selection process including (a) subscription rate, at time of compilation; (b) where it is indexed/abstracted; (c) whether available in microform; and (d) special features, etc. Immediately below each subject heading, there is a brief list of "Basic periodicals" in that field (at various levels), each of which is discussed in detail in the text that follows. Reviews of new magazines by Katz and his associates appear regularly in *Library Journal* to help us keep up with recent publications.

It is also likely that several of the serial indexes published by the H.W. Wilson Company can be used to aid a library. In a general collection, such as a public library, any of the ±185 titles indexed in their *Readers' Guide to Periodical Literature* (RGPL) can be viewed as a potential candidate for the subscription list. In such a context, RGPL, itself a serial, comes close to being "indispensable," and should be ordered. There are other Wilson indexes that selectively cover broad subject areas, e.g., biology and agriculture, humanities, social sciences, or more specific topics, e.g., art, business, law. Any of these that are relevant to a library's objectives will probably be ordered, and the lists of indexed titles provide a good list from which to select. Since Wilson indexes are sold on a service basis, budgeting for these can be a bit tenuous.

A committee of ALA's Reference and Adult Services Division recommends changes, additions and deletions, and advises H.W. Wilson in other matters relating to the various indexes. Clearly, the availability in a library of such an index will amplify patron demand for titles cited therein, reinforcing their importance. In some libraries, serials policy calls for adding and dropping subscriptions, according to the most recent addenda and subtracta. These changes are neither numerous nor frequent, but periodical publishers are understandably anxious while such decisions are pending. When announcement is made that a continuing title is to be dropped, there is often an anguished protest from the publisher who fears that there will be library cancellations. There may also be some frantic lobbying, sometimes successful, for reinstatement of an old favorite by a group of librarians.

For the more comprehensive collections in academic and research libraries, and/or where there is an intense concentration on a limited subject as in many special libraries, more exhaustive sources must be sought. Even where teaching and research staff have principal responsibility for selections, librarians can and should supply appropriate lists from which most choices ought to be made. Indexing and abstracting (I/A) periodicals are excellent sources for listings of the more important serials in the topics they cover. Since most I/As strive for comprehensive coverage, there will be considerable overlap and redundancy in their lists, especially in the sciences.

I/As are too numerous to attempt any listing of them here. Published reference guides and subject specialists on the staff can help to identify the most relevant I/As. If copies of those wanted as selection sources are not in hand, nor available for examination in nearby libraries, one can probably obtain them from the publishers as sample issues. If the library wants to maintain comprehensive and systematic coverage of recent publications, a good source would be the *New Serial Titles*. If evaluations are wanted, reviews in relevant professional publications, or advice of local experts who have had opportunity to inspect sample issues should prove helpful. With more and more libraries preparing/publishing lists of serial holdings, it is possible to utilize those that coincide well with the individual library's objectives, especially if the library chosen is known for the high quality of its collections.

GETTING DOWN TO CHOICES

Once the listings have been collected one must decide which titles are actually wanted. Some of the assembled listings will contain fewer titles than are needed in a given subject, and others will contain too many. For example, one might decide that the library should subscribe to all academic level magazines in Katz under the heading "Computers and Automation," and still want to add more. One can then turn to the more comprehensive *Ulrich's International Periodicals Directory*, seventeenth edition, 1977-1978 (R.R. Bowker); under "Computer Technology and Application" and find about 200 more serials than the 62 in Katz, and with a much higher proportion of foreign-language publications.

To reduce the number of offerings in Ulrich to more manageable dimensions, categories expected to be of least interest to the library's clientele can be eliminated and then the remaining titles can be considered. For example, one might omit any or all of the following, at least initially: (a) newsletters and/or tabloid format; (b) titles not known to be indexed or abstracted; (c) titles in specified foreign languages; (d) serials whose articles are included without refereeing; (e) commercially published serials requiring author payments, when this condition can be discovered; and (f) titles with less than 1,000 circulation. In this overall consideration, there is some merit in the argument that unindexed serials deserve extra consideration by reason of their exclusion, on grounds that articles cited in I/As are readily accessible via interlibrary loan and other cooperative arrangements.

Studies and analyses published in the scholarly and professional literature provide evaluations that use several different approaches. Their rankings are commonly based upon one or more of the following:
1. *Suffrage.* Tabulated votes/rankings of a select group of experts working in the discipline.
2. *Official Endorsement.* Evaluation under sponsorship of a learned society or professional association.
3. *Citation Analyses.* Approaches vary. Possibly a simple count of the number of times a serial is cited in other professional publications;

at other times, the tally is modified in some way, e.g., the number of times the title is cited during the review period divided by the total number of articles published; the survey may also be restricted to a few highly regarded serials in the same discipline.

4. *Use Studies.* Since many libraries do not maintain circulation records for periodicals, special efforts may be required to sample use under controlled conditions, during a limited time period, which can yield artificial evidence; we might also inspect unbound issues and ponder the "dilapidation factor."

With the plethora of I/As, the inclusion of a title in such a publication is no longer proof of quality, especially since many I/As go beyond reason in their coverage. Some included titles will scarcely produce a single relevant article in an entire year. Perhaps such I/A publishers expect that subscribers will confuse quantity of coverage with quality, and will therefore continue to pay the escalating rates without serious objection. All the same, information about a serial's I/A profile can indicate something. For example, a title such as *Simulation*, which is covered in six I/A publications, is more justified in its determined importance than some other established periodicals in the same subject that are in only one or two I/As.

It is somewhat easier to find an array of evaluative information for scientific serials than in most other areas, but determined researchers will be able to find useful studies and aids in nearly any field. For instance, in one study it was proposed that in a group of four neighboring libraries responsibility be assigned to each participant for a proportion of the religious titles on a composite list, so that at least one current subscription of each would be available in the library. A desiderata list was compiled by identifying titles that appeared in at least two of the following: *Catholic Periodicals Index*, *Index to Religious Periodicals*, and *Religious and Theological Abstracts*.

This circumstance suggests another consideration in choosing serials. If there are established libraries in the vicinity, with interests that are overlapping, it is worth extra effort to seek lists of their serial holdings, or preferably to compile a union list of serials received by those several libraries in the area. While a library most probably will subscribe to all of the affordable titles in higher priority groups, that same library might be able to rely on neighbors to maintain titles less in demand by its patrons. In consultation with the other libraries, responsibility can be established for acquisition of serials of interest to the group but not already received in the area. Lists of serials received by libraries, wherever located, whose objectives and size closely parallel each other can also be helpful in identifying important titles.

Sharing serial resources with other libraries is a complex topic, worthy of thorough separate treatment. At this point, however, it will suffice to simply note that this form of cooperation is increasing at all levels and in many areas throughout the world. Necessity has been the procreator of many useful formal and informal agreements that have been worked out between libraries. In some areas, traditional barriers to efficient interaction have been overcome, so that a consortium may include institutions of divergent size from both the public and private sectors. Interlibrary loan practices have been complicated and modified by the new copyright laws, but by now most libraries have learned to work within the new parameters without serious hindrance, for the benefit of all.

Quality and relevance to the library's objectives must be the foremost considerations in selecting serials, but the pragmatic question of cost cannot be ignored. Obviously, one cannot afford a standing order for Beilstein's *Handbuch der Organischen Chemie* nowadays if the annual serial allocation for the Chemistry Library is limited to $10,000—unless the library can do without *Chemical Abstracts* and quite a few other vital titles. Beyond this, care must be taken to ensure that each subscription chosen is more cost beneficial than others that are rejected. And in a given subject, if there are several expensive items of about equal value to the institution and they are nearly comparable in all respects except that one costs two or three times any of the others, the most expensive one will probably be the one to eliminate since it is the responsibility of selection officers to make the best possible use of the funds available.

In the section on maintaining and preserving serials some potential uses of microform were commented on. Depending on anticipated use within the institution, consideration should be given to the possible merits of microform as a substitute for paper, when permitted;

in addition to the paper copy, as a substitute for binding as a substitute for purchase of paper backfile. In addition to aspects relating to preservation, one must consider the elements of relative cost of both acquisitions expenditure and staff time, and immediate and long-range space requirements.

Decisions on purchase of serial backfiles are somewhat related to the selection of subscriptions and standing orders, although some desiderata in this category might have ceased publication by now. In connection with the active titles, concern must be expressed not only about which backfiles, but also how many volumes, in what sequence (i.e., which titles first), a few volumes of each of many titles in each of the three years of the backfile allocation, or longer runs of fewer, and in what formats.

To a degree, the schedule of priorities for serial commitments can identify titles whose backfiles will be important, but not entirely. In some science subjects, relatively short backfiles can serve most users needs. In other fields, researchers may insist that they cannot survive without complete runs of titles. Informed opinions should be sought on the above questions, and subsequent acquisitions attuned to budgets, including subject allocations. Since the anticipated use of backfiles is usually lower than for current issues, the potential for saving through sharing resources with other libraries can be quite promising.

MANAGING THE SERIALS BUDGET

Once it is known which serials are to be acquired, decisions must be made as to with whom orders are to be placed. The vendor choices must be cost-effective. In purchasing, libraries have two major alternatives: first, direct from a publisher, including societies and other agencies whose publishing activities may be incidental to other functions; or second, through agents who can supply/service serials on several publishers in various locations. To hold down the number of invoices that must be processed and payments to be made, both library acquisitions staff and institutional paymasters prefer that work be conducted through agents to whatever extent this is feasible.

In addition to affording greater efficiency in communications, agents can usually be persuaded to provide extra services for libraries that so request. The claiming of overdue serial parts from publishers is frequently performed by agents, especially those in foreign countries. In libraries where speed of delivery is judged to be crucial, an agent can obtain the wanted titles expeditiously and make bulk airfreight shipments at prearranged intervals. Of course, when such shipments come from overseas, the additional charges will increase the library's costs substantially.

In many libraries, higher authority requires that periodical renewals be awarded on a contract basis each year to the lowest bidder. When the total number is large, it may be advisable to separate the lot into several lists, probably by geographic area and/or possibly by broad subject. If subscriptions are let for bid, information and advice on reputations and performance of unfamiliar agents must be sought so that if serious questions remain unanswered their bids should not be solicited.

In some situations, municipal or other authorities may go so far as to require that all orders be sent at a specified time to a specific dealer, with no variations allowed. Even when not restricted in choices of vendor, one may find that prior experience is of little direct use in the vendor selection process. Different kinds of serials may warrant different treatment, and geographic locations may redirect attention from old favorites to other potential vendors. What is desired is the best combination of low cost and good service. When other factors are fairly equal—service charges, promptness in reporting and delivery, range of materials serviced, fees and discounts—the library may prefer to rely on a local firm for the largest share of business. It is relatively easy and inexpensive to communicate with them by telephone or a visit so that questions and problems can be resolved expeditiously. It is also advisable to consider ordering most foreign titles from selected overseas agents since their proximity to distant sources and language capacity is an advantage.

A few publishers will not supply their materials through a third party, and in those cases there is no option. It is also a reasonable alternative to order direct from publishers who issue a large number of serials that are needed. For a science collection, one might consider direct purchase from Academic Press, Elsevier-North Holland, McGraw-Hill, Springer Verlag, and Wiley-Interscience, to name only a few. If the quantity wanted from a given publisher is high, a discount that would be better than an agent could allow might be negotiated. Some publishers already have a policy that offers such advantages to direct purchasers under specified conditions. There certainly is no single method of purchase that works best in all situations and no institutional ordering pattern can be relied upon to operate at a high level of efficiency for an indefinite period.

Apart from purchase, an important method used in developing serial collections is to exchange materials, usually with other libraries. Exchange relationships should not be undertaken lightly. The supposed benefits, as viewed by protagonists not involved in working out details, can turn out to be illusory. If serial publications from within the institution are available to the library without charge, the contributors often want something in a related subject in exchange. The titles involved ought to be roughly comparable in quality, cost, frequency, format, and relevance to each receiving institution's needs. Since it is difficult to arrange such harmonious marriages, some institutions are often forced to accept and possibly offer materials that they would be unwilling to buy at any price if applying standard selection criteria. Records-keeping requirements are also increased at each end to obtain one title and exchange partners are obliged to set up separate claiming processes, thereby making the process both cumbersome and expensive despite its value.

It is sometimes thought to be a mixed blessing to be a depository for U.S. government publications, a state printing office, and/or any of several other agencies. However, many important serials are official publications, and many libraries that cannot get them without charge are purchasers. Gift subscriptions and standing orders may be offered by various agencies, commercial publishers, and individual donors. Whether to accept a subscription at all and, if so, what level of processing and maintenance is merited must be decided on the anticipated benefit in relation to costs. Declining to accept proferred but unwanted donations can be a bit touchy, and it is helpful to have a written policy that can be shown to impassioned would-be benefactors. Local politics and diplomatic requirements may dictate acceptance of an occasional marginal title. In such cases, losses can be cut by opting for the simplest possible processing. For example, issues of a monthly magazine can be sent directly to the current periodicals room, with no check-in or claim procedures and all but the most recent 12 issues can be discarded. Thus each issue is available for consultation for a year, processing costs are minimal, and binding costs eliminated. Many a paid subscription deserves this same unelaborate treatment.

Budget Analysis and Control

Many of the reference works cited above as selection aids provide cost information; the more frequently these appear, the more likely it is that the subscription rates shown will still apply. Reliable data are easiest to find for magazines. Major subscription agents can and will provide the latest price information on request. Some firms publish annual listings in early autumn, listing serials that they can supply and showing the expected rates for the coming year. Since publishers occasionally increase their prices late and without forewarning, suppliers usually recoup underpayments by sending additional billing to their customers later in the year.

Predicting the annual cost of serials is difficult at best, especially for titles published at irregular intervals and at varying prices for each part. For the more expensive serials, payment fluctuations can be great from one fiscal period to the next. Experienced agents may be able to supply reasonable estimates for a large block of serials, but the figures probably won't be of much use in managing each of a few dozen allocations. In addition, publishers' catalogs show a history of frequency of appearance and pricing patterns for their serials.

During recent years, book and periodical prices have risen at a steeper rate than most other domestic and foreign commodities. Serial budgets are more difficult to manage than book order expenditures because of the action that must be taken to end the standing commitment. Published projections of inflation, even when based on careful study and analysis by acknowledged experts, seem never to be quite what are expected. For one thing, the configuration of subscriptions and standing orders does not necessarily coincide with the sample analyzed, and inflation is only one factor to be considered. As a result budget adjustments are usually too little too late.

Comprehensive in-house inflation analyses are not easy to perform, even when recent and reliable cost data have been input for computer processing. But where computer processing of data cannot be undertaken, publisher catalogs provide a useful approach in sampling rates of inflation. The results, however, cannot safely be applied to other firms, even within the same country and subject specialty. Still, such studies can be quite revealing and meaningful in a limited way.

All libraries with a commitment to scholarly research in a wide range of subjects will likely include many foreign serials in their active lists. For them, 1979 renewal invoices issued in autumn 1978 brought a special kind of anguish when totals were translated into dollars. Libraries cannot blame other countries for dollar devaluation, but this absolution does not alleviate budgetary difficulties.

It is hard to cope with such radical financial perturbations when planning budgets and monitoring expenditures. Therfore, it is mandatory that agreements with vendors should be worked out carefully and in writing beforehand for the protection of both parties. Procedures to be followed must be acceptable to each. Discounts for serials may be allowed at stipulated percentages off publishers' list prices with discounts varying according to type of publication, geographic origin, and other factors.

It has already been observed that coping with substantial numbers of foreign serials is fraught with added complexities. U.S. libraries frequently need to be billed in dollars, but it is perfectly legitimate to request that suppliers stipulate the conversion rates used. As budget watchers, librarians need to be aware of fluctuations in values of foreign currencies, at least in those countries whose publications constitute a significant proportion of the acquisitions. If institutional payments overseas are slow, the dollar can have fallen significantly between the time of billing and arrival of our check. In such cases, libraries must be prepared to honor a supplemental billing if insufficient allowance has been made for the possibility. Conversely, should the dollar rise, one might inquire about a credit. When performing spot checks on invoices from abroad, allowances should be made of

2-3% variation in the dealer's favor, since the firm is not always able to obtain the bank rate at a given moment and will probably be required to pay a small fee each time dollars must be exchanged for local currency. We must remember that agents have problems too.

Defensive Measures

It is not unusual to find 60-65% of a university library's material expenditures earmarked for serial renewals. With such alarming gross increases in recent times, other purchase categories are reduced accordingly. If serials subscriptions must be canceled, on what bases is this done? In some libraries, candidates are chosen ad hoc: someone (library staff, teacher, patron) makes note of a title that appears to be superfluous to institutional objectives. If agreement can be reached by all parties on the essential point, the offending title is canceled. Another approach is to ask staff responsible for processing serial invoices to notify someone in authority whenever a price increase exceeds a certain amount or percentage over the previous payment. A good example of what could happen is that of *International Aerospace Abstracts* which increased in one year from $240 per year to $550, without benefit of dollar devaluation. Such a price reviewing procedure does not necessarily require cancellation at specific levels of increase, but it permits those responsible to take appropriate action.

It is also possible to single out specific categories of serials from which to select sacrificial offerings. Current newspaper subscriptions might be largely eliminated because interest and format are fleeting; their microform counterparts might be continued for their research potential. Newsletters and other publications used mainly for current awareness might be sacrificed to preserve other titles of more lasting value. Foreign language serials are probably less in demand in most disciplines, and might be subjected to close scrutiny. At various times and places, campaigns have been launched against such other categories as duplicate serials within a library system, loose-leaf services, titles in specified subjects where institutional interests may be waning, items priced above a certain limit, titles subject to high-level depredation even if not available in microform, monographic series whose parts might then be acquired on a selective basis, and many others. In short, there are as many possible reasons for de-selecting serials as for selecting them in the first place. Less wanted categories should go first, but one must not be too ritualistic in applying general rules. For example, some multiple subscriptions are both important and in heavy demand, and these duplicates will need to be maintained, even at the expense of unique titles. Decisions that may be sensible for a library with all materials in a central facility will not necessarily apply in a system with many branches. Care must always be taken to ensure that specific institutional needs and circumstances are taken into account.

Where budget increments have not kept pace with inflation or with the purchase implications of the recent informational explosion, it is sensible to adopt a steady-state policy with respect to serial allocations. Even before any extensive cancellations have been made, it might be an acceptable rule that no standing commitments can be added in a subject group until an equivalent dollar value has been eliminated. The trade-off must come before the renewals for cancel candidates have been paid, or the transaction must be postponed. If budgets are tight enough, the policy should be extended to require cancellations to balance extraordinary rate increases, although this will be more difficult to accomplish.

CONCLUSION

This discussion has gone full circle, from building up a serials collection to dismantling it. Consideration has been given to the nature of serials: definitions, characteristics, complexities of processing, problems of maintenance and preservation, and how they might be used. Approaches to selection and collection development have been discussed from several viewpoints and in various institutional environments. Management and control of serial commitments has been a growing concern in virtually every library in this country, and elsewhere, so that the professional literature on cancellation could soon outweigh articles on serials selection.

In retrospect, this entire process rather resembles one of the modern theories of cosmology: after explosive growth, the gravity of a library's situation is halting outward expansion in all directions, and the process of collapse and return to the primal condition has begun. It is hoped that this retrogression will eventually slow, and then stop well short of the ultimate solution.

Throughout, flexibility must be maintained. Even apart from the fiscal stagflation many libraries have been experiencing, serial commitments are subject to frequent change. Some titles will improve as the quality of others deteriorates, and serial birth rates seem to exceed deaths. Institutional programs and objectives are modified from time to time, and library adjustments must follow suit.

Many problems encountered in dealing with serials can be resolved easily and quickly; others are inherent in the breed, and while the effects of these may be alleviated, the old problems will always remain.

SELECTED READINGS

Although the following is not an exhaustive bibliography, it does include useful readings for those concerned with developing serials collections.

Two serials titles which are devoted to the subject are *Serials Librarians* (Haworth Press, 1976-) and *Serials Review* (Periam Press, 1975-).

In addition, several monographs, including two conferences, which address the issue are:

Blackwell's Periodical Conference, 2nd, *Economics of Serial Management* (Oxford, 1977).

Brown, Clara. *Serials: Acquisition and Management* (Birmingham, Ala.: EBSCO, n.d.).

Osborn, Andrew D. *Serials Publications: Their Place and Treatment in Libraries*, 2nd ed. (Chicago: ALA, 1973).

Spyers-Duran, Peter and Daniel Gore, eds. *Management Problems in Serials Work* (Westport, Conn.: Greenwood Press, 1974).

An annual review of what's happening with serials appears under the title of "Serials in Review" in *Library Resources and Technical Services*. Also one whole issue of *Drexel Library Quarterly* (July 1975) is devoted to "Current Issues in Serials Librarianship."

Other useful articles include the following:

Carson, Doris M., "What Is a Serial Publication?" *Journal of Academic Librarianship* 3 (Sept. 1977): 206-209.

Huff, William H., "The Acquisition of Serial Publications," *Library Trends* 18 (Jan. 1970): 294-317.

Smith, Katherine R., "Serials Agents/Serials Librarians," *Library Resources and Technical Services* 14 (Winter 1970): 5-30.

PART VI

NEW DIRECTIONS IN COLLECTION DEVELOPMENT

Collection Evaluation or Analysis:

Matching Library Acquisitions to Library Needs

Paul H. Mosher

INTRODUCTION

How good are our library collections? This perfectly reasonable question has proved extraordinarily difficult to answer with any meaning.
The literature of librarianship does not even agree on the meaning of
the term *good* with regard to collections, to say nothing of providing
us with ready techniques for analyzing or evaluating their quality.
Often we are told in response to the question how *good*, how *many*,
in the rather naive belief that quantity and quality are necessarily
equivalent terms when applied to library materials. To a considerable
extent, this approach has been adopted because of the sheer scale of
the problem: for example, how does one evaluate hundreds of

thousands of books in several libraries which may serve dozens of programs and thousands of patrons? The collections of a large library or group of branch libraries are a vast three-dimensional model not unlike the bead game in the Hermann Hesse novel.

Collection evaluation—the assessment of the utility of a library's collections to its users—is one of the essential functions of collection development. Since this process has as its ends the focusing of acquisitions expenditures on those materials most needed by library users and the maintenance of useful materials in the current stock, collection evaluation is an essential function of collection management as well.

EVALUATION FOLLOWS
PROGRAM AND GOAL SETTING

Assessment of the utility of library collections can effectively be planned and executed only if the library has set clear missions and goals for the management of its collections, goals which are consistent with and supportive of the missions and goals of the library's parent institution and user constituency. Evaluations are normally based on guidelines provided by a collection development policy statement, and are closely involved with financial goals or limits imposed upon a library's budget. A chief premise of collection management is that library collections should be developed economically and efficiently, with the end of minimizing the purchase, processing, and storage of unwanted materials in the library collections. Collection evaluations are thus also undertaken to identify unwanted duplicates and obsolete or very little used titles in order to control book stock growth and maximize the useful life of relatively high-cost active collection space. An ongoing plan of collection evaluation, carefully planned, efficiently executed, well reported, and acted upon can be a vital tool in controlling collection growth and assuring its continuing utility.

REASONS FOR
COLLECTION EVALUATION

Most academic library collections have grown, like Topsy, through long, unplanned, inconsistent, and uncoordinated processes of faculty selection, library approval or blanket plans, gift accumulation, and often inadequate and understaffed efforts in recent years to rectify this situation. It continues to be amazing that while most ARL libraries spend from one-quarter to one-third of their total budgets on acquisitions, many libraries still lack an effective collection development program—or any program at all—or staff even roughly proportional to program cost. Collection evaluations or assessments act as the radar or sonar of collection development programs, measuring and charting the surface contours of collections, skimming and sampling the upper layers, or drilling cores from carefully chosen sample areas to ascertain depth, and to measure the utility—either direct and immediate (for science/technology collections, for example), or more indirect or long-term (for hard-core humanities collections)—of collection for present and future users.

Evaluations of library collections are useful for many reasons. The following list includes some of the more important (1):

1. A more accurate understanding of the nature, shape, depth, and utility of collections.
2. Assessment of the effectiveness of collection development or acquisitions programs, methods, or sources.
3. The capacity of library collections to support research or curriculum of a specific program.
4. A guide or basis for collection planning, management, or pruning.
5. A means of ascertaining collection size, adequacy, or quality.
6. A way to measure the effectiveness of a collection development policy.
7. A means of discovering and rectifying gaps in library holdings.
8. A tool to focus human and monetary resources on areas most needing support rather than spreading effort indiscriminately over both areas of adequacy and inadequacy.
9. As an aid to the preparation of a collection development policy and assignment of collection intensity levels.

10. As a means of assessing whether collection intensity levels of a collection development policy are appropriate, or whether development effort has matched policy targets.
11. As a basis for and defense of book-budget request levels.
12. As a useful device to measure the potential value of resource sharing and to avoid unwanted duplication of materials with consortium partners.
13. As a device to measure the relative strength of collections for planning or allocation purposes.

The various reasons listed above may be summarized by the American Library Association's Resources and Technical Services Division guidelines on collection evaluation:

> ... assessments help determine whether a collection is meeting its objectives, how well it is serving its users, in what ways or areas it is deficient, and what remains to be done to develop the collection (2).

QUANTITATIVE OR QUALITATIVE, OBJECTIVE OR SUBJECTIVE?

A great deal of ink has been spilled (even in recent literature) over the issue of whether collection evaluations should be objective or subjective, and it is often assumed that quantified data are necessarily more objective than qualitative information. In fact, quantitative data is not necessarily more objective than qualitative or evaluative data. A statistic is just as capable of leading to misinterpretation or unsound conclusions as a judgment or evaluation based on insufficient information. On the other hand, an accurate, soundly based judgment, or even a perception based on long experience, may be as objective, or valid, as a set of statistics.

The work of any librarian involved in collection development or management consists of making a great many decisions and judgments. These decisions should be as well informed as possible, based on both quantitative and qualitative information, on faculty and specialist opinion, on analysis of teaching and research programs, on long-standing familiarity with the library's collections and goals. The issue is not one of subjective versus objective, but rather of the choice of the right methodological tools to produce the type and quality of result desired.

Most judgments are subjective. They may be made less so by the use of appropriate goals, criteria, policies, guidelines, tools, and procedures. Many methods are available to the librarian who wishes to evaluate library collections, and it is the librarian's business to ascertain on the basis of the institution's nature and mission, the parameters and perimeters set by the collection development policy statement, and the nature of the information needed, what evaluative tools and techniques will be most informative and useful.

APPROACHES TO COLLECTION EVALUATION

Collection evaluation is a term applied to a number of techniques used to achieve the ends listed above; it can be qualitative or quantitative, simple or complex, costly or inexpensive, time-intensive or time-economic, one-time or ongoing, and can be applied to the study of the collections or collection efforts of any type of library. Normally, as is the case with most evaluative or analytical examinations of library processes or functions, a program of collection evaluation will be most enlightening and useful if it combines more than one approach or method.

Like the closely related field of library materials use studies, collection evaluation is analogous to the work of an artillery observer or a signal directionfinder: a goal or target only becomes fully clear and accurately identified when more than one bearing has been established. Similarly, the findings of collection evaluations or analyses compound their yield if they can be grouped, and if, over time, various methods are used. For example, if a collection in Roman history, or in heat transfer, has 1500 titles, is this good or bad? Quantitative data from libraries having similar programs and goals improves the yield of data, and a check of holdings from a citation list from a significant recent book or journal article may reveal still more accurately the quality of a 1500-title collection *if* the book or article used for the evaluation is chosen on the basis of its relevance to teaching or research programs at the university or college housing the collection. In other words, collection size becomes more meaningful if levered off comparative or bibliographic data as well.

PREPARATION FOR EVALUATIONS

As we have said above, any collection assessment should follow from the mission and goals of a library, its parent institution, and its users. These should normally be summarized in a library's collection development statement, which should also include information on the nature of each program or academic department served, a conspectus of the program as set up and practiced locally, types, treatments, and collection intensity levels for materials collected, and at least a rough library call number classification sequence for materials collected (see the Dowd chapter on collection development policy statements). All of this information will be of use in planning or executing one or another type of evaluation.

Prior to beginning an evaluation, it will also be useful to review the ALA/RTSD collection development guidelines (2). Incipient collection evaluators will also benefit from scanning George Bonn's "Evaluation of the Collection," an article which appeared in *Library Trends* (3), and the chapter on collection evaluation in F.W. Lancaster's recent book on the measurement and evaluation of library services (4). The Bonn article is a catalog of methods by type of library which seeks to state the case for each type without evaluating its practical utility, and it is useful in suggesting appropriate methodologies. Lancaster studies collection assessment with the object of optimizing collection storage by placing the most-used materials in the most convenient and accessible space and storing other materials in less convenient and accessible locations; however, his treatment is very useful and thought provoking for planning evaluations. Both the Bonn article and the Lancaster chapter have substantial bibliographies of works which describe the theory and practice of collection evaluation in detail by type of library (5). An historical survey of collection evaluation and its chief ideas and methods may be found in the Mosher article, "Collection Evaluation in Research Libraries" (6).

The Office of Management Studies of the Association of Research Libraries also offers librarians assistance in establishing collection development programs and conducting collection assessments. Useful material from recent collection evaluations in ARL libraries is included in ARL SPEC kit No. 41, and results of a pilot collection analysis program are described in a pamphlet published in 1978 (7). The Office of Management Studies also sponsors a self-study type of program to assist non-ARL libraries in collection development and analysis efforts, using librarians from previously conducted projects as consultants (8).

METHODS OF EVALUATING COLLECTIONS

In the sections that follow, we have sought to review the most common forms and methods of collection evaluations and analyses. One will find some more useful than others depending on one's own inclinations and what it is one wants to find out about a collection. The methods are arranged more or less in order from the more simple to the more complex, and in each case some principal uses, advantages, and disadvantages are mentioned. Our principle has been to emphasize the useful, practical, and economical over the theoretical or abstract, and whenever possible to contradict the fashionable perception that the complex or obscure are more valuable than the simple or the obvious.

Surveys and Impressions

Shelf scanning—examination of materials on the shelves—is a simple and rewarding way of evaluating collections. It is valuable either when carried out by someone who knows the literature of the subjects covered, or by a less-experienced librarian who wishes to become familiar with existing collections. Surveys of this type may be enhanced by use of various tools: for example, adequacy of portions of the collections can be roughly ascertained by reference to the collection development policy statement, faculty and student subject interest profiles, or the appropriate subject classification schedules. Such an examination can outline size, scope, depth, currency and physical conditions of collections. It can be carried out relatively quickly and simply, and can be used on almost any portion of a library's collections. Findings can be used in preparing or amending a collection development policy statement, and can be used to prepare useful descriptions or surveys of the collections outlining the larger strengths and weaknesses. Results can also be useful in planning other, more substantial and documented forms of evaluation or analysis. The method can also identify candidates for restoration or preservation activity or for pruning.

Questioning Users

Most libraries should have regular programs of contact with users to ascertain how well the collections meet their needs. Experience has shown personal contact to be more successful in most cases than mailed questionnaires (return rates are low, concerns or dissatisfactions thus easily overlooked). Librarians often find it useful to have a standard form to record responses, and the forms can be used to standardize questions asked, to elicit responses for various types of services, and to create a lasting record of the responses. User perceptions of collection weakness or strength may be tested by using other methods, and this method, like shelf scanning, is a very useful starting point for other types of evaluations.

Numeric Counts

Count of volumes by subject classification breakdown, made from shelf list card count (measured in inches at about 100 volumes per inch), from shelf measurements (about 10 volumes per foot), or from automated data files, is a popular, relatively simple and useful measure, though it has significant drawbacks if used by itself as an evaluative tool.

Numeric counts alone can tell one how many books a library

processes in any given subject classification. The chief values of the method are its straightforwardness and clarify in gathering, representing, and interpreting data. Shelf list measurement data acquire meaning when compared with like data from other similar libraries: for example, it is easy to say, and to understand, that if library X has 10,000 titles in LC class J and library Y has 15,000, library Y has a better (larger) collection in political science. Furthermore, the data can be manipulated as finely as the capacity of a classification system to define its subjects. Data acquired in this way, if accurately interpreted—which is not always as easy as it seems—can be of use in ascertaining collection areas which need more, or less, collection effort, for justifying book-budget requests, for acquiring a general, or descriptive, view of a library's collections, and for planning cooperative collection development ventures. The validity and utility of the data can often be enhanced when used in conjunction with another evaluation technique.

Principal problems in using this method are: confusion arising from historical use of more than one classification system, inability of subject classifications accurately to describe programs or components of programs, meaninglessness of data if books were acquired uncritically, rates of duplication and obsolescence, and erroneous or obsolescent data. The method is not very helpful in making fine measurements, describing collection support for interdisciplinary, or "new," subjects (such as medieval studies or high-energy physics); nor does it tell one how "good" a collection is, or to what degree it can be expected to satisfy user need. The method also cannot tell the difference between textbooks, monographs, or source collections, for example. It is also good to remember that the Library of Congress system is more of a book address system than a classification of knowledge, and that data may be based on multiple shelf lists which contain a fair degree of duplication.

Statistical data are also normally used as a basis (if not *the* basis) for library standards. Numeric counts of collection size can be compared to these standards as a measure of rough collection adequacy, though not of quality.

Any academic library interested in using this technique will find both invaluable advice and comparative data in the most recent edition of the comparative shelf list measurement project sponsored by the ALA Discussion Group of Chief Collection Development Officers of Large Research Libraries. Available from the University of California, Berkeley General Library, this document publishes approximate comparative collection sizes according to a LC class breakdown by 490 classes for 27 ARL libraries (9).

Formulas and Standards

Predicated on the assumption that there is a necessary correlation between a library collection's adequacy and its collection size, Clapp and Jordan, and others, have devised formulas for determining the minimal adequacy of an academic library's collection to provide support for user needs, or against which probable adequate program support by a library's collections can be measured. Formulas attempt to assign quantities to various programmatic factors such as the numbers of faculty and students in various categories, and the numbers of undergraduate or graduate subjects or degree programs (10). These formulas were designed primarily to establish basic target collection sizes for libraries in the new colleges and universities established in this country in the fifties and sixties. They, and the figures, often given in library evaluation standards, make no attempt to indicate the quality of collections, but only minimum adequate size to support a group of programs. Essentially, most formulas seek to establish a core undergraduate collection size after some model (e.g., Clapp-Jordan use Lamont Library at Harvard) and add increments per faculty member, student, and program. Library standards, devised for accreditation purposes, also establish minimally adequate collection sizes for certain types of libraries.

Interlibrary Loan Analysis

A relatively simple means of measuring collection adequacy against user demand is analysis of a reasonably large random sample of interlibrary loan requests. Counted by subject or program, publication date, language (or country) of publication, and format (document, book, serial, etc.), interlibrary loan requests can identify areas of collection weakness or unmet user need, whether there is unmet demand for current or out-of-print materials, whether there is need for attention to publications of a particular region, and if the library is giving inadequate attention to a particular format. Like any data, the results are susceptible to varying interpretation; certainly the library's missions and goals and the collection development policy statement should be used in interpreting the findings.

Bibliographic Checking

Most collection evaluation methods are aimed at description of size, estimating acquisitions budget needs, allocating book budgets, or identifying materials for storage or discard. The checking of bibliographies against library holdings is one of few methods that can be used to ascertain collection quality or excellence, rather than collection size or ability to meet user demand. Quality is here used to mean long-term utility of or need for library materials. While the method itself is not intrinsically difficult, the planning and follow-through required by this method call for judgment and discrimination and a good knowledge of user programs and supporting bibliography (11). Bibliographies must be well chosen, samplings must be decided on, and results must be interpreted, reported, and acted on; it is a method which should usually be designed by or with the close counsel of subject bibliographers or specialists, either from within the library or carefully chosen from user groups.

The comparison of a library's holdings against lists or bibliographies is one of the oldest forms of collection evaluation. The method has been used both to test the adequacy of an individual library collection and to evaluate comparatively the holdings of a number of libraries for various purposes, including resource sharing and coordinated collection development planning, and the bibliography covering its methodology is well developed.

When a carefully chosen group of bibliographies is used to test and enrich the results of surveys, user impressions and reports, and numeric counts, a very useful topography of collection strengths and weaknesses can be obtained. Use of a variety of complementary methods invariably provides a truer and more useful picture of collections than a single method used in isolation.

Evaluation against bibliographies is also a method that can be very helpful in focusing materials budgets on areas most deserving or needful of development effort, while limiting funds spend on materials or areas of lower priority. It is especially useful in libraries that need to build to improve retrospective collections, or that need to evaluate the effectiveness over time of collection development or acquisitions techniques.

The methodology of a collection analysis using bibliographic checking usually begins with the library's users, with reference librarians or subject specialists within the library, as the result of shelf scanning, or purchase-request analysis. It can also take place as a systematic testing of collections supporting a range of programs, program by program, over time. Most frequently this form of analysis follows from some indication of unmet need or collection inadequacy and the method is used to discover whether or not the perceived problem is real, and to identify specific materials or types of materials which, if acquired, would correct the inadequacy. Bibliography checking can also be used with the opposite intent: to verify that collections perceived to be strong in a particular area are, in fact, adequate or strong, and that reallocation of resources is appropriate.

Once the need or desire for such an evaluation is established, it is necessary to identify a useful bibliography, determine an appropriate sample, locate a searcher, train the searcher if necessary, conduct the evaluation, prepare a report summarizing the findings, determine whether action is required as the result of findings, and finally, take the action called for.

There are four basic techniques used in evaluating academic library collections by use of bibliographic checking. These techniques can be adapted to serve the needs of most other types of libraries as well.

1. A check of a sampling chosen from one or more accepted, important subject or field bibliographies, or bibliographies which would support the particular programs under examination;
2. a check of one or more monographic or journal article bibliographies or citation lists from works of significance to local users or programs;

3. checks of basic lists of most-used, most-cited titles—from reading lists, graduate field reading lists, or departmental bibliographies to determine basic collection adequacy; and
4. more comprehensive searches of titles in bibliographies or lists in areas where weaknesses were revealed by any of the above methods.

Practice has shown that samples should usually be weighted rather than statistically random. Searching should concentrate on most significant or useful titles, and can be done by librarians or support staff. In the extensive program undertaken by Stanford University, graduate students have been hired and trained to do the work, and a manual has been produced to help train them and to serve as a ready reference tool to answer basic questions they may have.

Checking Against Catalogs of Other Libraries
This method is carried out much like the one above, and an appropriate catalog must be selected with as much care as an appropriate bibliography. There are, however, fundamental problems which may be inherent in this method: does the catalog reflect holdings of an institution sufficiently like the one being studied, of similar size, mission, goals, and clientele? Have selection criteria of that institution always, consistently been of high quality? If the collection represented by the catalog aspires to comprehensiveness, is it selective enough to tell what one wants to know?

Use Studies
Other methods of collection evaluation seek to measure unmet demand (interlibrary loan analysis), or the adequacy of the collection to meet present or future needs. Use studies measure the adequacy of collections by measuring circulations and in-house use of library materials. This method is most familiar in connection with pruning or weeding collections (see Mosher's chapter on "Managing Library Collections: The Process of Review and Pruning"), but is also a form of evaluating collection utility. Findings can also be used to indicate

collection areas of little or no use, which may in turn suggest changes in collection development policy, acquisitions patterns, or in approval plan profiles. Heavy use may also suggest the desirability of higher duplication rates of most-used items.

As is true of other collection evaluation methods, use studies are most effective when more than one technique is used—whatever single method one chooses has something wrong with it (e.g., book pockets or checkout slips were inconsistently used or are sometimes missing or obliterated, in-house use accounts for a significant part of collection use but is difficult to record, etc.).

Use studies are also especially helpful in dealing with serials as a category, both in evaluation and pruning. The most common techniques for studying use are the following, which is covered in the chapters on "Citation and Use Studies."

1. *Circulation Frequency.* How often, if ever, has a volume been circulated? Has circulation frequency declined or increased markedly?

2. *In-House Use.* This is measured by counting reshelvings, by asking users to mark a slip on a volume each time it is used, or by slipping each volume so that the slip falls out if the volume is consulted.

3. *Citation Study.* Does the library have books or journals most frequently cited by one or another group of significant users? The study can be made against any appropriate standard citation index, against the citations of publications by a local user group, or against the citations in a standard or significant journal. In this case, use does not mean measurement of consultation by the local user population, but specific, cited use by writers who publish in a specific sample of publications.

4. *Questioning Users.* In this case, a sampling of users, by category, are questioned on the use of library materials, either through personal interviews or questionnaires, and the results are then tabulated, interpreted, and reported.

The classic book on library materials use is Fussler and Simon's *Patterns in the Use of Books in Large Research Libraries* (12). William McGrath, Philip Morse, G.J. Snowball, and Richard Trueswell are all involved in the development of models and formulas to aid in the study of library use or to predict its behavior given certain variables, and have published suggestive and useful articles on the subject (13).

Analysis of Machine-Readable Cataloging Data

An interesting variant of the shelf list measurement evaluation method has been developed by a team of librarians working out of the SUNY Central Administration Office of Library Services. In an effort to develop collection comparison tools, which would help the SUNY library system set up a coordinated collection development program and to allocate materials funds equitably within a library system, they have written a group of programs to perform collection analyses on library catalog data contained on OCLC archival tapes (14).

The system matches the 490 LC class breakdown used by the *National Shelflist Count* (see [9]) to the NCES Higher Education General Information Survey taxonomy used by academic institutions to report program registrations by academic discipline by most American universities and colleges. The idea is to provide computer-produced analyses of collection sizes by academic program in a structure more sensitive to standard academic program organization than is allowed by a straight LC shelf list count. Problems remain, for the HEGIS and LC structure matching may still not always produce a wholly accurate measure of collection size by academic program or discipline—but the program is the most sophisticated computer collection analysis system yet devised, and SUNY seeks to develop it as an exportable system that can be used to analyze the collections of any library possessing OCLC archival tapes.

AFTER THE EVALUATION

The results of any evaluation should be clearly and concisely reported, including data which may need to be checked, summarized, or recalculated at some future date, or which may be needed as the basis for remedial collection development work on preparation of desiderata lists. The report should include data such as the following:

1. the reason why the evaluation was conducted;
2. the nature and goal of the evaluation;
3. the source of method used;
4. problems encountered;
5. general comments about the collection;
6. a summary of specific strengths or weaknesses;
7. suggestions for additional analyses and recommended methods;
8. peripheral discoveries or observations of use to the library;
9. a plan or campaign of action to improve collections in areas of *undesirable* weakness, with lists of specific items or types of materials needed, and cost estimates for the campaign if appropriate.

Since reports can be long and complex, it is often useful to maintain a file of report summaries for use in future reporting, budget justifications, or discussion of findings with other librarians or faculty. A sample summary from an evaluation is included in the Appendix.

Record keeping is an important aspect of collection evaluation. Programs of analysis are likely to go on over a long period of time as need, concern, funding, and staffing dictate, and good reports and summaries lead to improvement in methodology and technique. Furthermore, it is sometimes beneficial to repeat one or more collection evaluations after the passage of some years to measure and guide the library's efforts to improve collections on the basis of findings.

Together with planning of collections, materials selection, allocation of materials budgets, the construction of establishment of approval plans, and review of collections for discard, storage, and preservation, collection evaluation is a basic tool of collection management and is one of the functions of collection development in any library.

APPENDIX

A Sample Evaluation Summary

SUL Collection Development Office
Collection Evaluation Summary

L. Golomb, 1976

Anthropology: Adequacy and Availability of the Collections at Stanford

Departments/
Fields:

Anthropology
Sociology
History
Economics

Sampling:

250 titles based on titles in Anthropology Graduate field and course bibliographies.

Findings:

Stanford possesses 249 of the 250 titles checked (over 99%). 236 titles were found in the Main Library, and 13 uniquely in branch libraries. Three titles (1%) were never located and were presumed missing.

During a busy-period shelf check, 84% of the titles were available on the shelves of one or more campus libraries; another 14.4% were in circulation and could readily be recalled. Main Library use, considered alone, was more intense: of 348 copies of the Main Library's 236 titles, 57.5% were available on the shelves during the busy-period check, 28.7% were on loan, and 13.8% were unavailable (or could not be found).

There have been complaints of low-availability of high-priority Social Science materials in the

Stanford libraries. Data from this study would suggest that these complaints are ill-founded, and that the problem may be elsewhere: problems perceived by the social science user in negotiating the system to find his book. Many users in these fields may possess inadequate bibliographic or library instruction, or may lack the patience to seek materials in decentralized locations. This study indicates that a user-orientation and training program should be developed for Social Science patrons—especially graduate students—in bibliography and library use. The effect of such a program may well be the better and fuller use by library patrons in this broad area.

NOTES AND REFERENCES

1. A number of these points were taken from my article, "Collection Evaluation in Research Libraries: The Search for Quality, Consistency and System in Collection Development," *LRTS* 23 (1979): 17.

2. American Library Association/Resources and Technical Services Division, *Guidelines for the Evaluation of Library Collections.* (Chicago: American Library Association, 1979.)

3. George S. Bonn, "Evaluation of the Collection." *Library Trends* 22 (1974): 265-304.

4. F.W. Lancaster, *The Measurement and Evaluation of Library Service.* (Washington, D.C.: Information Resources Inc., 1977), pp. 165-206.

5. Bonn, "Evaluation . . .," pp. 297-304; Lancaster, *Measurement . . .* , pp. 203-206.

6. Paul H. Mosher, "Collection Evaluation in Research Libraries," pp. 16-32.

7. ARL SPEC Kit, Association of Research Libraries, Office of University Library Management Studies, Systems and Procedures Exchange Center, *Collection Assessment*, SPEC Kit 41, February 1978.

8. *Collection Analysis in Research Libraries; An Interim Report on a Self-Study Process.* (Association of Research Libraries, Office of Library Management Studies, Washington, D.C.: 1978.)

9. *Titles Classified by the Library of Congress Classification: National Shelflist Count, 1977 Edition.* (Berkeley, General Library, University of California, 1979.)

10. Verner Clapp and R.T. Jordan, "Quantitative Criteria for Adequacy of Academic Library Collections." *College and Research Libraries* 26 (1965): 371-380. Corrected in *CRL* 27 (1966): 72. There is a useful commentary on the Clapp-Jordan formula, with the construction of a rather different formula approach to adequate collection sizes for Australian college libraries in E.J. Wainwright and J.E. Dean, *Measures of Adequacy for Library Collections in Australian Colleges and Advanced Education; Report of a Research Project Conducted on Behalf of the Commission on Advanced Education*, (Perth: Western Australian Institute of Technology, 1976), vol. 2, pp. 42-50.

11. Techniques recently used for this method at Stanford University and the University of Nebraska are described in ARL OMS SPEC Kit 41 cited above.

12. H.H. Fussler and J.L. Simon, *Patterns in the Use of Books in Large Research Libraries*. (Chicago: University of Chicago Press, 1969.)

13. Among these are W.E. McGrath, "The Significance of Books Used According To a Classified Profile of Academic Departments," *College and Research Libraries* 33 (1972): 212-219; Philip M. Morse, "Measures of Library Effectiveness," *Library Quarterly* 42 (1972): 15-30; G.J. Snowball, "Use Survey of Social Sciences and Humanities Periodicals in an Academic Library," *CACUL Newsletter* 3 (1971): pp. 39-67; R.W. Trueswell, "Some Behavioral Patterns of Library Users: The 80/20 Rule," *Wilson Library Bulletin* 43 (1979): 458-461.

14. Glyn T. Evans, "The Cost of Information about Library Acquisitions Budgets." *Collection Management* 2 (1978): 19-20.

Creativity in Collection Management and Development

George B. Miller, Jr.

INTRODUCTION

For more than three decades there has been an increasing interest in creativity. It is now generally recognized that there can be creativity in most of our daily activities. Creativity is not simply relegated to the fine arts. It can be found in business, child rearing, cooking, hobbies, repair work, athletics, private moments; and yes, indeed, in librarianship.

Sitting at one's desk in a library, one can solve what had previously seemed an insurmountable problem by the use of a little creativity—perhaps a fleeting idea; but it takes conviction. A free-flowing, flexible mind also helps.

A conversation in a drawing room in Paris many years ago between Einstein and the French poet Paul Valéry might serve to illustrate the point:

> Valéry's mania was to say that he was more interested in the process of creation than in the actual opus which came out of this creative process . . . and he started asking questions of Einstein, about how he worked.
>
> "How do you work, and could you tell us something of this?" Einstein was very vague about it.
>
> He said, "Well, I don't know . . . I go out in the morning and take a walk."
>
> "Oh," said Valéry, "interesting, and of course you have a notebook and whenever you have an idea you write it out in your notebook."
>
> "Oh," said Einstein, "no, I don't."
>
> "Indeed, you don't?"
>
> "Well, you know an idea is so rare."
>
> That is really as much as I think can be said as to really great creativity (1).

At the end of *A Portrait of the Artist as a Young Man*, James Joyce wrote: "Welcome, O life! I go to encounter for the millionth time the reality of experience, to forge in the smithy of my soul the uncreated conscience of my race" (2).

In commenting on this passage, Rollo May wrote:

> What a rich and profound statement that is . . . In other words, every creative encounter is a new event; every time requires another assertion of courage. And to encounter "the reality of experience" is surely the basis for all creativity (3).
>
> We cannot *will* to have insights. We cannot *will* creativity. But we can *will* to give ourselves to the encounter with intensity of dedication and commitment (4).

Watching and hearing Artur Rubinstein play the Grieg Piano Concerto at the age of ninety teaches one something about the expanses of creativity. It is simple, it is enriching, it is perhaps the highest goal. But more than that, there is an important distinction between the originator and the interpreter, although each is creative in his or her own way, whatever that may be.

The creative process is a mystery. Ideas spring upon one. The receptivity must be there, the willingness; but as May writes, the encounter with reality is essential. To apply creativity to libraries, and particularly to collection development, one must perhaps loosen up a bit.

NONTRADITIONAL FUNDING

Special Yearly Funding
Over and above traditional yearly fundings, sometimes, on a regular basis, year-end funding may be tapped from various sources. Some highly placed officers of an institution often have discretionary funds for contingencies or for entertaining dignitaries, which may not have been exhausted. If the library maintains desiderata lists, these lists may be employed to expend funds with dispatch. The telephone can be used, with a follow-up formal purchase order; and the library can thus be assured a delivery within the fiscal year—a boost to the budget.

Intra-Institutional Supplements
Windfalls do occur from time to time. Library officials need to apprise, or even to cultivate, higher administrative officers so that those officers realize the library is a logical repository for benefactions, particularly unrestricted gifts.

Capital-Outlay Funding
Creativity can be used to develop various methods of supplementary funding. If one is going to seek capital-outlay funding for library materials from a governmental agency, one needs to obtain a legal opinion. Probably, in the case of state and municipal jurisdictions, that opinion would have to be written by the attorney general or the city attorney. The opinion should designate that library materials are indeed a capital investment. This is fairly easy to prove, and there are precedents.

For example, in 1972, the electorate of the State of New Mexico, after an extremely well-organized campaign, voted to grant ten million dollars to the 17 tax-supported academic libraries of the state to be spent over a five-year period in order to bring those libraries up to national standards, as articulated in the Clapp-Jordan formula (5). The campaign was carefully coordinated among student leaders, academic librarians, and public information officers. The students, briefed in considerable detail with background information, statistics and charts, made all the presentations at the legislative hearings. Academic officials, including librarians, stayed in the background; the students were largely instrumental in reaching the collective ear of both houses of the legislature. The vote in favor of putting a bond issue up to a vote at the next general election passed unanimously. The following fall, the bond issue passed overwhelmingly.

A coda: in order to carry out such a campaign to fruition, a dedicated group of representatives of all the institutions involved must maintain constant vigilance. One person must coordinate the campaign, almost on a full-time basis, particularly as the pace of the campaign picks up. Pockets of resistance need to be identified and countermanded with reasonable arguments. Above all, publicity, which includes not only press releases but also brochures, radio broadcasts, telecasts, and public speechmaking, should be carefully orchestrated. It is extremely important that the campaign not peak too early or, for that matter, too late. The witness of New Mexico should be an encouragement to those libraries or groups of libraries that want to try for supplementary funding. It can be done, even in these days of California's Proposition 13; but success requires a gargantuan effort, great dedication, and good coordination, but mostly a conviction that it *can* be done.

In some states another possibility for capital-outlay funding is what is usually called the severance tax, which is a tax on the removal of minerals or other natural resources from the land in the state. Customarily, these funds are used for capital funding as they accumulate. The stewardship of these funds lies with the legislature, although the funds may be administered through a state agency. The important point is that access to these funds is through legislation. Action on such a library bill does not have to go to the electorate, as is the case with a bond issue.

Grants

Substantial opportunities for grants to libraries from both private and public agencies are often overlooked. Grant applications have to be carefully thought out, planned, and documented. Realistic, justified budgets must be submitted.

It is sad to contemplate that sometimes funds, available to libraries, are returned to the national or state funding agencies, because too few libraries applied, or because those libraries that did apply spent too little time on carefully preparing their applications.

The National Endowment for the Humanities, the National Endowment for the Arts, the National Science Foundation and, of course, the Council on Library Resources, to mention only a few, are possible sources for library funding. Private foundations are another source. *The Foundation Directory* contains valuable information on interests, size, and location of these foundations (6).

Almost exclusively, agencies and foundations will award grants only for programmatic projects with terminal dates; on-going projects are rarely funded and then only for the short term.

Research Overhead

Contracts to institutions for research, whether governmental or private, include a component called research overhead (7, 8). This covers space, heating, lighting and cleaning; but all too rarely is the library, which also provides a research service, included (9, 10). The reason for this is, unfortunately, ignorance or lack of initiative on the part of library administrators, or administrators of parent institutions are reluctant to relinquish control of the research-overhead funds.

Nevertheless, increasingly these funds are becoming available to libraries, particularly those with more assertive library administrators or more sympathetic managers in the parent institution.

The University of Washington reports that it spends 76% of its monies for library materials to support faculty and graduate research (11, 12). Much of that support for library collection development can justifiably come from research overhead.

Friends Groups

Additional nontraditional funding may come from friends or associates groups. The effectiveness of this kind of program depends, of course, on the degree of commitment of the groups and the coordination within the library itself, because it should always be remembered that these good people are donating their own free time and should be accordingly appreciated and acknowledged.

Sometimes friends groups are legally incorporated outside the institution they are supporting. This arrangement often allows greater flexibility in handling their own finances, although the business office or the accounting department of the parent institution will usually process the invoices, using friends funds.

It is also a good idea for the friends to have a permanent executive director, full time if possible. He or she should maintain constant contact with the library administration, not only to keep up but also to support and develop creative ideas.

GIFTS

Gifts, as a source of creative supplementary funding, although traditional in libraries, are greatly underutilized. Customarily, there are two types of gifts: restricted and unrestricted. The latter, of course, is preferable, although a restricted gift can reinforce an area of strength in the collections, particularly if the donor continues to contribute to that area.

Policies

It is ironic that in these days of reduced budgets, some libraries are cutting back on their gifts and exchange efforts or even eliminating the units. The pursuit of gifts would seem to be an obvious alternative for creative collection development in the face of diminished funding. However, there are everywhere chief administrators of libraries who are unfamiliar with some aspects of collection development; or even, in some cases of most aspects of collection development.

Gifts and exchange sections are often merely passive recipients and processors of gifts and long-term exchanges. Active solicitation of gifts, to approach the situation from a different point of view, can be a very time consuming but nevertheless rewarding activity.

It is important that the library have a written gift policy and also a policy for exchanges. These policies should be cleared with the library attorney. A sample policy can be found in Rogers and Weber (*13*).

Scouting and Being Social

The most effective gift program usually involves the active participation of all members of the library staff and, in the case of academic libraries, of teaching faculty. However, there almost needs to be a full-time coordinator who is free to examine all offers of gifts and who will take care of acknowledgments. That person should be tactful and adventuresome, but also persuasive.

Librarians should always be aware of the legal implications of gift acceptances and should carefully follow procedures.

One gift often leads to another. Librarians and staff members who are active in the community and who are alert to library needs can be extremely helpful in leading prospective donors to the proper person in the library who is charged with that responsibility.

For libraries serving a research function, whether public or academic, the active and continuing solicitation of manuscripts and papers of local authors, public officials, musicians, and artists can be invaluable. Lists should be made and responsibility assigned for contacting possible donors of papers.

VOLUNTEERS

The resourceful tapping of the good will of potential volunteers, especially young people, retired persons, or simply people with free time, can on occasion solve staffing problems. Moving of library materials is one example; short-term projects is another. Some training and good supervision is usually necessary.

Honorary Consultants

If the community has people with specialized knowledge or people of reputation, it is surprising how many of them are willing to donate their time for book selection, for assistance in writing policies, or even for advising staff on reference questions. Formally appointed as honorary consultants, they probably should be given some special prerogatives in the library: a carrell, extended borrowing privileges, and even a parking permit.

Book Fairs

Many libraries hold an annual book fair. Volunteers are a *sine qua non* for these affairs. Books need to be sorted, moved, priced, arranged, carried, sold, rearranged, and repacked. The friends, service groups, staff members, and students often volunteer. Again, supervision is important.

PUBLIC RELATIONS

Publicity

Press releases are the lifeblood of a library. The John Cotton Dana Award of the H.W. Wilson Company rewards particularly imaginative public relations campaigns or projects every year. Releases can also be issued about tax forms available in libraries from the Internal Revenue Service or from the State Division of Taxation and Revenue or about special purchases of note. Releases can also be issued about staff or faculty appointments and about special gifts, special events, library-sponsored awards or exhibits, or about new acquisitions of a regular nature. Press releases should be distributed internally, to the public the library serves, and/or to the library profession at large, as appropriate.

If the parent institution has a public relations or public information office, the library officer in charge of public relations or communications should maintain very close liaison with that office. More often than not, that office has procedures, forms, and contacts that can be of great assistance to the library and can advise on problems of a public relations nature.

Special Events

Some libraries sponsor lecture series, using both staff members and outside experts. The lectures may also be published in a library lecture series.

Autograph parties in the library for local or regional authors can be held. Concerts by community musicians or performances by acting or dancing groups can be sponsored. The library may eventually request the papers of those individuals or groups. The contacts are invaluable.

Banquets honoring major donors or special events, such as the acquisition of the millionth volume (or any other significant number), can be organized.

Exhibits are particularly important—on a regular basis if possible. It is a good idea to have a library exhibits committee in order to spread the work load. Those staff members with artistic talents should always be included on the committee. The library should also have a written policy on exhibits and, for that matter, on special events in general. It is important to be able to exclude as well as to include, and the written policy provides that rationale.

Publications

In addition to the publication of a library lecture series, other projects might be considered. Through the friends group, grants for the publication of limited editions of works by local authors might be a possibility; e.g., the friends might commission or cosponsor a history of the town or city, a history of the parent institution, or a history of the library. Finely printed keepsakes could also be commissioned for special occasions, e.g., the friends annual banquet, the occasion of a major acquisition, the retirement of a distinguished librarian, or a longevity anniversary of a colleague's service to the library.

PURCHASES

Rather than simply be a follower and passive recipient of requests for materials, an aggressive library collection development officer, with good judgment and imagination, should seize every opportunity for the library to assume a leadership role in the institution he or she serves. For example, if a particularly rich collection is offered to an academic library, either as a gift or a purchase, and if the collection is not directly relevant to courses being offered at that particular time, with proper consultation, the library by acquiring that collection could be providing for future programs and not just the present-day needs. In other words, a library builds also for the future and not just for the present. *Carpe diem* sometimes is the best course. Great libraries have never been built by timid souls.

Bargaining

Many librarians do not realize the bargaining power they have, even if they have only small budgets. Discounts are available, at least in the United States, delayed payments can be arranged, prices can be held against artificial deadlines if one assures the purchase and has a good reputation in the book market. Good and ethical relations with bookdealers are extremely important. However, sometimes one has to be a tough trader.

Trading

On the subject of trading, libraries on occasion face the problem of unneeded *blocks* of books and serials in their stacks. A professor may have left the university, and his or her subject is no longer being taught. A program may have been eliminated. An ethnic group may have moved from the area of a branch public library; people speaking another language may have moved in. What does the librarian do then? Rather than house unneeded materials one needs to seek out where those materials are most needed. Some dealers will purchase such materials, but one should be careful to ascertain the going market price. It is also possible to trade with another library. If the legal or financial officer will allow such a transaction, a library can build up a standing account with another library. Then, one can draw on that account as the other library has material available, but every arrangement must be carefully spelled out in written form and approved by higher authorities and notarized.

Disposal of Unneeded Materials

From time to time, collection development officers are offered collections that contain material both very valuable and appropriate under the collection development policies of the library, but that also contain material not needed. If the collection must be bought *en bloc*, then the unit cost must be carefully negotiated. In so doing, the following points should be considered: Can the library process the volume of material? Has the collection development officer consulted all the people who should be involved? If the library is paying a unit cost of X number of dollars and the library wants only 60% of the collection, is the overall cost of the material the library wants fair market value? Can the library afford to dispose of the unwanted material?

What are the methods of disposal? Again, here the librarian needs strict legal guidance in tax-supported institutions, because one is dealing with public property. Following proper procedures, one can offer the material for sale to dealers. The library can also put it up for public bidding or hold a book sale. However, the most important aspect of all this is that one should keep in mind the cost benefits and the value of the material. In the case of rarity and appropriateness of material, one might have to make the adventurous decision to go ahead with the purchase and tighten the belt in another area of the budget.

CONCLUSION

Creativity in library collection development requires conviction as well as a thorough knowledge of subject matter. On occasion, it also requires boldness.

The greater the dedication of those responsible, and the more thorough and imaginative the response to the need for collection development, the greater will be the library that emerges: a citadel of learning and research, a sanctuary.

REFERENCES

1. J. Monod, in *The Creative Process in Science and Medicine*, H.A. Krebs and J.H. Shelley, eds. (New York: Elsevier, 1975.)
2. James Joyce, *A Portrait of the Artist as a Young Man.* (New York: Viking Press, 1916; Compass Books, 1956), p. 253.
3. Rollo May, *The Courage to Create.* (New York: Bantam Books, 1976), p. 20.
4. Ibid., p. 46.
5. Verner Clapp and Robert T. Jordan, "Quantitative Criteria for Adequacy of Academic Library Collections." *College and Research Libraries* 26 (1965): 371-380.
6. *The Foundation Directory.* (New York: The Foundation Center, 1977.)
7. "Determining Indirect Cost Rates in Research Libraries," in Association of Research Libraries, Systems and Procedures Exchange Center, SPEC KIT No. 34 (Washington, D.C.: ARL, July 1977.)
8. Peat, Marwick, Mitchell and Co., *Study of Indirect Cost Rates of Organizations Performing Federally Sponsored Research.* (New York: Peat, Marwick, Mitchell and Co., November 1977.)
9. "Cost Principles for Educational Institutions," *ARL OMB Circular* No. A-21.
10. Association for Research Libraries, *ARL Newsletter* No. 91, p. 5.
11. Letter to the author from Peter H. Stevens, Head, Acquisitions Division, University of Washington Libraries, Seattle, Wash. May 22, 1978.
12. Letter to the author from Peter H. Stevens, June 7, 1978, including a report "Library Survey—Autumn 1977" by Takayoshi Okamoto.
13. Rutherford D. Rogers and David C. Weber, *University Library Administration.* (New York: H.W. Wilson Company, 1971), Appendix V, p. 374.

Education for Collection Development

Charles B. Osburn

INTRODUCTION

A study completed in 1966 reached the uninspiring conclusion that, in general, library school graduates did a better job of selecting materials than nongraduates and that the difference between the two groups was statistically significant (1). While it is good to know that the profession's positive assumptions about the value of professional education can be supported, it is at the same time troubling to learn that the difference separating the selection performance of those who have received professional schooling from those who have not is not more striking. In consideration of the increasing complexity of matching collections with their respective communities, this conclusion is indeed quite humbling and should have rendered the profession less complacent about the articulation of its education and practice divisions. Clearly, the time has come when a substantial theoretical base for collection management and development must be established and offered through the formal mechanism of professional library education. Much more serious attention should be given to the relationship between education and practice in collection management and development than we have seen heretofore, and the author wishes to suggest some relevant considerations.

It is true that librarians, as all professionals, learn through practice; but it is also true that they are equipped to do this well only after they have acquired the appropriate foundation of knowledge and theory. Since the quality of entering professionals is controlled by the library science programs through which the status of librarian is conferred, the nature and quality of these programs are crucial in determining the role of the library profession in society. The present chapter proceeds from a brief consideration of the past and current place of collection development in the library profession, and some of the past and current difficulties of maintaining a useful dialog between education and practice that have worked against the institution of a solid academic program for collection development. This is followed by a consideration of the rationale behind an expanded substantive approach to education for collection development in the context of the development of library science and the evolution of society.

THE MAJOR ISSUES OF
LIBRARY EDUCATION

The educational part of a profession is responsible to a considerable extent for both reflecting concerns of that profession and giving guidance in its directions. Consequently, the literature of library education should serve as the record of these concerns and directions during the past two decades. At the risk of missing some major issues and misrepresenting others, the chief categories of the library literature of the past 20 years seem to be: accreditation, Ph.D. programs, identification of a core curriculum, integration of computer technology into the curriculum, the need to update and upgrade curriculum generally, censorship, the need to define a theory of librarianship, specialization versus generalization, for need to emphasize *science* in library science, enrollment and recruitment as part of the nationwide abundance of professional vacancies and later as part of the diminished job market. It is not surprising that collection development is not to be found among these categories, except perhaps by broad implication, for the literature of library science generally exhibits little interest in that function.

Now, a library may be many things to many people, and the variety of activities in any library certainly has increased in the past century; but the *sine qua non* of any library, lest we forget, is a collection of recorded materials whose primary purpose is to serve a given community. These may be relatively safe views to expound in public, but when considered in conjunction with the place of collection development in library education and literature, they underline a paradox. Responsible for the paradox are two quite different views of collection development that have been influential in recent decades. One says simply that collection development is an art that cannot be taught; there are those who have it and those who do not, and it cannot be acquired in library school. Opposing this view are those who seem to hold an unspoken assumption that the selection of library materials is an inherent privilege of the profession, and, therefore, that conferral of the professional degree automatically carries with it the license and know-how to develop collections. While certain guidelines are, indeed, offered in selection courses in library school, they too seldom are examined in depth and so remain almost platitudinous; for example: "know your community," or "the right book for the right person," or "a collection for all time," or even "the right to read." (If any aspect of collection development is studied in depth it may be the censorship question because it lends itself well to discussion, case study, and both historical and sociological approaches.) These are all very important guidelines, but rarely are they grounded in the kind of substantive knowledge that renders them meaningful and implementable.

There may have been a time when the selection process in libraries was straightforward and uncomplicated, and when the education of prospective librarians was quite properly focused on the routines of specific operations and on the inculcation of professional principles. That time passed, however, the the publication explosion, with the rise of professionalization of librarianship, and with general changes in a society that has been more and more aggressively self-deterministic. The publications universe is much more vast and varied than it was just two decades ago, the community has assumed a new identity, and the user population has evolved into a new configuration. These developments bear profound and far-reaching implications for the development of collections intended to best serve any given community, but the educational foundation to do this adequately is not presently available in the profession.

IMPEDIMENTS TO EDUCATION
FOR COLLECTION DEVELOPMENT

Conditions in library education and practice have generally not been conducive to the establishment of an educational program incorporating a solid foundation for collection development officers. This is due in part to the slowness of the profession at large to distinguish collection development as a decision-making and planning process apart from acquisitions. As recently as 1964, the dean of the Graduate Library School of the University of Chicago posed the question: "Should a library school curriculum include courses on book selection? (2)" Because libraries traditionally have tended to respond to changing conditions, usually with a considerable time lag, rather than involve themselves directly with, or give direction to, those changing conditions, collections have evolved largely as a result of the passive function of acquisitions. To the contrary, the concept of collection development, which is relatively recent terminology in library science, makes explicit that there is to be planning behind the growth or maintenance of collections, and that collections at any given time in the future should be the result of development rather than evolution. The concept implies that collection response to changing conditions is to be part of a predetermined, definable system of relating the collection to the community, managed by the librarian. Library education has in its turn mirrored the confounding of development and acquisitions and thus has exhibited a degree of ambivalence toward the collection development aspect of the professional program that suggests neglect.

The slowness of librarianship to distinguish collection development as a decision-making and planning process apart from acquisitions is related to two other problems in the profession that have fundamental implications for education. The history of American library practice and education evinces a strong emphasis on form and an off-setting lack of interest in content. Certainly the profession has had its share of thinkers, and the literature is spotted with admonitions about the dominance of form over content. Nonetheless, priorities have been ordered by the physical confrontation of daily routines in such a way that manning the desk, filing the order, and forestalling a variety of backlogs have been viewed as the mainstay of the library occupation. Efforts to avoid reflecting this strong current in library practice have not been notably successful in library education. The second problem in practice that has implications for education reinforces the first: that is, the failure of librarianship to upgrade itself by upgrading paraprofessional work with appropriate swiftness. The reasons behind the pervasive hesitancy to upgrade would, by themselves, constitute a most thought-provoking sociological study. However, it may be sufficient for the purposes of the present chapter to conclude that the major curricular changes encouraged by library education can be consumed by the profession only to the extent that the professional positions it incorporates are designed for a level that really can make full, effective use of an educational foundation that captures the professional ideal.

There have been several other major impediments to the advancement of education for collection development. Not the least of these is the lack of experience of those who teach collection development. Because the theory behind collection development and the organization of collection development have been so diverse throughout the United States—even within similar types of libraries—and because the definition of collection development still is not widely understood, it is not surprising that the pool of knowledgeable, experienced librarians has not been adequate for the purposes of formal training. A more general problem has to do with the preparedness and expectations of the beginning students. This applies, of course, to the greater part of the spectrum of library education, if not to its entirety. This problem refers to motivation for entering the profession and its relationship to perceptions about the nature of the profession. One has the distinct impression, for example, that little is known about the profession from outside, that much of what little is known is incorrect, and that much of what little is correct may not coincide with the professional ideal (assuming that there is a collective professional ideal). In that case, it could be expected that of those students who finally work out well in librarianship many or most do so only because of some fortunate statistical probability. If changes in the essence of library practice and library education—along the lines of those to be suggested later specifically for collection development— are really to be effected, the movement toward change will be merely a boot-strap operation, if it is not accompanied by the infusion of a new kind of librarian into the profession. As noted earlier, professional education both responds to and provides guidance to the profession, and considerably more emphasis should be placed on the guidance aspect than it has been heretofore.

LEADERSHIP FROM LIBRARY EDUCATION IN ADVANCING THE FUNDAMENTALS OF COLLECTION DEVELOPMENT

The library profession is sorely in need of leadership. Consider the debate of whether or not there is a theory of librarianship and the need becomes evident. With the advent of the publication explosion, followed by relatively rich library funding, library education rallied to respond to the identified need of library practice to control a vast influx of bibliographic data. Advanced computer technology was employed to turn an almost overwhelming problem for the profession into a stimulating challenge. Since then, much attention has been given to the place of technology in libraries. It was primarily because a large number of library school faculty were drawn from other disciplines that library education was not only able to respond to a crisis, but also to provide leadership in the field. What seems to remain in the solution to the problem of physically coping with vast amounts of bibliographical data is to implement existing knowledge and to effect some refinement. The part of the crisis that library education can properly be expected to address with special force has passed. A different area where leadership is particularly needed now presents itself.

When the discipline of documentation was joined with an analysis of the application of computer technology to library management, information science emerged as a discipline. Although the definition of information science is not definitive or always clear, what is clear is that its implications for all of librarianship are profoundly significant. Consequently, one should explore more closely the implications of information science for collection development and the place of collection development in librarianship, and one might do this in the context of a general recommendation that library education become more aggressive and realistic, but imaginative in its monitoring and guidance of the profession.

The most fundamental knowledge and capabilities required in collection development can be summarized as follows: knowlege of the information and publication universe, ability to control that information bibliographically, knowledge of the community related to publication and information, understanding of the likely causes of change in the information universe, understanding of the likely causes of change in the community, ability to monitor the information universe and community, knowledge of signs of change in each, ability to adjust policy and procedures, knowledge of quality control methods, ability to effectively integrate collection development policy and procedures into library operations.

The preceding outline of the characteristics of library collection development describes a system, and it is above all the system concept in operations research that information science has to offer of value to collection development. By understanding the collection development function as a system, objective analysis can be applied to it so that collections will result from planned development rather than from uncontrolled evolution, or from a librarian's preconceptions that have little relation to the interactions of the information universe and the community. For purposes of the present discussion, the term *information universe* refers to that part of recorded human expression and communication that is affected by or is of interest to the community; the term *community* refers to any definable group of people who have the potential to affect or be interested in the information universe. Information science also has been largely responsible for bringing into library education the knowledge and techniques of a variety of related disciplines, a trend that doubtless is essential in applying the system concept to any complex human activity. In the aim of basing the study of collection development on a system concept as described above, however, some related disciplines will have to be studied in much greater depth than they have been heretofore, and new disciplines for the purpose of library education may have to be designed from the merger of others.

Largely through information science, librarianship has borrowed most heavily, thus far, from the applied sciences. As a consequence, the procedures of librarianship are well advanced technologically, the potential for further refinement or wider use constrained primarily by inadequate funding rather than by an extraordinary shortage of educated professionals. Meanwhile, the relationship between community and library collections continues to change, but the potential of information science for policymaking and planning related to this fundamental aspect of librarianship has barely been explored. The awakening of consciousness about the management function in librarianship was stimulated—among other conditions—by the technology infused into the profession via information science. This was certainly a progressive step. However, library education and, especially, library practice have now reached a plateau or stagnation point whose outstanding feature is an exaggerated preoccupation with efficiency. Here is a case where library education could well take the lead in guiding the profession toward greater concern for the effectiveness of library service, giving primacy to the goal of matching collections with community needs and interests.

Turning to the desirable characteristics of a collection development librarian, one can begin to get a better idea of the kind of educational program that would be most useful; and by use of the word *program*, far more than an isolated course or two is intended. In terms of aptitude and psychological makeup, the collection development librarian should be endowed with the kind of intellectual curiosity that facilitates conceptualization rather than the tracking of details. This person should be interested in planning, and in formulating policy, but have the capacity to reassess goals, plans, and policy. In terms of skills, the new collection development librarian needs to be a communicator who understands the full implications of the systems concept in collection development, and needs to be able to deal effectively as an equal with those in the community who place the greatest demand on the collections. In terms of knowledge, the new collection development librarian will have to know the historical background behind relevant sociological concepts and phenomena of the community well enough to be able to manage the collection development function as a service system for human progress.

Clearly, library education will have to undertake some major innovations if professionals with these characteristics are to be produced. Looking at these changes broadly, a new program for education in collection development will require the recognition of collection development as central to library operations and pivotal in library-community relations, and it will require the advancement of theoretical and interdisciplinary studies with a sociological concentration. The systems approach, which heretofore has been applied to the internal library organization, now must be applied to the library as nerve center between information universe and community, with the sociological aspects of information and library science as the connectors and substance. Leadership in this direction seems naturally to reside in the province of library education.

A NEW CORE PROGRAM

The success of the kind of collection development operation suggested above will require the profession to adopt a solid academic or scientific orientation toward establishing goals, planning policy procedure, evaluating success, and testing new hypotheses. These are the processes of collection development. Those upon whom is conferred the professional status of librarian must have the theoretical and knowledge foundation that qualifies them to occupy positions at a decision-making level of greater organizational and community impact than can be expected today. Translated into a broad goal for library education this means an understanding of the function of libraries within the social dynamism of recorded human expression and communication, and implementation of this knowledge by academic or scientific methods.

Giving structure to the educational program there must be a strong emphasis on research and writing, and on the importance of continued professional education in a variety of forms. The purpose of this emphasis on an academic approach is to guarantee that future librarians will have an understanding of the full range of implications of library materials as an element in the social system, so that they can give direction to change in the system rather than merely respond to changing elements in the system. From another point of view, since planning is the essence of collection development, the new program should emphasize that activity and de-emphasize the problem-solving activity now characteristic of much of librarianship.

The kind of educational program for collection development that can best meet these goals has as its nucleus the sociology of recorded human expression and communication (3). This is the study of the interrelationships of the recorded universe, parts of society, and society generally; the effects of one on the others. It is historical, descriptive, analytical, and projective. It has to do with the motivation and production of recorded expression and communication, the reasons and ways of its transmission, the organization and parameters of the system and its parts. It analyzes the ways in which the system develops and evolves. It examines the past in order to understand the present and uses this knowledge to plan the future.

Some of this knowledge has been a traditional part of the professional education, but not in the context of a systems view of the sociology of recorded human expression and communication. Still other relevant knowledge exists but either has not been made a core element in library science or has not been included at all. Still other parts of the knowledge required have not yet been organized to the point that they are immediately suitable to an educational program.

As examples, the history of writing and printing traditionally has been a part of library education, although usually disconnected from relevant sociological implications; the sociology of science, including scientific communication, has been developed primarily within the last two decades with very great potential for collection development education, but it has as yet had little impact on any aspect of librarianship. Examples of areas that have not yet been well developed are the sociology of humanistic scholarship and the sociology of mass reading tastes and information needs (4).

A core program concentrating on the sociology of recorded human expression and communication would require the blending of knowledge gained from both historical and social science research. In most cases, the rudiments of this kind of core program have been established in use and citation studies and various aspects of psychology, sociology, history, communications, bibliography, and documentation. There remains above all the matter of applying the pertinent parts of these disciplines and activities to the establishment of a cohesive program of education for library collection development. The systems view implies that change is evolutionary and developmental, so that an analysis of this system from an historical perspective is important in designing a model that conveys an understanding of how change can both be effected and accommodated. One of the major aims in studying the system and parts of the system related directly to the student's type-of-library specialization is to gain insight into the community's perception of the system—for that is crucial in learning how modification in the system may be conceived, modeled, and carried forward. It will be necessary for the program to draw on the methodology developed in historical and social science research, as well as upon the knowledge accumulated in those areas. All librarians may not be expected to use all methodologies, of course, but their learning experience should make them aware of the appropriate methodologies for given situations or concepts, realistic expectations for the research product and how to use it, alternative methodologies, the training and background required of those who may carry out the research, and how to keep abreast of new developments in research techniques.

Other substantive matters are related to putting this knowledge and skill to work in library collection development. Primarily, they are public relations, policy and planning, decision-making and communications. Naturally, an understanding of the role of all media—not just printed media—is essential to the study of the sociology of recorded human expression and communication. In a research and writing orientation, the place of a thesis for the masters degree is evident.

Just as the mounting of this kind of core program requires teaching faculty of diverse training and background (ranging through child psychology, urban sociology, and sociology of scholarship, for example), it also places special demands on the qualities of the students. To attract the students who are best suited to this kind of program, library schools will have to become active in recruitment from colleges and graduate schools, and perhaps start as early as the high school level, when students are contemplating their career possibilities. However, if recruitment efforts are to be launched successfully by individual library schools, the whole profession will systematically and on a large scale have to begin marketing a new image for librarianship. Enough has been written about the image of librarianship and its negative influence on the development of the profession that it need not be described here. But amazingly little seems to have been done in a concerted effort to diminish this major impediment to progress. Even to start such a campaign would cost a great deal, both in time and dollars. Nonetheless, the importance of information of all kinds in contemporary and future society must by this time be sufficiently understood in most quarters that the price might be considered justified by the product. If so, the idea that the quality of information is commensurate with the quality of the profession that handles it should be marketable to the public. As a profession, librarianship has done little to condition public attitude, while popular television series dramatize the life-death decisions of the medical and legal professions—decisions which, after all, hinge frequently on the quality of information made available to the practitioner.

Entrance standards could be tightened not simply by raising required grade point averages and test scores, but perhaps even more significantly by careful consideration of the prospective student's expressed interest in librarianship and the substance of that student's academic background relative to the new core program. Following entrance into the professional program, a sustained, systematic plan for career counseling—perhaps involving practitioners in the profession—is necessary to ensure that the student's aptitudes, abilities, and knowledge are drawn upon to their potential by the curriculum. As recruitment improves, the prospective student's knowledge about the profession will increase, so that the intensity of continued career counseling may diminish. For those students who follow a path leading toward a collection development position, the advantages in this kind of program of requiring a second graduate degree in a relevant field and the completion of a thesis are evident. An apprenticeship of some kind can be especially useful in producing a collection development officer. This experience can probably be arranged through a work-study plan, an intern program, or perhaps even through institutes or a series of workshops in which practicing collection development officers are participants. In any case, it is very advantageous to bring together the student and the practitioner in a controlled teaching-learning situation, provided the practitioner and the library school are in agreement about the fundamental theory behind collection development.

CONCLUSION

In the present assessment of education for collection development, concentration has been on the perspective from which library collection development can most effectively be addressed in practice and, in doing so, inferences have been drawn about the characteristics of education and training that seem most likely to deliver the appropriate knowledge foundation. The intention has been to make these considerations generalizable to collection development in the setting of all types of libraries serving their respective kinds of cummunities. Library collection development requires more than perspective, of course, since it is a practical function. But without this theory, or this foundation or holistic perspective, the special knowledge and skills that distinguish the school library selector from the Slavic bibliographer and both from the adult fiction selector in a medium-sized public library cannot be employed to the fullest benefit of the respective communities. It has been stressed that professional library education must create and transmit this kind of knowledge for the purpose of educating future collection development librarians.

If much of what is written in these pages seems to apply not just to library collection development but also to the profession generally, that is because it is written in the beliefs that the essence of librarianship is to be found in the dynamics of community and collection, and that the collection ideally is a microcosm of the community's intellectual processes. The nucleus of education for collection development combines a conception of these social dynamics as a system with the related knowledge that is required to develop collections effectively in that context.

REFERENCES AND NOTES

1. John Anthony McCrossan, "Library Science Education and Its Relationship to Competence in Adult Book Selection in Public Libraries" (Ph.D. dissertation, University of Illinois, 1966), p. 164.

2. Don R. Swanson, ed., *The Intellectual Foundations of Library Education. The Twenty-Ninth Annual Conference of the Graduate Library School, July 6-8, 1964* (Chicago: University of Chicago Press, 1965), p. 5.

3. I am describing here what I believe is the equivalent of Jesse Shera's concept of "social epistemology." There may be some difference, however, since my understanding of the word *epistemology* makes of it only a part of the sociology I advocate, albeit a very large part. See the relevant sections of his book *The Foundations of Education for Librarianship* (New York: Becker and Hayes, 1972), pp. 112-115 and 128-134. Shera applies the concept to the whole of librarianship, whereas I see it as the heart of collection development.

4. It has been only very recently that the first comprehensive consumer research study of book readers and buyers was carried out. See the *Consumer Research Study on Reading and Book Purchasing* (Darien, Conn.: Book Industry Study Group, 1978).

Toward a Theory of Collection Development

William E. Hannaford

In 1961 American Sociologist William Goode declared: "I am doubtful that the librarians will become full-fledged professionals" (*1*). The reason for this, we are told, had to do with the lack of a corpus of theoretical knowledge essential to librarianship.

> The central gap is of course the failure to develop a general body of scientific knowledge ... in the way that the medical profession with its auxiliary scientific fields has developed an immense body of knowledge with which to cure human diseases. While the general knowledge embodied in professional library curriculums is likely to be communications theory, the sociology or psychology of mass communications, or the psychology of learning as it applies to reading, most day-to-day professional work

utilizes rather concrete, rule-of-thumb, local regulations and rules, and a major cataloguing system. The problems of selection and organization are dealt with on a highly empiricist basis, concretely, with little reference to general scientific principles. Moreover little if any of the current research in librarianship attempts to develop such general principles (2)

Yet, 14 years later, reassurance still did not come from Ralph Edwards who claimed that "progress has been made in the development of relevant theory and knowledge since Goode wrote. Research in information science and user studies has added a good deal to the core of knowledge, and yet it must be admitted that what Goode said about the day-to-day work of the typical librarian is still true" (3).

The professional status issue aside, even today it is not entirely clear that Goode's view about the lack of a body of scientific knowledge in librarianship does not hold true. Whether such a body of knowledge has been or is being developed is partly an empirical issue and one not easily solved. It is partly empirical because certain kinds of evidence either for or against the existence of scientific knowledge in librarianship can be given. It is a difficult issue because it is not clear how much knowledge is necessary to constitute a corpus. Further, the issue is not entirely empirical because what scientific knowledge is or comes to be is not itself an empirical matter. In any event, the interesting question is not whether librarians have or will develop a corpus of scientific knowledge. Rather, it is whether scientific knowledge itself is possible in the field of library science.

Here the objection might be raised that the empirical question of whether librarianship has or will have a body of scientific knowledge is rapidly being answered by books such as the present one and a multitude of others along with journal articles. Taking the argument one step further, it follows from the fact that a body of scientific knowledge is being produced in librarianship that such a body is possible (4). That is, since it is, it is possible.

A glance at a good bibliography demonstrates that librarianship does, indeed, have a body of knowledge (5). It can be shown that this knowledge is scientific and the body sufficient, then it can be safely assumed that librarianship does have a body of scientific knowledge. This chapter will attempt to articulate what scientific knowledge is and to see if the knowledge of librarianship, particularly that of collection development, might be scientific. The primary purpose, however, is to give an argument for the possibility of scientific knowledge in collection development, a step which is logically, though obviously not chronologically, prior to the development of such knowledge. If such knowledge is possible, and if a working definition of scientific knowledge can be constructed, then the only part of the proof—that collection development has constructed or is constructing a body of scientific knowledge—remaining is the empirical part of comparing scientific knowledge with knowledge in collection development.

Scientific knowledge is a term used with a good deal of ease, and yet, it is not often clearly understood. When it is defined not one but many definitions are given. Let us look at several of these to see if scientific knowledge might be appropriate to librarianship. In the discussion that follows a cluster of concepts—scientific knowledge, science, and theory—will be considered. Throughout, the words *scientific* and *theoretical* will be used interchangeably.

In the same article where he doubts that librarians will ever attain professional status, Goode states that scientific knowledge "must first of all be organized in abstract principles, and cannot consist of mere details however vast in quantity. The principles must be applicable to concrete problems" (6). A working definition of theory is given by Kenneth Whittaker in an article about a theory of reference service: "I mean the formulation of concepts through the study of ideas, attitudes, and practices . . . (7)" The *Oxford English Dictionary* defines *science* as a "branch of study which is concerned either with a connected body of demonstrated truths or with observed facts systematically classified and more or less colligated by being brought under general laws . . . (8)" and *theory* as "a scheme or system of ideas or statements, held in an explanation or account of facts or phenomena; a hypothesis that has been confirmed by observation or experience . . . a statement of what are held to be the general laws, principles, or causes of something known or observed" (9).

All of these definitions, which are basically those of ordinary usage, have in common that scientific knowledge is theoretical (abstract, conceptual, made up of principles and laws) in nature and connected in some way to the practical (concrete problems, observed facts). The connection between the theoretical and the practical is usually called explanation. In short, the theoretical is seen as an explanation, in some sense or other, of the practical.

The above definitions, though they reflect ordinary usage, also closely approximate those given by scientists, logicians, and philosophers of science. For example, Michael Scriven, a philosopher, gives the following definition of scientific theory: "typically a system of propositions which organizes the evidence internally and in relation to other propositions of the system which contain certain (possibly hypothetical) entities or states; so that we can see it as a consistent and connected whole, where the connection consists of explanation (not necessarily deduction) in the direction . . . to (propositions describing the phenomena) and of inference (not necessarily induction in the narrow sense) in the other direction" (10). Thomas Kuhn in his well-known book on scientific revolutions defined science in terms of paradigms. He states that by choosing the term *paradigm* it is meant "to suggest that some accepted examples of actual scientific practice—examples which include law, theory, application, and instrumentation together—provide models from which spring particular coherent traditions of scientific research" (11). For Einstein and Infeld "science is not just a collection of laws, a catalogue of unrelated facts. It is a creation of the human mind, with its freely invented ideas and concepts. Physical theories try to form a picture of reality and to establish its connection with the wide world of sense impressions. Thus the only justification for our mental structures is whether and in what way our theories form such a link" (12).

As was true for the first set of definitions, this second set emphasizes the connection between the theoretical and the practical. Scientific knowledge is not a collection of facts, but neither is it just an assemblage of theories and laws. It is both, with theory explaining the phenomena of the world of sense.

Explanation is one of the key concepts in any discussion of scientific knowledge. In fact, it has been said that "the distinctive aim of the scientific enterprise is to provide systematic and responsibly supported explanations" (13). To put it another way, the main business of science is to construct theories which adequately picture reality. Explanation provides the glue in one of the most commonly held views of modern science. In this view, science consists of several tiers: theory, law, and observation. Briefly and simplistically, theories explain laws or other theories which, in turn, explain observation. An example of this hierarchical picture of scientific explanation in the field of physics is the theory of relativity: general relativity explains special relativity explains Newtonian mechanics explains observations of planetary motions (14).

In the discussion of scientific knowledge above, the model of science elaborated is that most often applied to the physical sciences. Similar models are increasingly being applied to the social sciences (15). It is questionable whether any such model has been effectively applied to library science. Since the primary interest here is in showing that scientific knowledge is possible in librarianship, no attempt will be made here to show conclusively that librarianship does lend itself to some such model of science. However, this author does believe that librarianship in general and collection development in particular can be scientific in one form or another.

More and more collection development, taken as a body of knowledge, does contain the ingredients requisite for being scientific. It does put forth, for example, various theories and principles which can be translated into practices. Just as psychological theory explains how human beings can and do behave, collection development theory explains how library collections can be and are being built.

It might be objected that no part of librarianship can be a science because there is a lack of clarity, at this point in time, concerning just what phenomena it is to explain. As Fodor points out, this is a harmless objection because "the properties a phenomenon must have in order to fall within the domain of the theory are specified ex post facto by reference to the conceptual mechanisms that the theory employs" (16). In short, the theory comes first; only later is the domain clearly articulated. This process, of course, clearly demarcates just what phenomena do and do not belong within the domain of the theory.

Although it is important for several reasons, the issue of whether scientific knowledge is possible in collection development still has not been successfully addressed. If it can be shown that such knowledge is possible for collection development, similar arguments might hold for other areas within librarianship. Further, the issue bears on other matters such as improving practices in the field and adding to the arguments bearing on the professional status issue. Also, in showing that collection development can be scientific some of the theory itself might be laid out.

In order to understand precisely what is at stake in asking whether scientific knowledge is possible in collection development, it might be helpful to phrase the issue in several different ways. It is essentially the same issue as whether collection development is at all scientific or theoretical in nature, whether there can be a theory of collection development, or whether it is merely limited to a number of practices. If it is only the latter, then it has no claim to having theories and principles with which to guide everyday activities. To deny the possibility of scientific knowledge is to deny that there can be a theory, and to affirm limitation to the particular.

The argument that scientific knowledge is possible in collection development takes the form of a conceptual analysis. In Kantian language, such an analysis would be called a deduction, and the title of this chapter, then, would be something like "A Prolegomenon to Any Future Possibility of Systematic Knowledge in Collection Development" (17). A conceptual analysis or Kantian deduction of collection development amounts to showing that it is a coherent concept, i.e., that it has a possible application (18). To put it another way, if collection development is not a coherent or logical concept, then it has no possible application and no theory is possible. Logically, this analysis proves the possibility of and must precede any articulation of a theory of collection development.

Before beginning this analysis, an example of an analysis of another concept might be helpful in order to show just how the process is not empirical in nature. If one were asked to analyze the concept of God, one would not be able to "look around" for any clues. God is not the sort of creature found under rocks. Thus, the analysis of the concept of God must proceed a priori in a rational manner, not a posteriori in an empirical one. It could be argued that the concept of God includes omniscience and omnipotence, i.e., that God is omniscient and omnipotent. Neither of these features of God is induced from any empirical evidence. Rather, they were deduced from the concept of God itself. Put another way, the concept of God includes at least these two, and possibly other, facets.

Such an analysis can also be applied to the concept of unicorn. It is known that a unicorn is a horselike animal with a single horn protruding from the front of its head. The concept unicorn includes single horn. Even though no one has ever seen a real unicorn, and even though there is serious question of their existence, the concept unicorn is a coherent one. If one were asked to search for a unicorn, one would at least know what to look for, and there is always the remote possibility that one might be found.

On the other hand, suppose one were asked to search the world high and low for a square circle. Before beginning the search it should be recognized that such a search is futile for no square circles can exist. The feature of the two contradict, because a square is, by definition, not circular. Thus, the concept square circle is incoherent or illogical.

The concept of collection development is certainly not like that of square circle because it contains no apparent or even hidden contradictions. That is, it appears to be a coherent concept, one that has a possible application. It might be argued that even though the concept of collection development, like that of God and unicorn, is not incoherent or illogical, it is somewhat ambiguous and unclear. The conceptual analysis which follows is intended to be a contribution to the process of unpacking and clarifying the concept of collection development.

Collection development is one of the most discussed and still least well-known areas within librarianship. Just what is collection development? Though it is often confused with the acquisition or selection of library materials, it is neither. The acquisition of materials refers to the technical routines libraries use to acquire materials, i.e., searching, ordering and paying. Nor is it just the selection of materials, though this is one part of the total picture. Collection development is the overall molding or development of a collection for a purpose to suit a group of users. In short, collection development is the building of the best collection possible given certain conditions. The conditions obviously differ greatly for different libraries.

Collection development is implemented in library settings in almost every imaginable way. Libraries budget and select using a host of different methods. Organizational patterns also differ greatly. In small libraries often every librarian is involved at least in part in collection development. In large research libraries there are often subject or area specialists, called bibliographers, selectors, or collection development officers, who are specifically charged with developing the collection. These concerns are not going to be discussed in this chapter, since they are, at least logically, secondary to the concept of collection development itself and have already been discussed elsewhere.

Just as the concept of God can be analyzed into omniscience and omnipotence, and the concept of unicorn into single horn, four-legged, and horselike, to name a few of their features, the concept of collection development can be analyzed into its parts. It can be argued that there are at least four parts that capture the concept of collection development: selection, de-selection or weeding, evaluation and funding. Each of these parts when properly balanced, and when coupled with the various subsidiary interests, should produce the best possible collection.

The argument, or deduction itself, can be given briefly as follows. In order to fully develop the best possible collection, the collection has to be carefully molded and shaped. That is, certain additions to and deletions from the collection have to be made. To do this the collection should first, logically, have been evaluated. That is, what should be added to and taken from the collection has to be known before additions and deletions are actually made. This evaluation acts, in effect, as part of a master plan for developing the collection. The funding aspect should be fairly obvious. To develop a collection requires money. The time, effort, and cost of planning and evaluating a collection, as well as adding and removing materials from that collection on an on-going basis, are extensive. Also, the expertise required in each part is expensive.

An analogy might be somewhat useful here. When asked to plan a building, an architect first visits the site and only later draws up the plans. These plans are changed, i.e., certain additions and deletions are made, due to various existing conditions. Funding for the building is obtained, and the building grows. During the actual building, many changes are made in the plans and thus in the building itself. The entire process is usually quite flexible. Building a building is not unlike building a collection.

Since collection development involves each of the four parts mentioned above, they need to be examined briefly to see how each fits into the whole. This exercise should complete the deduction at least in schematic form, showing the possible application of the concept of collection development.

Logically, the first step in molding a collection is the evaluation of the collection itself. The evaluation leads to a knowledge of the specific strengths and weaknesses of the collection. This knowledge, coupled with the external constraints of the purpose of the collection and the type of user, helps produce a picture of what has to be done to the collection to make it what it should or could be.

Once a clear idea of the strengths and weaknesses of the collection is known, a master plan can be developed. This plan, like the architect's drawing, must show what the collection should be while remaining sufficiently flexible. The next step is to seek the funds to implement the plan. Selection and de-selection enter at this point. Some materials will need to be added to and others removed from the collection in order to make it what it should be. De-selection, of course, includes not only weeding but also storage. The process of adding and deleting materials from a collection is ongoing and can never ideally be complete unless the collection is closed. The shaping and molding accomplished by adding and deleting materials for the collection must be rational. That is, materials must be added to and taken from the collection only after there is a clear idea of what the collection should be.

The four parts of collection development form one whole. If any one of the four is missing the whole suffers and, in effect, is no longer complete. For example, with no funding, no shaping or molding of the collection is possible. If the collection is never evaluated, then no real shaping and molding can occur because there is no vision of what is being shaped and molded. Analogously, an architect cannot build a structure unless some fairly clear idea of what the structure is to look like exists.

The deduction is complete, i.e., it has been shown that collection development is a concept with possible application. This means that the concept of collection development is coherent and that scientific knowledge in collection development is, indeed, possible. As a result, it follows that collection development can be a science.

A deduction such as the one given above is intended to show possibility rather than actuality. In this particular case it has been argued that collection development can be scientific, not that it is. In actual fact, collection development may not be scientific, i.e., it may not have a body of theoretical knowledge. Rather than being guided by principles (rational, well-thought-out plans) much collection development is probably done on a day-to-day basis. What this means, of course, is that collections are not really being developed, though they are being added to, deleted from, and the like. Using the analogy of the architect one more time, what would it be like to construct a building using no plans?

The attempt in this chapter at what might be called meta-theory is only a beginning, one that needs to be greatly refined and more comprehensively developed. The very fact that meta-theoretical issues in the field of library science are now possible and beginning to be discussed is evidence of the growth of a body of scientific knowledge in the field.

REFERENCES

1. William J. Goode, "The Librarian: From Occupation to Profession." *Library Quarterly* 34 (1961): 307.
2. Ibid., pp. 212-213.
3. Ralph M. Edwards, "The Management of Libraries and the Professional Functions of Librarians." *Library Quarterly* 45 (1975): 157.
4. For an example of the knowledge currently being produced, see *Library Resources and Technical Services* 23 (Winter 1979).
5. For a good recent bibliography in collection development, see *Advances in Librarianship*, vol. 8 (New York, 1978), pp. 40-54.

6. Goode, "The Librarian . . .," p. 308.

7. Kenneth Whittaker, "Towards a Theory for Reference Service." *Journal of Librarianship* 9 (1977): 57.

8. *The Compact Edition of the Oxford English Dictionary* (London: Clarendon Press, 1971), p. 2668.

9. Ibid., p. 3284.

10. Michael Scriven, "A Possible Distinction Between Traditional Scientific Disciplines and the Study of Human Behavior." In *The Foundations of Science and the Concepts of Psychology and Psychoanalysis*, Minnesota Studies in the Philosophy of Science, vol. 1 (Minneapolis, 1956), p. 333.

11. Thomas S. Kuhn, *The Structure of Scientific Revolution*. (Chicago: University of Chicago Press, 1962), p. 10.

12. Albert Einstein and Leopold Infeld, *The Evolution of Physics*. (New York: Simon & Schuster, 1961), p. 294.

13. Ernest Nagel, *The Structure of Science*. (New York: Harcourt, Brace and World, 1961), p. 15.

14. For a full discussion of the hierarchical view, see J.J.C. Smart, *Between Philosophy and Science* (New York: Humanities Press, 1968), pp. 78- .

15. For good discussions of the social sciences as science, see the following two books: Peter Winch, *The Idea of a Social Science* (London: Humanities Press, 1965); Jerry Fodor, *Psychological Explanation: An Introduction to the Philosophy of Psychology* (New York: Random House, 1968).

16. Fodor, *Psychological Explanation . . .*, p. 12.

17. Immanuel Kant, *Critique of Pure Reason*. (New York: Doubleday, 1965.)

18. For a similar argument applied to social and political con epts, see Robert Paul Wolff, *The Poverty of Liberalism* (Boston: Beacon Press, 1968).

AUTHOR INDEX

SUBJECT INDEX